Teaching Stories: An Anthology on the Power of Learning and Literature

Bruce Springsteen's America

Lives of Moral Leadership

The Moral Intelligence of Children

Children of Crisis, I: A Study of Courage and Fear

Still Hungry in America

The Image Is You

Uprooted Children

Teachers and the Children of Poverty

Wages of Neglect (*with Maria Piers*)

Drugs and Youth (*with Joseph Brenner and Dermont Meagher*)

Erik H. Erikson: The Growth of His Work

The Middle Americans (*with Jon Erikson*)

The Geography of Faith (*with Daniel Berrigan*)

Migrants, Sharecroppers, Mountaineers (*Volume II of* Children of Crisis)

The South Goes North (*Volume III of* Children of Crisis)

Farewell to the South

Twelve to Sixteen: Early Adolescence (*with Jerome Kagan*)

A Spectacle unto the World: The Catholic Worker Movement (*with Jon Erikson*)

The Old Ones of New Mexico (*with Alex Harris*)

The Buses Roll (*with Carol Baldwin*)

The Darkness and the Light (*with Doris Ulmann*)

Irony in the Mind's Life: Essays on Novels by James Agee, Elizabeth Bowen, and George Eliot

William Carlos Williams: The Knack of Survival in America

The Mind's Fate: Ways of Seeing Psychiatry and Psychoanalysis

Eskimos, Chicanos, Indians (*Volume IV of* Children of Crisis)

Privileged Ones: The Well-Off and the Rich in America (*Volume V of* Children of Crisis)

A Festering Sweetness (*poems*)

The Last and First Eskimos (*with Alex Harris*)

Women of Crisis, I: Lives of Struggle and Hope (*with Jane Coles*)

Walker Percy: An American Search

Flannery O'Connor's South

Women of Crisis, II: Lives of Work and Dreams (*with Jane Coles*)

Dorothea Lange

The Doctor Stories of William Carlos Williams (*editor*)

Agee (*with Ross Spears*)

The Moral Life of Children

The Political Life of Children

Simone Weil: A Modern Pilgrimage

Dorothy Day: A Radical Devotion

In the Streets (*with Helen Levitt*)

Times of Surrender: Selected Essays

Harvard Diary: Reflections on the Sacred and the Secular

That Red Wheelbarrow: Selected Literary Essays

The Child in Our Times: Studies in the Development of Resiliency (*edited with Timothy Dugan*)

Anna Freud: The Dream of Psychoanalysis

Rumors of Separate Worlds (*poems*)

The Spiritual Life of Children

The Call of Stories: Teaching and the Moral Imagination

Their Eyes Meeting the World: The Drawings and Paintings of Children (*with Margaret Sartor*)

The Call of Service: A Witness to Idealism

Doing Documentary Work

The Secular Mind

When They Were Young

FOR CHILDREN
Dead End School
The Grass Pipe
Saving Face
Riding Free
Headsparks

POLITICAL LEADERSHIP

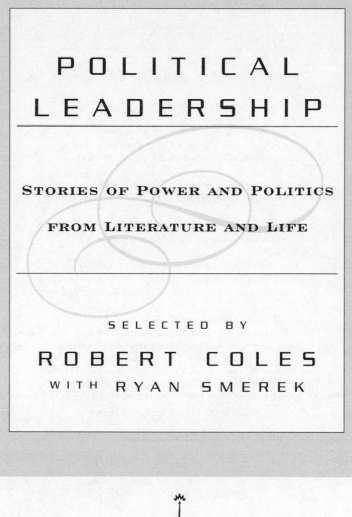

POLITICAL LEADERSHIP

STORIES OF POWER AND POLITICS

FROM LITERATURE AND LIFE

SELECTED BY

ROBERT COLES

WITH RYAN SMEREK

THE MODERN LIBRARY

NEW YORK

Published in the United States by Modern Library,
an imprint of The Random House Publishing Group,
a division of Random House, Inc., New York.

MODERN LIBRARY and the TORCHBEARER Design
are registered trademarks of Random House, Inc.

Permission acknowledgments to reprint from previously
published materials can be found on page 301.

LIBRARY OF CONGRESS CATALOGING-IN-PUBLICATION DATA
Political leadership: stories of power and politics from literature
and life / selected by Robert Coles with Ryan Smerek.
p.   cm.
ISBN 0-8129-7170-1
1. Political leadership.   2. Political leadership in literature.   3. Power
(Social sciences)   4. Power (Social sciences) in literature.
I. Coles, Robert.   II. Smerek, Ryan.

JC330.3.P643 2005   303.3'4—dc22   2005047226

Printed in the United States of America

www.modernlibrary.com

246897531

Book design by JoAnne Metsch

To America's citizens,
and to those who have been, and will be,
a great nation's political leaders

CONTENTS

Contents

INTRODUCTION

The idea for this anthology was given to a group of us college students by Perry Miller, a professor of literature much interested in the Puritans, who bore down so hard morally, and too, politically, on the seventeenth- and eighteenth-century American settlers of what is now Massachusetts. Our professor reminded us that religiously minded individuals are not without political interests, strategies, activities, going back, of course, to biblical times; and he went on to mention novelists and playwrights who have had similar inclinations to look long and hard at who has power to do what—where, and why, and with which consequences. In particular, we were asked to read Tolstoy, Dostoevsky, George Eliot, and too, we were pointed back to Sophocles—even as, at that time, French philosophical novelists such as Camus and Sartre were wondering (in the wake of the terrible murderousness of Hitler) what to conclude about the future of mankind. We had much to learn from certain storytellers of yore, Miller kept insisting—"novelists who wanted to understand the workings of politics, and the way certain individuals wield power, become leaders, practitioners of political leadership."

Yes, most of us averred, there was a lot to be learned from the greatly ambitious novels of the English or Russian nineteenth-century masters (even from some more recently alive writers of fiction), but our chief task was to respond to the teaching remarks of our literature professors, who by and large were interested in figuring out literary plots, their devices and hidden meanings, not to mention their respective places in one or another chronology. Politics, history, they were for the social sciences—to which we ought go, if we wanted to know about rulers, their hopes and maneuvers, their manner of exerting the authority they had managed to acquire (through the choice of voters, through stealth, through the accidents and incidents of time).

Years later, in medical school, I would hear an emphatic echo of Perry Miller's once rather singular assertions—now spoken by an extraordinarily astute clinician whose stethoscope always graced his neck: Yale Kneeland knew how to attend the noises of the heart, figure out the significance of certain neurological reflexes, but also take heed of the stories our patients send our way as we ask them questions, try understanding what has befallen them, gone awry in their bodily (and psychological) everyday life. Again and again he sent us over to bookstores and libraries so that we would, as he kept putting it, "learn about life from those who know how to present it in words to others who know how to read"—such a single, direct, unpretentious manner of rendering what might happen when a person who has put ideas on paper is attended by a reader with willing diligence.

Sometimes, Dr. Kneeland moved from a soaring rhetoric, with the intent of stirring us, to the specificity of a particular sentence, even a paragraph, all put before our waiting eyes through the application of chalk to a blackboard usually taken with numbers, biological and chemical abbreviations, and theoretical formulations meant to get our apprentice medical minds going strong. We learned of Dr. Lydgate, of course, in George Eliot's *Middlemarch,* but we also were told of Eliot's *Felix Holt, the Radical*—her effort to indicate the workings of political life as it gets embedded in the personal inclinations and interests (and too, the social dealings) of those who take the lead in matters political. "You might want to think of history as enabled by the politics that brings it participants, moves it along, so you might want to turn to Leo Tolstoy and Fyodor Dostoevsky and George Eliot"—then, just as we had taken in the enormity of the suggestion (the urgent request, actually), a lowered voice, seemingly stating a hurried afterthought, intoned, "and Mr. Trollope too."

I think it fair to say that more of us had scant knowledge of Anthony Trollope's writing career (never mind his interest in the way politics worked in nineteenth-century England), but Dr. Kneeland knew that in medicine, details count a lot, and he wanted to extend that kind of immediate analytic (and psychoanalytic) thinking to our lives as members of his audience. He set before us authors and the names of their books, and he also got to us more trenchantly by mentioning two names we well knew, that of President (and General) Dwight D. Eisenhower, and that of Britain's Winston Churchill. Not that we were in for a spell of partisan politics or ideology— rather, we were asked this: "You might want to imagine a novelist going about Eisenhower's life, or Churchill's" (or even, he noted, the life of a twentieth-century incarnation of the devil, the German *führer,* Adolf Hitler, whose life had become a big part of our recent life just a few decades earlier). For sure, we may have silently assented (while shuffling our feet, and awaiting our return to the cardiovascular or pulmonary or renal lecture matter now so noticeably set aside out of the fancy or whim of our erudite physician become literary scholar and lecturer).

Suddenly a hand waving in the air, belonging to one of us—and we all were jolted! Dr. Kneeland took notice, said, "Yes?" The student, with embarrassment, hesitation, gave his comment in the form of a question. "I don't understand how all this connects with medicine, sir." Silence, and some heads nodding, while some eyes looked left and right in search of a knowing, agreeing ocular meeting. Finally, a broad smile from our lecturer, and in a second or two this reply: "We are here to understand *lives*—the troubles, the pain, the worries, of our patients, who teach us all the time as they tell us what hurts them. Every day all of life comes to our eyes and ears, our thinking, wondering minds, and that same life (including our own) lives in neighborhoods, in nations, which certain individuals manage, control, direct, govern, rule—in one fashion or another, lead. You might say (dare I do so?) that political leadership, in Washington or London or wherever, has a kind of life in our clinics, hospital rooms, private offices, where people have come looking for advice, help with instructions, recommendations, prescriptions, to be sure, but we might also regard such an initiative on their part as a search for leadership (even 'political leadership'): the suffering one asking the healing one to mend things, to say yes or no, many affirmations, not a few remonstrances." Some of us were quickly admiring, grateful recipients of such remarks sent to us so surprisingly in such an atmosphere, while some of us were impatient, even irritated—yet again the description passed on, over the years, from class to class, rings true: Yale Kneeland, the English professor who somehow got to be a physician, and a professor of medicine, no less.

Still, not a few of Dr. Kneeland's students went to purchase some of the books he mentioned, their titles on the notepaper we kept readily at hand to help us get closer to being knowing doctors, or the tape recording of his lecture. Indeed, weeks later some of those books became familiar to a few, even recommended to friends, family members. How well, for instance, do I recall some quite similar reactions to President Eisenhower's triumph over Adlai Stevenson: "Twice—the stuff of Tolstoy or George Eliot!" We had learned our lesson from our medical teacher, and after those few words gained the extended reflection that signaled a willingness to think of a moment of history, of politics, with a narrator's guidance: the drama of it all, the ironies and paradoxes, the stories of yearning and defeat, of unquestionable good (as seen by some) in a struggle with the unappealing, even the sinister or outright bad (as regarded by others). Literature had become the stuff of political introspection—of a politics we citizens of a great and powerful democracy were daily observing, attempting to fathom.

Twenty years later found me in South Africa, where I was working with white children of English or Afrikaner background in Cape Town, in Johannesburg, and with darker-skinned children living in neighborhoods kept apart from those of their white fellow citizens. I had, before then, lived and worked in our American South, observed the last-ditch struggle to end segregationist dominance of that region, and now, many thousands of miles away, across an ocean, on a different continent, was visiting homes and schools where children and their parents and teachers were at pains to figure out a nation's tumultuous history, its direfully fought politics. Such abstractions became for me clinical challenges, struggles: how to do justice to "the political life of children"—in my daily life of research, speaking with boys and girls, their families, in the hope of acquiring some sense of how their lives were unfolding, with what accomplishments, what setbacks.

One day, in Cape Town, as I discussed my work with a group of sociologists and psychologists, Nadine Gordimer came up—her novel *My Son's Story* is a vigorously discerning and subtle probe, through a story, into the life of a nation (its politics) as it came relentlessly to bear on the life of a child, on a boy's knowledge of a world, what it allows, what it adamantly refuses to let happen (without a sternly punishing admonition). Soon enough I was reading the novel, and was yet once more back in my mind to Professors Miller and Kneeland, to their eager embrace of literature as a decided assist in the comprehension of politics, in the parallel pursuit of moral reflection. In a sense, Gordimer's use of dark skin asked this about people with white skin, "Why do some people give orders, and other people get down on their knees and say yes, yes, yes?" A novel's fourteen-year-old lad posed inquiries, one after the other, offering a vividly affecting description of a present-day political reality—one which brought to my mind some of the starkly stated questions I'd heard in Alabama and Mississippi during the early 1960s: a prelude to the new politics that arrived in 1964 with the adoption, finally, of the voting rights bill of the Congress, and with that outcome a new political reality, a new political leadership in towns, in counties, in city and state offices, across a region. In America's South, I'd been told to call upon novelists for help in getting closer to a region's human truths, and now in South Africa, I was pointedly being directed toward a novelist to get a clear idea of how a country's political leadership gives shape to so many nuances of a people's lived life.

Years later, also, I was trying to teach college students and graduate students about "Politics and the Good"—about the trials and tribulations that can come upon those who take part in political life, become sometime followers of this or that person, party, program, sometime advocates of a particular agenda. I began college teaching, working alongside Erik H. Erikson, who was much interested in leadership—not only that of Luther and Gandhi (discussed in his books) but the leadership, as he once described it in a lecture, "of those who take a step out of the ordinary, and in time, become themselves extraordinary": men or women, he was asserting, who get followed out of admiration that becomes devotion— leaders for followers eager to have ideas addressed as ideals that summon commitment. When asked for a course's syllabus of my own teaching, I turned to memories of Perry Miller and Yale Kneeland, their advocacy of literature as a repository (among many things) of political reflection, even, at times, wisdom. I also turned to twentieth-century writers who had dared contemplate the way politics works—the pitfalls or breakthrough times that go with leadership exerted in a given nation's political life. George Orwell, Carl Sandburg, Robert Penn Warren, became for us in a seminar, introspective or suggestive guides—helpful, indeed, as storytelling or lyrical observers, and occasionally provocateurs, ready to confront us readers with authority become compliance obtained, or disagreement vigorously disputed.

There were additional times of musing—encounters with individuals who in their ongoing political lives had very much become leaders (elected to be a governor, a senator), and thereby held high by many, or conversely, derided insistently by others: political leadership as a defining divide that prompts a pro, a con, from countless others who go to the polls, or answer pollsters with opinions of applause or decided dislike. How well I recall Georgia's then (1967) governor Lester Maddox telling me, during a meeting, that I ought to talk to those who had rallied around him over the years. "You've got to have followers if you're going to be a leader," he remarked quite pointedly as I kept going after *him,* his beliefs, his policies, his political way of self-preservation—and belatedly, after writing about him for those who read the pages of a magazine, I took his advice, heard from (a few times) self-described followers who gave their explicit, and often quite touching and revealing, reasons for "falling in line," as one Georgia citizen called it, who explained his own decision to say yes to Lester, even if there was a no or two in his mind: "You have to raise your hand and say to yourself that this guy's

got you (got to you), or no sir, he's not for you (you're following his line, or you're walking away, and shaking your head
with a *no way* look on your face). That's how it goes in this
life, you follow the leader or you turn to another leader, so the
people asking questions, about who you're for or against, hear
you say 'nope' to someone, or 'You bet, I'll buy the goods he's
peddling in his speeches!' "

Living the life of leadership means linking arms with those
many others who avidly seek a given person's sponsorship, attention, passion—the ability to speak for followers, earn from
them a trust that turns, ultimately, to boxes checked, levers
pulled, at the voting place, and before then, after then, feelings accepted, words addressed to oneself in silence, to others in the course of a family's life, a neighborhood or working
place occupied. No wonder Robert F. Kennedy once remarked that "it takes two to tango," and then used a
metaphor pursued further, considered in its practical application to political leadership as it all the time becomes enacted, then taken to heart by others: "Part of leadership is
getting yourself across to others, so they're willing to sign on
the dotted line, say they're enough with you, for you, to be on
your side, your team. (It's an agreement, a little like a dance,
you could say—the political candidate going down the aisles,
or streets in his city or state, and some will look and listen
and say *sure thing,* and others will say *not for me. I want no
part of that!*)" Living political leadership is someone stepping
briskly, adroitly, in response to rhythms of thought and conviction, of want and apprehension, of need and alarm—so
that the walker, the person living a political life that aims at

political leadership, is eventually held to, even held up high—the followers' embrace become the successful office-holder's sure ticket to a public esteem, signaled over many years through repeated victories at the hands of a persuaded (occasionally enamored) electorate. So the pages ahead, in their respective ways, imply, signal us to keep in mind.

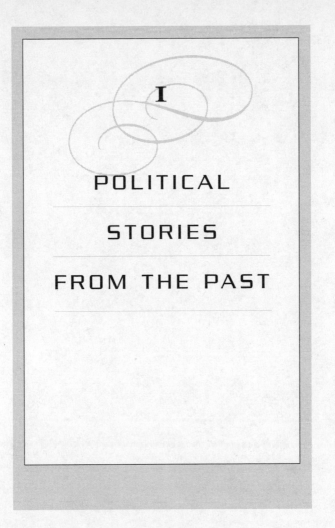

I

POLITICAL

STORIES

FROM THE PAST

WE LIVE IN history, its heritage a powerful force in our present-day lives. And so it goes with nations as well. Past political errors or breakthroughs inform the way we think about nationhood and how we act as citizens in the country we call our own.

In the following political stories of the past, we see how the process of politics is enacted by those who rule, and how it impacts those who follow. Through the eyes of tragedians of long ago, such as Sophocles, and later through the words of nineteenth-century novelists of England and Russia, such as George Eliot and Dostoevsky, we learn how average people tried to live, and tried to make do, in families and neighborhoods. But these same introspective writers were also attempting to render the political side of our lives—depicting the leaders to whom we acquiesce, and the doubt (even, at times, outright disapproval or disdain) we have with respect to them.

Here, then, are political moments of the past, given the suggestive life high art can convey to a reader's later time. Through them, we see how politics works—we witness the manipulations of power and ambition, the art of compromise, the rise and fall of political careers, and the desire to conquer. In short, the past becomes the teacher of the present.

GEORGE ELIOT

George Eliot (1819–80), the pseudonym of Mary Ann Evans, is regarded as one of the great Victorian novelists, especially noted for her insightful psychological characterizations. Her best-known novel, *Middlemarch* (1871–72), follows the emotional and intellectual frustrations of Dorothea Brooke. As Oscar Wilde once remarked in 1897, Eliot "is the embodiment of philosophy in fiction."

In *Felix Holt, the Radical,* written in 1866, Eliot observes that progressive reformers can be even more self-interested than their conservative opponents. Young Harold Transome returns to England from the American colonies with a self-made fortune, then scandalizes his district by running for Parliament as a Radical.

This excerpt from *Felix Holt* introduces the concept of "political consciousness," which can be understood as a continuing and acute sense of the role politics plays in everyday life. Through Felix Holt's actions, George Eliot shows us how average people are affected by politics—how their values and daily activities are connected to, and shaped by, government.

For George Eliot, the political process articulated a given country's social values—it provided public expression for the customs and conflicts of daily life. The theater of politics becomes, then, an affirmation of a citizenry's values, concerns, and aspirations.

From FELIX HOLT, THE RADICAL

Thus Treby Magna, which had lived quietly through the great earthquakes of the French Revolution and the Napoleonic wars, which had remained unmoved by the "Rights of Man," and saw little in Mr. Cobbett's "Weekly Register" except that he held eccentric views about potatoes, began at last to know the higher pains of a dim political consciousness; and the development had been greatly helped by the recent agitation about the Reform Bill. Tory, Whig, and Radical did not perhaps become clearer in their definition of each other; but the names seemed to acquire so strong a stamp of honour or infamy, that definitions would only have weakened the impression. As to the short and easy method of judging opinions by the personal character of those who held them, it was liable to be much frustrated in Treby. It so happened in that particular town that the Reformers were not all of them large-hearted patriots or ardent lovers of justice; indeed, one of them, in the very midst of the agitation, was detected in using unequal scales—a fact to which many Tories pointed with disgust as showing plainly enough, without further argument, that the cry for a change in the representative system was hollow trickery. Again, the Tories were far from being all oppressors, disposed to grind down the working classes into serfdom; and it was undeniable that the inspector at the tape manufactory, who spoke with much eloquence on the extension of the suffrage, was a more tyrannical personage than openhanded Mr. Wace, whose chief political tenet was, that it was all nonsense giving men votes when they had no stake in the country. On the other hand, there were some Tories who gave themselves a great deal of leisure to abuse hypocrites, Radicals, Dissenters, and atheism generally, but whose inflamed faces, theistic swearing, and frankness in expressing a wish to borrow, certainly did not mark them out strongly as holding opinions likely to save society.

The Reformers had triumphed: it was clear that the wheels were going whither they were pulling, and they were in fine spirits for exertion. But if they were pulling towards the country's ruin, there was the more need for others to hang on behind and get the wheels to stick if possible. In Treby, as elsewhere, people were told they must "rally" at the coming election; but there was now a large number of waverers— men of flexible, practical minds, who were not such bigots as to cling to any views when a good tangible reason could be urged against them; while some regarded it as the most neighbourly thing to hold a little with both sides, and were not sure that they should rally or vote at all. It seemed an invidious thing to vote for one gentleman rather than another.

These social changes in Treby parish are comparatively public matters, and this history is chiefly concerned with the private lot of a few men and women; but there is no private life which has not been determined by a wider public life, from the time when the primeval milkmaid had to wander with the wanderings of her clan, because the cow she milked was one of a herd which had made the pastures bare. Even in that conservatory existence where the fair Camellia is sighed for by the noble young Pineapple, neither of them needing to care about the frost or rain outside, there is a nether apparatus of hot-water pipes liable to cool down on a strike of the gardeners or a scarcity of coal. And the lives we are about to look back upon do not belong to those conservatory species; they are rooted in the common earth, having to endure all the ordinary chances of past and present weather. As to the weather of 1832, the Zadkiel of that time had predicted that the electrical condition of the clouds in the political hemisphere would produce unusual perturbations in organic existence, and he would perhaps have seen a fulfilment of his remarkable prophecy in that mutual influence of dissimilar destinies which we shall see gradually unfolding itself. For if the mixed political conditions of Treby Magna had not been acted on by the passing of the Reform Bill, Mr. Harold Transome would not have presented himself as a candidate for North Loamshire, Treby would not have been a polling-place, Mr. Matthew Jermyn would not have been on affable terms with a Dissenting preacher and his flock, and the venerable town would not have been placarded with handbills, more or less complimentary and retrospective—conditions in this case essential to the "where," and the "what," without which, as the learned know, there can be no event whatever.

. . . .

How Harold Transome came to be a Liberal in opposition to all the traditions of his family, was a more subtle inquiry than he had ever cared to follow out. The newspapers undertook to explain it. The *North Loamshire Herald* witnessed with a grief and disgust certain to be shared by all persons who were actuated by wholesome British feeling, an example of defection in the inheritor of a family name which in times past had been associated with attachment to right principle, and with the maintenance of our constitution in Church and State; and pointed to it as an additional proof that men who had passed any large portion of their lives beyond the limits of our favoured country, usually contracted not only a laxity of feeling towards Protestantism, nay, towards religion itself—a latitudinarian spirit hardly distinguishable from atheism—but also a levity of disposition, inducing them to tamper with those institutions by which alone Great Britain had risen to her pre-eminence among the nations. Such men, infected with outlandish habits, intoxicated with vanity, grasping at momentary power by flattery of the multitude, fearless because godless, liberal because un-English, were ready to pull one stone from under another in the national edifice, till the great structure tottered to its fall. On the other hand, the *Duffield Watchman* saw in this signal instance of self-liberation from the trammels of prejudice, a decisive guarantee of intellectual pre-eminence, united with a generous sensibility to the claims of man as man, which had burst asunder, and cast off, by a spontaneous exertion of energy, the cramping out-worn shell of hereditary bias and class interest.

But these large-minded guides of public opinion argued

from wider data than could be furnished by any knowledge of the particular case concerned. Harold Transome was neither the dissolute cosmopolitan so vigorously sketched by the Tory *Herald,* nor the intellectual giant and moral lobster suggested by the liberal imagination of the *Watchman.* Twenty years ago he had been a bright, active, good-tempered lad, with sharp eyes and a good aim; he delighted in success and in predominance; but he did not long for an impossible predominance, and become sour and sulky because it was impossible. He played at the games he was clever in, and usually won; all other games he let alone, and thought them of little worth. At home and at Eton he had been side by side with his stupid elder brother Durfey, whom he despised; and he very early began to reflect that since this Caliban in miniature was older than himself, he must carve out his own fortune. That was a nuisance; and on the whole the world seemed rather ill-arranged, at Eton especially, where there were many reasons why Harold made no great figure. He was not sorry the money was wanting to send him to Oxford; he did not see the good of Oxford; he had been surrounded by many things during his short life, of which he had distinctly said to himself that he did not see the good, and he was not disposed to venerate on the strength of any good that others saw. He turned his back on home very cheerfully, though he was rather fond of his mother, and very fond of Transome Court, and the river where he had been used to fish; but he said to himself as he passed the lodge-gates, "I'll get rich somehow, and have an estate of my own, and do what I like with it." This determined aiming at something not easy but clearly possible, marked the direction in which Harold's nature was strong; he had the energetic will and muscle, the self-confidence, the quick perception, and the narrow imagination which make what is admiringly called the practical mind.

Since then his character had been ripened by a various experience, and also by much knowledge which he had set himself deliberately to gain. But the man was no more than the boy writ large, with an extensive commentary. The years had nourished an inclination to as much opposition as would enable him to assert his own independence and power without throwing himself into that tabooed condition which robs power of its triumph. And this inclination had helped his shrewdness in forming judgments which were at once innovating and moderate. He was addicted at once to rebellion and to conformity, and only an intimate personal knowledge could enable any one to predict where his conformity would begin. The limit was not defined by theory, but was drawn in an irregular zigzag by early disposition and association; and his resolution, of which he had never lost hold, to be a thorough Englishman again some day, had kept up the habit of considering all his conclusions with reference to English politics and English social conditions. He meant to stand up for every change that the economical condition of the country required, and he had an angry contempt for men with coronets on their coaches, but too small a share of brains to see when they had better make a virtue of necessity. His respect was rather for men who had no coronets, but who achieved a just influence by furthering all measures which the common sense of the country, and the increasing self-assertion of the majority, peremptorily demanded. He could be such a man himself.

. . . .

"It is such a beautiful day," he said, "it would do you good to go into the air. Let me take you along the river towards Little Treby, will you?"

"I will put my bonnet on," said Esther, unhesitatingly, though they had never walked out together before.

It is true that to get into the fields they had to pass through the street; and when Esther saw some acquaintances, she reflected that her walking alone with Felix might be a subject of remark—all the more because of his cap, patched boots, no cravat, and thick stick. Esther was a little amazed herself at what she had come to. So our lives glide on: the river ends we don't know where, and the sea begins, and then there is no more jumping ashore.

When they were in the streets Esther hardly spoke. Felix talked with his usual readiness, as easily as if he were not doing it solely to divert her thoughts, first about Job Tudge's delicate chest, and the probability that the little white-faced monkey would not live long; and then about a miserable beginning of a night-school, which was all he could get together at Sproxton; and the dismalness of that hamlet, which was a sort of lip to the coalpit on one side and the "public" on the other—and yet a paradise compared with the wynds of Glasgow, where there was little more than a chink of daylight to show the hatred in women's faces.

But soon they got into the fields, where there was a right of way towards Little Treby, now following the course of the river, now crossing towards a lane, and now turning into a cart-track through a plantation.

"Here we are!" said Felix, when they had crossed the wooden bridge, and were treading on the slanting shadows made by the elm trunks. "I think this is delicious. I never feel less unhappy than in these late autumn afternoons when they are sunny."

"Less unhappy! There now!" said Esther, smiling at him with some of her habitual sauciness, "I have caught you in self-contradiction. I have heard you quite furious against puling, melancholy people. If I had said what you have just said, you would have given me a long lecture, and told me to go home and interest myself in the reason of the rule of three."

"Very likely," said Felix, beating the weeds, according to the foible of our common humanity when it has a stick in its hand. "But I don't think myself a fine fellow because I'm melancholy. I don't measure my force by the negations in me, and think my soul must be a mighty one because it is more given to idle suffering than to beneficent activity. That's what your favourite gentlemen do, of the Byronic-bilious style."

"I don't admit that those are my favourite gentlemen."

"I've heard you defend them—gentlemen like your Rénes, who have no particular talent for the finite, but a general sense that the infinite is the right thing for them. They might as well boast of nausea as a proof of a strong inside."

"Stop, stop! You run on in that way to get out of my reach. I convicted you of confessing that you are melancholy."

"Yes!" said Felix, thrusting his left hand into his pocket, with

13

a shrug; "as I could confess to a great many other things I'm not proud of. The fact is, there are not many easy lots to be drawn in the world at present; and such as they are I am not envious of them. I don't say life is not worth having: it is worth having to a man who has some sparks of sense and feeling and bravery in him. And the finest fellow of all would be the one who could be glad to have lived because the world was chiefly miserable, and his life had come to help some one who needed it. He would be the man who had the most powers and the fewest selfish wants. But I'm not up to the level of what I see to be best. I'm often a hungry discontented fellow."

"Why have you made your life so hard then?" said Esther, rather frightened as she asked the question. "It seems to me you have tried to find just the most difficult task."

"Not at all," said Felix, with curt decision. "My course was a very simple one. It was pointed out to me by conditions that I saw as clearly as I see the bars of this stile. It's a difficult stile too," added Felix, striding over. "Shall I help you, or will you be left to yourself?"

"I can do without help, thank you."

"It was all simple enough," continued Felix, as they walked on. "If I meant to put a stop to the sale of those drugs, I must keep my mother, and of course at her age she would not leave the place she had been used to. And I had made up my mind against what they call genteel businesses."

"But suppose every one did as you do? Please to forgive me for saying so; but I cannot see why you could not have lived as honourably with some employment that presupposes education and refinement."

"Because you can't see my history or my nature," said Felix, bluntly. "I have to determine for myself, and not for other men. I don't blame them, or think I am better than they; their circumstances are different. I would never choose to withdraw myself from the labour and common burthen of the world; but I do choose to withdraw myself from the push and the scramble for money and position. Any man is at liberty to call me a fool, and say that mankind are benefited by the push and the scramble in the long-run. But I care for the people who live now and will not be living when the long-run comes. As it is, I prefer going shares with the unlucky."

Esther did not speak, and there was silence between them for a minute or two, till they passed through a gate into a plantation where there was no large timber, but only thin-stemmed trees and underwood, so that the sunlight fell on the mossy spaces which lay open here and there.

"See how beautiful those stooping birch-stems are with the light on them!" said Felix. "Here is an old felled trunk they have not thought worth carrying away. Shall we sit down a little while?"

"Yes, the mossy ground with the dry leaves sprinkled over it is delightful to one's feet." Esther sat down and took off her bonnet, that the light breeze might fall on her head. Felix, too, threw down his cap and stick, lying on the ground with his back against the felled trunk.

"I wish I felt more as you do," she said, looking at the point of her foot, which was playing with a tuft of moss. "I can't help caring very much what happens to me. And you seem to care so little about yourself."

"You are thoroughly mistaken," said Felix. "It is just because I'm a very ambitious fellow, with very hungry passions, wanting a great deal to satisfy me, that I have chosen to give up what people call worldly good. At least that has been one determining reason. It all depends on what a man gets into his consciousness—what life thrusts into his mind, so that it becomes present to him as remorse is present to the guilty, or a mechanical problem to an inventive genius. There are two things I've got present in that way: one of them is the picture of what I should hate to be. I'm determined never to go about making my face simpering or solemn, and telling professional lies for profit; or to get tangled in affairs where I must wink at dishonesty and pocket the proceeds, and justify that knavery as part of a system that I can't alter. If I once went into that sort of struggle for success, I should want to win—I should defend the wrong that I had once identified myself with. I should become everything that I see now beforehand to be detestable. And what's more, I should do this, as men are doing it every day, for a ridiculously small prize—perhaps for none at all—perhaps for the sake of two parlours, a rank eligible for the churchwardenship, a discontented wife and several unhopeful children."

Esther felt a terrible pressure on her heart—the certainty of her remoteness from Felix—the sense that she was utterly trivial to him.

"The other thing that's got into my mind like a splinter," said Felix, after a pause, "is the life of the miserable—the spawning life of vice and hunger. I'll never be one of the sleek dogs. The old Catholics are right, with their higher rule and their lower. Some are called to subject themselves to a harder discipline, and renounce things voluntarily which are lawful for others. It is the old word—'necessity is laid upon me.' "

"It seems to me you are stricter than my father is."

"No! I quarrel with no delight that is not base or cruel, but one must sometimes accommodate oneself to a small share. That is the lot of the majority. I would wish the minority joy, only they don't want my wishes."

Again there was silence. Esther's cheeks were hot in spite of the breeze that sent her hair floating backward. She felt an inward strain, a demand on her to see things in a light that was not easy or soothing. When Felix had asked to walk, he had seemed so kind, so alive to what might be her feelings, that she had thought herself nearer to him than she had ever been before; but since they had come out, he had appeared to forget all that. And yet she was conscious that this impatience of hers was very petty. Battling in this way with her own little impulses, and looking at the birch-stems opposite till her gaze was too wide for her to see anything distinctly, she was unaware how long they had remained without speaking. She did not know that Felix had changed his attitude a little, and was resting his elbow on the tree-trunk, while he supported his head, which was turned towards her. Suddenly he said, in a lower tone than was habitual to him.

"You are very beautiful."

She started and looked round at him, to see whether his face would give some help to the interpretation of this novel speech. He was looking up at her quite calmly, very much as a reverential Protestant might look at a picture of the Virgin, with a devoutness suggested by the type rather than by the image. Esther's vanity was not in the least gratified: she felt that, somehow or other, Felix was going to reproach her.

"I wonder," he went on, still looking at her, "whether the subtle measuring of forces will ever come to measuring the force there would be in one beautiful woman whose mind was as noble as her face was beautiful—who made a man's passion for her rush in one current with all the great aims of his life."

Esther's eyes got hot and smarting. It was no use trying to be dignified. She had turned away her head, and now said, rather bitterly, "It is difficult for a woman ever to try to be anything good when she is not believed in—when it is always supposed that she must be contemptible."

"No, dear Esther"—it was the first time Felix had been prompted to call her by her Christian name, and as he did so he laid his large hand on her two little hands, which were clasped on her knees. "You don't believe that I think you contemptible. When I first saw you—"

"I know, I know," said Esther, interrupting him impetuously, but still looking away. "You mean you did think me contemptible then. But it was very narrow of you to judge me in that way, when my life had been so different from yours. I have great faults. I know I am selfish, and think too much of my own small tastes and too little of what affects others. But I am not stupid. I am not unfeeling. I can see what is better."

"But I have not done you injustice since I knew more of you," said Felix, gently.

"Yes, you have," said Esther, turning and smiling at him through her tears. "You talk to me like an angry pedagogue.

Were *you* always wise? Remember the time when you were foolish or naughty."

"That is not far off," said Felix, curtly, taking away his hand and clasping it with the other at the back of his head. The talk, which seemed to be introducing a mutual understanding, such as had not existed before, seemed to have undergone some check.

"Shall we get up and walk back now?" said Esther, after a few moments.

"No," said Felix, entreatingly. "Don't move yet. I dare say we shall never walk together or sit here again."

"Why not?"

"Because I am a man who am warned by visions. Those old stories of visions and dreams guiding men have their truth: we are saved by making the future present to ourselves."

"I wish I could get visions, then," said Esther, smiling at him, with an effort at playfulness, in resistance to something vaguely mournful within her.

"That is what I want," said Felix, looking at her very earnestly. "Don't turn your head. Do look at me, and then I shall know if I may go on speaking. I do believe in you; but I want you to have such a vision of the future that you may never lose your best self. Some charm or other may be flung about you—some of your atta-of-rose fascinations—and nothing but a good strong terrible vision will save you. And if it did save you, you might be that woman I was thinking of a little while ago when I looked at your face: the woman whose beauty makes a great task easier to men instead of turning them away from it. I am not likely to see such fine issues; but they may come where a woman's spirit is finely touched. I should like to be sure they would come to you."

"Why are you not likely to know what becomes of me?" said Esther, turning away her eyes in spite of his command. "Why should you not always be my father's friend and mine?"

"O, I shall go away as soon as I can to some large town," said Felix, in his more usual tone,—"some ugly, wicked, miserable place. I want to be a demagogue of a new sort; an honest one, if possible, who will tell the people they are blind and foolish, and neither flatter them nor fatten on them. I have my heritage—an order I belong to. I have the blood of a line of handicraftsmen in my veins, and I want to stand up for the lot of the handicraftsman as a good lot, in which a man may be better trained to all the best functions of his nature than if he belonged to the grimacing set who have visiting-cards, and are proud to be thought richer than their neighbours."

"Would nothing ever make it seem right to you to change your mind?" said Esther (she had rapidly woven some possibilities out of the new uncertainties in her own lot, though she would not for the world have had Felix know of her weaving). "Suppose, by some means or other, a fortune might come to you honourably—by marriage, or in any other unexpected way—would you see no change in your course?"

"No," said Felix, peremptorily; "I will never be rich. I don't count that as any peculiar virtue. Some men do well to accept riches, but that is not my inward vocation: I have no fellow-feeling with the rich as a class; the habits of their lives are odious to me. Thousands of men have wedded poverty because they expect to go to heaven for it; I don't expect to go to heaven for it, but I wed it because it enables me to do what I most want to do on earth. Whatever the hopes for the world may be—whether great or small—I am a man of this generation; I will try to make life less bitter for a few within my reach. It is held reasonable enough to toil for the fortunes of a family, though it may turn to imbecility in the third generation. I choose a family with more chances in it."

Esther looked before her dreamily till she said, "That seems a hard lot; yet it is a great one." She rose to walk back.

"Then you don't think I'm a fool," said Felix, loudly, starting to his feet, and then stooping to gather up his cap and stick.

"Of course you suspected me of that stupidity."

"Well—women, unless they are Saint Theresas or Elizabeth Frys, generally think this sort of thing madness, unless when they read of it in the Bible."

"A woman can hardly ever choose in that way; she is dependent on what happens to her. She must take meaner things, because only meaner things are within her reach."

"Why, can you imagine yourself choosing hardship as the better lot?" said Felix, looking at her with a sudden question in his eyes.

"Yes, I can," she said, flushing over neck and brow.

Their words were charged with a meaning dependent entirely on the secret consciousness of each. Nothing had been said which was necessarily personal. They walked a few yards along the road by which they had come, without further speech, till Felix said gently, "Take my arm." She took it, and they walked home so, entirely without conversation. Felix was struggling as a firm man struggles with a temptation, seeing beyond it and disbelieving its lying promise. Esther was struggling as a woman struggles with the yearning for some expression of love, and with vexation under that subjection to a yearning which is not likely to be satisfied. Each was conscious of a silence which each was unable to break, till they entered Malthouse Lane, and were within a few yards of the minister's door.

"It is getting dusk," Felix then said; "will Mr. Lyon be anxious about you?"

"No, I think not. Lyddy would tell him that I went out with you, and that you carried a large stick," said Esther, with her light laugh.

Felix went in with Esther to take tea, but the conversation was entirely between him and Mr. Lyon about the tricks of canvassing, the foolish personality of the placards, and the probabilities of Transome's return, as to which Felix declared himself to have become indifferent. This scepticism made the minister uneasy: he had great belief in the old political watchwords, had preached that universal suffrage and no ballot were agreeable to the will of God, and liked to believe that a visible "instrument" was forthcoming in the Radical Candidate who had pronounced emphatically against Whig finality. Felix, being in a perverse mood, contended that universal suffrage would be equally agreeable to the devil; that he would change his politics a little, have a larger traffic, and see himself more fully represented in Parliament.

"Nay, my friend," said the minister, "you are again sporting with paradox; for you will not deny that you glory in the name of Radical, or Root-and-branch man, as they said in the great times when Nonconformity was in its giant youth."

"A Radical—yes; but I want to go to some roots a good deal lower down than the franchise."

"Truly there is work within which cannot be dispensed with; but it is our preliminary work to free men from the stifled life of political nullity, and bring them into what Milton calls 'the liberal air,' wherein alone can be wrought the final triumphs of the Spirit."

"With all my heart. But while Caliban is Caliban, though you multiply him by a million, he'll worship every Trinculo that carries a bottle. I forget, though—you don't read Shakespeare, Mr. Lyon."

"I am bound to confess that I have so far looked into a volume of Esther's as to conceive your meaning; but the fantasies therein were so little to be reconciled with a steady contemplation of that divine economy which is hidden from sense and revealed to faith, that I forbore the reading, as likely to perturb my ministrations."

Esther sat by in unusual silence. The conviction that Felix willed her exclusion from his life was making it plain that something more than friendship between them was not so thoroughly out of the question as she had always inwardly asserted. In her pain that his choice lay aloof from her, she was compelled frankly to admit to herself the longing that it had been otherwise, and that he had entreated her to share his difficult life. He was like no one else to her: he had seemed to bring at once a law, and the love that gave strength to obey the law. Yet the next moment, stung by his independence of her, she denied that she loved him; she had only longed for a moral support under the negations of her life. If she were not to have that support, all effort seemed useless.

Esther had been so long used to hear the formulas of her father's belief without feeling or understanding them, that they had lost all power to touch her. The first religious experience of her life—the first self-questioning, the first voluntary subjection, the first longing to acquire the strength of greater motives and obey the more strenuous rule—had come to her through Felix Holt. No wonder that she felt as if the loss of him were inevitable backsliding.

But was it certain that she should lose him? She did not believe that he was really indifferent to her.

. . . .

The group round the speaker in the flannel shirt stood at the corner of a side-street, and the speaker himself was elevated by the head and shoulders above his hearers, not because he was tall, but because he stood on a projecting stone. At the opposite corner of the turning was the great inn of the Fox and Hounds, and this was the ultra-Liberal quarter of the High Street. Felix was at once attracted by this group; he liked the look of the speaker, whose bare arms were powerfully muscular, though he had the pallid complexion of a man who lives chiefly amidst the heat of furnaces. He was leaning against the dark stone building behind him with folded arms, the grimy paleness of his shirt and skin standing out in high relief against the dark stone building behind him. He lifted up one forefinger, and marked his emphasis with it as he spoke. His voice was high and not strong, but Felix recognized the fluency and the method of a habitual preacher or lecturer.

"It's the fallacy of all monopolists," he was saying. "We know what monopolists are: men who want to keep a trade all to themselves, under the pretence that they'll furnish the public with a better article. We know what that comes to: in some countries a poor man can't afford to buy a spoonful of salt, and yet there's salt enough in the world to pickle every living thing in it. That's the sort of benefit monopolists do to mankind. And these are the men who tell us we're to let politics alone; they'll govern us better without our knowing anything about it. We must mind our business; we are ignorant; we've no time to study great questions. But I tell them this: the greatest question in the world is, how to give every man a man's share in what goes on in life—"

"Hear, hear!" said Felix, in his sonorous voice, which seemed to give a new impressiveness to what the speaker had said. Every one looked at him: the well-washed face and its educated expression along with a dress more careless than that of most well-to-do workmen on a holiday, made his appearance strangely arresting.

"Not a pig's share," the speaker went on, "not a horse's share, not the share of a machine fed with oil only to make it work and nothing else. It isn't a man's share just to mind your pin-making, or your glass-blowing, and higgle about your own wages, and bring up your family to be ignorant sons of ignorant fathers, and no better prospect; that's a slave's share; we want a freeman's share, and that is to think and speak and act about what concerns us all, and see whether these fine gentlemen who undertake to govern us are doing the best they can for us. They've got the knowledge, say they. Very well, we've got the wants. There's many a one would be idle if hunger didn't pinch him; but the stomach sets us to work. There's a fable told where the nobles are the belly and the people the members. But I make another sort of fable. I say, we are the belly that feels the pinches, and we'll set these aristocrats, these great people who call themselves our brains, to work at some way of satisfying us a bit better. The aristocrats are pretty sure to try and govern for their own benefit; but how are we to be sure they'll try and govern for ours? They must be looked after, I think, like other workmen. We must have what we call inspectors, to see whether the work's well done for us. We want to send our inspectors to Parliament. Well, they say—you've got the Reform Bill; what more can you want? Send your inspectors. But I say, the Reform Bill is a trick—it's nothing but swearing-in special constables to keep the aristocrats safe in their monopoly; it's bribing some of the people with votes to make them hold their tongues about giving votes to the rest. I say, if a man doesn't beg or steal, but works for his bread, the poorer and the more miserable he is, the more he'd need have a vote to send an inspector to Parliament—else the man who is worst off is likely to be forgotten; and I say, he's the man who ought to be first remembered. Else what does their religion mean? Why do they build churches and endow them that their sons may get paid well for preaching a Saviour, and making themselves as little like Him as can be? If I want to believe in Jesus Christ,

I must shut my eyes for fear I should see a parson. And what's a bishop? A bishop's a parson dressed up, who sits in the House of Lords to help and throw out Reform Bills. And because it's hard to get anything in the shape of a man to dress himself up like that, and do such work, they give him a palace for it, and plenty of thousands a-year. And then they cry out—'The Church is in danger,'—'the poor man's Church.' And why is it the poor man's Church? Because he can have a seat for nothing. I think it *is* for nothing; for it would be hard to tell what he gets by it. If the poor man had a vote in the matter, I think he'd choose a different sort of a Church to what that is. But do you think the aristocrats will ever alter it, if the belly doesn't pinch them? Not they. It's part of their monopoly. They'll supply us with our religion like everything else, and get a profit on it. They'll give us plenty of heaven. We may have land *there*. That's the sort of religion they like— a religion that gives us working men heaven, and nothing else. But we'll offer to change with 'em. We'll give them back some of their heaven, and take it out in something for us and our children in this world. They don't seem to care so much about heaven themselves till they feel the gout very bad; but you won't get them to give up anything else, if you don't pinch 'em for it. And to pinch them enough, we must get the suffrage, we must get votes, that we may send the men to Parliament who will do our work for us; and we must have Parliament dissolved every year, that we may change our man if he doesn't do what we want him to do; and we must have the country divided so that the little kings of the counties can't do as they like, but must be shaken up in one bag with us. I say, if we working men are ever to get a man's share, we must have universal suffrage, and annual Parliaments, and the vote by ballot, and electoral districts."

"No!—something else before all that," said Felix, again startling the audience into looking at him. But the speaker glanced coldly at him and went on.

"That's what Sir Francis Burdett went in for fifteen years ago; and it's the right thing for us, if it was Tomfool who went in for it. You must lay hold of such handles as you can. I don't believe much in Liberal aristocrats; but if there's any fine carved gold-headed stick of an aristocrat will make a broomstick of himself, I'll lose no time but I'll sweep with him. And that's what I think about Transome. And if any of you have acquaintance among county voters, give 'em a hint that you wish 'em to vote for Transome."

At the last word, the speaker stepped down from his slight eminence, and walked away rapidly, like a man whose leisure was exhausted, and who must go about his business. But he had left an appetite in his audience for further oratory, and one of them seemed to express a general sentiment as he turned immediately to Felix, and said, "Come, sir, what do you say?"

Felix did at once what he would very likely have done without being asked—he stepped on to the stone, and took off his cap by an instinctive prompting that always led him to speak uncovered. The effect of his figure in relief against the stone background was unlike that of the previous speaker. He was considerably taller, his head and neck were more massive, and the expression of his mouth and eyes was something very different from the mere acuteness and rather hard-lipped antagonism of the trades-union man. Felix Holt's face had the look of habitual meditative abstraction from objects of mere personal vanity or desire, which is the peculiar stamp of culture, and makes a very roughly-cut face worthy to be called "the human face divine." Even lions and dogs know a distinction between men's glances; and doubtless those Duffield men, in the expectation with which they looked up at Felix, were unconsciously influenced by the grandeur of his full yet firm mouth, and the calm clearness of his grey eyes, which were somehow unlike what they were accustomed to see along with an old brown velveteen coat, and an absence of chin-propping. When he began to speak, the contrast of voice was still stronger than that of appearance. The man in the flannel shirt had not been heard—had probably not cared to be heard—beyond the immediate group of listeners. But Felix at once drew the attention of persons comparatively at a distance.

"In my opinion," he said, almost the moment after he was addressed, "that was a true word spoken by your friend when he said the great question was how to give every man a man's share in life. But I think he expects voting to do more towards it than I do. I want the working men to have power. I'm a working man myself, and I don't want to be anything else. But there are two sorts of power. There's a power to do mischief—to undo what has been done with great expense and labour, to waste and destroy, to be cruel to the weak, to lie and quarrel, and to talk poisonous nonsense. That's the sort of power that ignorant numbers have. It never made a joint stool or planted a potato. Do you think it's likely to do much towards governing a great country, and making wise laws, and giving shelter, food, and clothes to millions of men? Ignorant power comes in the end to the same thing as wicked power; it makes misery. It's another sort of power that I want us working men to have, and I can see plainly enough that our all having votes will do little towards it at present. I hope we, or the children that come after us, will get plenty of political power some time. I tell everybody plainly, I hope there will be great changes, and that some time, whether we live to see it or not, men will have come to be ashamed of things they're proud of now. But I should like to convince you that votes would never give you political power worth having while things are as they are now, and that if you go the right way to work you may get power sooner without votes. Perhaps all you who hear me are sober men, who try to learn as much of the nature of things as you can, and to be as little like fools as possible. A fool or idiot is one who expects things to happen that never can happen; he pours milk into a can without a bottom, and expects the milk to stay there. The more of such vain expectations a man has, the more he is of a fool or idiot. And if any working man expects a vote to do for him what it never can do, he's foolish to that amount, if no more. I think that's clear enough, eh?"

"Hear, hear," said several voices, but they were not those of the original group; they belonged to some strollers who had been attracted by Felix Holt's vibrating voice, and were Tories from the Crown. Among them was Christian, who was smoking a cigar with a pleasure he always felt in being among people who did not know him, and doubtless took him to be something higher than he really was. Hearers from the Fox and Hounds also were slowly adding themselves to the nucleus. Felix, accessible to the pleasure of being listened to, went on with more and more animation:

"The way to get rid of folly is to get rid of vain expectations, and of thoughts that don't agree with the nature of things. The men who have had true thoughts about water, and what it will do when it is turned into steam and under all sorts of circumstances, have made themselves a great power in the world: they are turning the wheels of engines that will help to change most things. But no engines would have done, if there had been false notions about the way water would act. Now, all the schemes about voting, and districts, and annual Parliaments, and the rest, are engines, and the water or steam—the force that is to work them—must come out of human nature—out of men's passions, feelings, desires. Whether the engines will do good work or bad depends on these feelings; and if we have false expectations about men's characters, we are very much like the idiot who thinks he'll carry milk in a can without a bottom. In my opinion, the notions about what mere voting will do are very much of that sort."

"That's very fine," said a man in dirty fustian, with a scornful laugh. "But how are we to get the power without votes?"

"I'll tell you what's the greatest power under heaven," said Felix, "and that is public opinion—the ruling belief in society about what is right and what is wrong, what is honourable and what is shameful. That's the steam that is to work the engines. How can political freedom make us better, any more than a religion we don't believe in, if people laugh and wink when they see men abuse and defile it? And while public opinion is what it is—while men have no better beliefs about public duty—while corruption is not felt to be a damning disgrace—while men are not ashamed in Parliament and out of it to make public questions which concern the welfare of millions a mere screen for their own petty private ends,—I say, no fresh scheme of voting will much mend our condition. For, take us working men of all sorts. Suppose out of every hundred who had a vote there were thirty who had some soberness, some sense to choose with, some good feeling to make them wish the right thing for all. And suppose there were seventy out of the hundred who were, half of them, not sober, who had no sense to choose one thing in politics more than another, and who had so little good feeling in them that they wasted on their own drinking the money that should have helped to feed and clothe their wives and children; and another half of them who, if they didn't drink, were too ignorant or mean or stupid to see any good for themselves better than pocketing a five-shilling piece when it was offered them. Where would be the political power of the thirty sober men? The power would lie with the seventy drunken and stupid votes; and I'll tell you what sort of men would get the power—what sort of men would end by returning whom they pleased to Parliament."

Felix had seen every face around him, and had particularly noticed a recent addition to his audience; but now he looked before him without appearing to fix his glance on any one. In spite of his cooling meditations an hour ago, his pulse was getting quickened by indignation, and the desire to crush what he hated was likely to vent itself in articulation. His tone became more biting.

"They would be men who would undertake to do the business for a candidate, and return him: men who have no real opinions, but who pilfer the words of every opinion, and turn them into a cant which will serve their purpose at the moment; men who look out for dirty work to make their fortunes by, because dirty work wants little talent and no conscience; men who know all the ins and outs of bribery, because there is not a cranny in their own souls where a bribe can't enter. Such men as these will be the masters wherever there's a majority of voters who care more for money, more for drink, more for some mean little end which is their own and nobody else's, than for anything that has ever been called Right in the world. For suppose there's a poor voter named Jack, who has seven children, and twelve or fifteen shillings a-week wages, perhaps less. Jack can't read—I don't say whose fault that is—he never had the chance to learn; he knows so little that he perhaps thinks God made the poor-laws, and if anybody said the pattern of the workhouse was laid down in the Testament, he wouldn't be able to contradict them. What is poor Jack likely to do when he sees a smart stranger coming to him, who happens to be just one of those men that I say will be the masters till public opinion gets too hot for them? He's a middle-sized man, we'll say; stout, with coat upon coat of fine broadcloth, open enough to show a fine gold chain: none of your dark, scowling men, but one with an innocent pink-and-white skin and very smooth light hair—a most respectable man, who calls himself by a good, sound, well-known English name—as Green, or Baker, or Wilson, or, let us say, Johnson—"

FYODOR DOSTOEVSKY

Fyodor Dostoevsky (1821–81), born in Moscow, was a Russian novelist, journalist, and short-story writer whose work is best known for its psychological penetration into the human soul. He was arrested in 1849 due to his affiliation with a group of utopian socialists, and was sentenced to death. At the moment of facing the firing squad, his sentence was commuted to imprisonment in Siberia, where he spent the next four years. Released from prison and military service by 1858, Dostoevsky began a fourteen-year period of intensely committed writing in which he published many significant texts. Among these was *Crime and Punishment* (1866), a novel in which Dostoevsky first develops the theme of redemption through suffering.

In 1880, a year before his death, Dostoevsky published *The Brothers Karamazov,* a family drama viewed by many as one of the great works of literature for its existentialist probing into life's meaning. Within the novel, Dostoevsky debates the notion of mankind's ability to handle freedom in "The Grand Inquisitor": freedom, ironically, as a source of anxiety, even a threat, as opposed to a gift of human possibility.

Throughout his writing life, Dostoevsky put into storytelling what he had personally experienced—a nation's citizen becoming its close observer, insistent critic, and earnest advocate of change. He saw politics as both an opportunity and a danger. In his fiction, Dostoevsky offers protagonists who ask the reader to consider his or her obligation to the world; and he forces us to consider what moral or spiritual purposes we act upon. Politics, then, becomes an arena for human expression, argument, introspection.

From THE BROTHERS KARAMAZOV

" 'Decide yourself who was right: you or the one who questioned you then? Recall the first question; its meaning, though not literally, was this: "You want to go into the world, and you are going empty-handed, with some promise of freedom, which they in their simplicity and innate lawlessness cannot even comprehend, which they dread and fear—for nothing has ever been more insufferable for man and for human society than freedom! But do you see these stones in this bare, scorching desert? Turn them into bread and mankind will run after you like sheep, grateful and obedient, though eternally trembling lest you withdraw your hand and your loaves cease for them." But you did not want to deprive man of freedom and rejected the offer, for what sort of freedom is it, you reasoned, if obedience is bought with loaves of bread? You objected that man does not live by bread alone, but do you know that in the name of this very earthly bread, the spirit of the earth will rise against you and fight with you and defeat you, and everyone will follow him exclaiming:

"Who can compare to this beast, for he has given us fire from heaven!" Do you know that centuries will pass and mankind will proclaim with the mouth of its wisdom and science that there is no crime, and therefore no sin, but only hungry men? "Feed them first, then ask virtue of them!"—that is what they will write on the banner they raise against you, and by which your temple will be destroyed. In place of your temple a new edifice will be raised, the terrible Tower of Babel will be raised again, and though, like the former one, this one will not be completed either, still you could have avoided this new tower and shortened people's suffering by a thousand years—for it is to us they will come after suffering for a thousand years with their tower! They will seek us out again, underground, in catacombs, hiding (for again we shall be persecuted and tortured), they will find us and cry out: "Feed us, for those who promised us fire from heaven did not give it." And then we shall finish building their tower, for only he who feeds them will finish it, and only we shall feed them, in your name, for we shall lie that it is in your name. Oh, never, never will they feed themselves without us! No science will give them bread as long as they remain free, but in the end they will lay their freedom at our feet and say to us: "Better that you enslave us, but feed us." They will finally understand that freedom and earthly bread in plenty for everyone are inconceivable together, for never, never will they be able to share among themselves. They will also be convinced that they are forever incapable of being free, because they are feeble, depraved, nonentities and rebels. You promised them heavenly bread, but, I repeat again, can it compare with

earthly bread in the eyes of the weak, eternally depraved, and
eternally ignoble human race? And if in the name of heavenly
bread thousands and tens of thousands will follow you, what
will become of the millions and tens of thousands of millions
of creatures who will not be strong enough to forgo earthly
bread for the sake of the heavenly? Is it that only the tens of
thousands of the great and strong are dear to you, and the remaining millions, numerous as the sands of the sea, weak but
loving you, should serve only as material for the great and the
strong? No, the weak, too, are dear to us. They are depraved
and rebels, but in the end it is they who will become obedient. They will marvel at us, and look upon us as gods, because we, standing at their head, have agreed to suffer
freedom and to rule over them—so terrible will it become for
them in the end to be free! But we shall say that we are obedient to you and rule in your name. We shall deceive them
again, for this time we shall not allow you to come to us. This
deceit will constitute our suffering, for we shall have to lie.
This is what that first question in the wilderness meant, and
this is what you rejected in the name of freedom, which you
placed above everything. And yet this question contains the
great mystery of this world. Had you accepted the "loaves,"
you would have answered the universal and everlasting anguish of man as an individual being, and of the whole of
mankind together, namely: "before whom shall I bow down?"
There is no more ceaseless or tormenting care for man, as
long as he remains free, than to find someone to bow down to
as soon as possible. But man seeks to bow down before that
which is indisputable, so indisputable that all men at once

would agree to the universal worship of it. For the care of these pitiful creatures is not just to find something before which I or some other man can bow down, but to find something that everyone else will also believe in and bow down to, for it must needs be *all together*. And this need for *communality* of worship is the chief torment of each man individually, and of mankind as a whole, from the beginning of the ages. In the cause of universal worship, they have destroyed each other with the sword. They have made gods and called upon each other: "Abandon your gods and come and worship ours, otherwise death to you and your gods!" And so it will be until the end of the world, even when all gods have disappeared from the earth: they will still fall down before idols. You knew, you could not but know, this essential mystery of human nature, but you rejected the only absolute banner, which was offered to you to make all men bow down to you indisputably—the banner of earthly bread; and you rejected it in the name of freedom and heavenly bread. Now see what you did next. And all again in the name of freedom! I tell you that man has no more tormenting care than to find someone to whom he can hand over as quickly as possible that gift of freedom with which the miserable creature is born. But he alone can take over the freedom of men who appeases their conscience. With bread you were given an indisputable banner: give man bread and he will bow down to you, for there is nothing more indisputable than bread. But if at the same time someone else takes over his conscience—oh, then he will even throw down your bread and follow him who has seduced his conscience. In this you were right. For the mystery of man's being is not only in living, but in what one lives for. Without a firm idea of what he lives for, man will not consent to live and will sooner destroy himself than remain on earth, even if there is bread all around him. That is so, but what came of it? Instead of taking over men's freedom, you increased it still more for them! Did you forget that peace and even death are dearer to man than free choice in the knowledge of good and evil? There is nothing more seductive for man than the freedom of his conscience, but there is nothing more tormenting either. And so, instead of a firm foundation for appeasing human conscience once and for all, you chose everything that was unusual, enigmatic, and indefinite, you chose everything that was beyond men's strength, and thereby acted as if you did not love them at all—and who did this? He who came to give his life for them! Instead of taking over men's freedom, you increased it and forever burdened the kingdom of the human soul with its torments. You desired the free love of man, that he should follow you freely, seduced and captivated by you. Instead of the firm ancient law, man had henceforth to decide for himself, with a free heart, what is good and what is evil, having only your image before him as a guide—but did it not occur to you that he would eventually reject and dispute even your image and your truth if he was oppressed by so terrible a burden as freedom of choice? They will finally cry out that the truth is not in you, for it was impossible to leave them in greater confusion and torment than you did, abandoning them to so many cares and insoluble problems. Thus you yourself laid the foundation for the destruction of your own kingdom, and do not blame anyone else for it. Yet is this what was offered you? There are three powers, only three powers on earth, capable of conquering and holding captive forever the conscience of these feeble rebels, for their own happiness—these powers are miracle, mystery, and authority. You rejected the first, the second, and the third, and gave yourself as an example of that.' "

ANTHONY TROLLOPE

Anthony Trollope (1815–82) was born in London, England. He wrote forty-seven novels and five volumes of short stories, as well as travel books, biographies, and collections of short sketches. Due to poverty and debt, Trollope's childhood was acutely unhappy and his education was continually disrupted. In 1834, at the age of nineteen, he became a junior clerk in the General Post Office in London. Working most of his professional life in the postal service, Trollope traveled abroad frequently until he resigned in 1867. A year later, Trollope was defeated in his single attempt to enter Parliament as a Liberal.

He is best known for the "Barsetshire" series (*Barchester Towers, Doctor Thorne, Framley Parsonage, The Small House at Allington,* and *The Last Chronicle of Barset*), as well as the six "Palliser"—or "political"—novels, a series about a fictional family of nobles that includes *Can You Forgive Her? Phineas Finn, The Eustace Diamonds, Phineas Redux, The Prime Minister,* and *The Duke's Children.*

Trollope's work offers an unsurpassed portrait of the professional and landed classes of Victorian England. To my mind, he was the ideal political novelist; Trollope ran for political office, was an astute writer, and he had a kind of political concentration that others did not have. Trollope knew personally of what he wrote—his stories are a documentary portrayal of political life as it plays out in daily dealings among political leaders; an unfolding saga with characters who contemplate, connive, win or lose.

In these selections from *The Prime Minister,* Trollope's fictitious prime minister contemplates his first month in office and how ill-suited he is for the position; he fears being a *fainéant,* or do-nothing, leader. In the fourth selection, the old duke describes the attributes of a good prime minister: "One wants in a Prime Minister a good many things, but not very great things." And later, the wife of the prime minister describes what she considers to be good political leadership: "When I see a man who is supposed to have earned the name of a statesman, and been high in the councils of his sovereign, induced by personal jealousy to do as he is doing, it makes me feel that an honest man should not place himself where he may have to deal with such persons."

From THE PRIME MINISTER

At about nine the Duke had returned, and was eating his very simple dinner in the breakfast-room—a beefsteak and a potato, with a glass of sherry and Apollinaris water. No man more easily satisfied as to what he eat and drank lived in London in those days. As regarded the eating and drinking he dined alone, but his wife sat with him and waited on him, having sent the servant out of the room. "I have told her Majesty that I would do the best I could," said the Duke.

"Then you are Prime Minister."

"Not at all. Mr. Daubeny is Prime Minister. I have undertaken to form a ministry, if I find it practicable, with the assistance of such friends as I possess. I never felt before that I had to lean so entirely on others as I do now."

"Lean on yourself only. Be enough for yourself."

"Those are empty words, Cora;—words that are quite empty. In one sense a man should always be enough for himself. He should have enough of principle and enough of conscience to restrain him from doing what he knows to be wrong. But can a shipbuilder build his ship single-handed, or the watchmaker make his watch without assistance? On former occasions such as this, I could say, with little or no help from without, whether I would or would not undertake the work that was proposed to me, because I had only a bit of the ship to build, or a wheel of the watch to make. My own efficacy for my present task depends entirely on the co-operation of others, and unfortunately upon that of some others with whom I have no sympathy, nor have they with me."

"Leave them out," said the Duchess boldly.

"But they are men who will not be left out, and whose services the country has a right to expect."

"Then bring them in, and think no more about it. It is no good crying for pain that cannot be cured."

"Co-operation is difficult without community of feeling. I find myself to be too stubborn-hearted for the place. It was nothing to me to sit in the same Cabinet with a man I disliked when I had not put him there myself. But now—. As I have travelled up I have almost felt that I could not do it! I did not know before how much I might dislike a man."

"Who is the one man?"

"Nay;—whoever he be, he will have to be a friend now, and therefore I will not name him, even to you. But it is not one only. If it were one, absolutely marked and recognized, I might avoid him. But my friends, real friends, are so few! Who is there besides the Duke on whom I can lean with both confidence and love?"

"Lord Cantrip."

"Hardly so, Cora. But Lord Cantrip goes out with Mr. Gresham. They will always cling together."

"You used to like Mr. Mildmay."

"Mr. Mildmay,—yes! If there could be a Mr. Mildmay in the Cabinet this trouble would not come upon my shoulders."

"Then I'm very glad that there can't be a Mr. Mildmay. Why shouldn't there be as good fish in the sea as ever were caught out of it?"

"When you've got a good fish you like to make as much of it as you can."

"I suppose Mr. Monk will join you."

"I think we shall ask him. But I am not prepared to discuss men's names as yet."

"You must discuss them with the Duke immediately."

"Probably;—but I had better discuss them with him before I fix my own mind by naming them even to you."

"You'll bring Mr. Finn in, Plantagenet?"

"Mr. Finn!"

"Yes;—Phineas Finn,—the man who was tried."

"My dear Cora, we haven't come down to that yet. We need not at any rate trouble ourselves about the small fishes till we are sure that we can get big fishes to join us."

"I don't know why he should be a small fish. No man has done better than he has; and if you want a man to stick to you—"

"I don't want a man to stick to me. I want a man to stick to his country."

"You were talking about sympathy."

"Well, yes;—I was. But do not name anyone else just at present. The Duke will be here soon, and I would be alone till he comes."

"There is one thing I want to say, Plantagenet."

"What is it?"

"One favour I want to ask."

"Pray do not ask anything for any man just at present."

"It is not anything for any man."

"Nor for any woman."

"It is for a woman,—but one whom I think you would wish to oblige."

"Who is it?" Then she curtseyed, smiling at him drolly, and put her hand upon her breast. "Something for you! What on earth can you want that I can do for you?"

"Will you do it,—if it be reasonable?"

"If I think it reasonable, I certainly will do it."

Then her manner changed altogether, and she became serious and almost solemn. "If, as I suppose, all the great places about her Majesty be changed, I should like to be Mistress of the Robes."

"You!" said he, almost startled out of his usual quiet demeanour.

"Why not I? Is not my rank high enough?"

"You burden yourself with the intricacies and subserviences, with the tedium and pomposities of Court life! Cora, you do not know what you are talking about, or what you are proposing for yourself."

"If I am willing to try to undertake a duty, why should I be debarred from it any more than you?"

"Because I have put myself into a groove, and ground myself into a mould, and clipped and pared and pinched myself all round,—very ineffectually as I fear,—to fit myself for this thing. You have lived as free as air. You have disdained,—and though I may have grumbled I have still been proud to see you disdain,—to wrap yourself in the swaddling bandages of Court life. You have ridiculed all those who have been near her Majesty as Court ladies."

"The individuals, Plantagenet, perhaps; but not the office. I am getting older now, and I do not see why I should not begin a new life." She had been somewhat quelled by his unexpected energy, and was at the moment hardly able to answer him with her usual spirit.

"Do not think of it, my dear. You asked whether your rank was high enough. It must be so, as there is, as it happens, none higher. But your position, should it come to pass that your husband is the head of the Government, will be too high. I may say that in no condition should I wish my wife to be subject to other restraint than that which is common to all married women. I should not choose that she should have any duties unconnected with our joint family and home. But as First Minister of the Crown I would altogether object to her holding an office believed to be at my disposal." She looked at him with her large eyes wide open, and then left him without a word. She had no other way of showing her displeasure, for she knew that when he spoke as he had spoken now all argument was unavailing.

The Duke remained an hour alone before he was joined by the other Duke, during which he did not for a moment apply his mind to the subject which might be thought to be most prominent in his thoughts,—the filling up, namely, of a list of his new government. All that he could do in that direction without further assistance had been already done very easily. There were four or five certain names,—names that is of certain political friends, and three or four almost equally certain of men who had been political enemies, but who would now clearly be asked to join the ministry. Sir Gregory Grogram, the late Attorney-General, would of course be asked to resume his place; but Sir Timothy Beeswax, who was up to this moment Solicitor-General for the Conservatives, would also be invited to retain that which he held. Many details were known, not only to the two dukes who were about to patch up the ministry between them, but to the political world at large,—and were facts upon which the newspapers were able to display their wonderful foresight and general omniscience with their usual confidence. And as to the points which were in doubt,—whether or not, for instance, that consistent old Tory, Sir Orlando Drought, should be asked to put up with the Post-office or should be allowed to remain at the

Colonies,—the younger Duke did not care to trouble himself till the elder should have come to his assistance. But his own position and his questionable capacity for filling it,—that occupied all his mind. If nominally first he would be really first. Of so much it seemed to him that his honour required him to assure himself. To be a *fainéant* ruler was in direct antagonism both to his conscience and his predilections. To call himself by a great name before the world, and then to be something infinitely less than that name, would be to him a degradation. But though he felt fixed as to that, he was by no means assured as to that other point, which to most men firm in their resolves as he was, and backed up as he had been by the confidence of others, would be cause of small hesitation. He did doubt his ability to fill that place which it would now be his duty to occupy. He more than doubted. He told himself again and again that there was wanting to him a certain noble capacity for commanding support and homage from other men. With things and facts he could deal, but human beings had not opened themselves to him. But now it was too late! and yet,—as he said to his wife,—to fail would break his heart! No ambition had prompted him. He was sure of himself there. One only consideration had forced him into this great danger, and that had been the assurance of others that it was his manifest duty to encounter it. And now there was clearly no escape,—no escape compatible with that cleanhanded truth from which it was not possible for him to swerve. He might create difficulties in order that through them a way might still be opened to him of restoring to the Queen the commission which had been entrusted to him. He might insist on this or that impossible concession. But the memory of escape such as that would break his heart as surely as the failure.

When the Duke was announced he rose to greet his old friend almost with fervour. "It is a shame," he said, "to bring you out so late. I ought to have gone to you."

"Not at all. It is always the rule in these cases that the man who has most to do should fix himself as well as he can where others may be able to find him." The Duke of St. Bungay was an old man, between seventy and eighty, with hair nearly white, and who on entering the room had to unfold himself out of various coats and comforters. But he was in full possession not only of his intellects but of his bodily power, showing, as many politicians do show, that the cares of the nation may sit upon a man's shoulders for many years without breaking or even bending them. For the Duke had belonged to ministries nearly for the last half century. As the chronicles have also dealt with him, no further records of his past life shall now be given.

He had said something about the Queen, expressing gracious wishes for the comfort of her Majesty in all these matters, something of the inconvenience of these political journeys to and fro, something also of the delicacy and difficulty of the operations on hand which were enhanced by the necessity of bringing men together as cordial allies who had hitherto acted with bitter animosity one to another, before the younger Duke said a word. "We may as well," said the elder, "make out some small provisional list, and you can ask those you name to be with you early to-morrow. But perhaps you have already made a list."

"No indeed. I have not even had a pencil in my hand."

"We may as well begin then," said the elder facing the table when he saw that his less-experienced companion made no attempt at beginning.

"There is something horrible to me in the idea of writing down men's names for such a work as this, just as boys at school used to draw out the elevens for a cricket match." The old stager turned round and stared at the younger politician. "The thing itself is so momentous that one ought to have aid from heaven."

Plantagenet Palliser was the last man from whom the Duke of St. Bungay would have expected romance at any time, and, least of all, at such a time as this. "Aid from heaven you may have," he said, "by saying your prayers; and I don't doubt you ask it for this and all other things generally. But an angel won't come to tell you who ought to be Chancellor of the Exchequer."

"No angel will, and therefore I wish that I could wash my hands of it." His old friend still stared at him. "It is like sacrilege to me, attempting this without feeling one's own fitness for the work. It unmans me,—this necessity of doing that which I know I cannot do with fitting judgment."

"Your mind has been a little too hard at work to-day."

"It hasn't been at work at all. I've had nothing to do, and have been unable really to think of work. But I feel that chance circumstances have put me into a position for which I am unfit, and which yet I have been unable to avoid. How much better would it be that you should do this alone,—you yourself."

"Utterly out of the question. I do know and think that I always have known my own powers. Neither has my aptitude in debate nor my capacity for work justified me in looking to the premiership. But that, forgive me, is now not worthy of consideration. It is because you do work and can work, and because you have fitted yourself for that continued course of lucid explanation which we now call debate, that men on both sides have called upon you as the best man to come forward in this difficulty. Excuse me, my friend, again, if I say that I expect to find your manliness equal to your capacity."

"If I could only escape from it!"

"Psha;—nonsense!" said the old Duke, getting up. "There is such a thing as a conscience with so fine an edge that it will allow a man to do nothing. You've got to serve your country. On such assistance as I can give you you know that you may depend with absolute assurance. Now let us get to work. I suppose you would wish that I should take the chair at the Council."

"Certainly;—of course," said the Duke of Omnium, turning to the table. The one practical suggestion had fixed him, and from that moment he gave himself to the work in hand with all his energies. It was not very difficult, nor did it take them a very long time. If the future Prime Minister had not his names at his fingers' ends, the future President of the Council had them. Eight men were soon named whom it was thought well that the Duke of Omnium should consult early in the morning as to their willingness to fill certain places.

"Each one of them may have some other one or some two whom he may insist on bringing with him," said the elder

Duke; "and though of course you cannot yield to the pressure in every such case, it will be wise to allow yourself scope for some amount of concession. You'll find they'll shake down after the usual amount of resistance and compliance. No;—don't you leave your house to-morrow to see anybody unless it be Mr. Daubeny or her Majesty. I'll come to you at two, and if her Grace will give me luncheon, I'll lunch with her. Good night, and don't think too much of the bigness of the thing. I remember dear old Lord Brock telling me how much more difficult it was to find a good coachman than a good Secretary of State."

The Duke of Omnium, as he sat thinking of things for the next hour in his chair, succeeded only in proving to himself that Lord Brock never ought to have been Prime Minister of England after having ventured to make so poor a joke on so solemn a subject.

. . . .

The Prime Minister at this moment was sitting in his own particular room at the Treasury Chambers, and before the entrance of his friend had been conscientiously endeavouring to define for himself, not a future policy, but the past policy of the last month or two. It had not been for him a very happy occupation. He had become the Head of the Government,—and had not failed, for there he was, still the Head of the Government, with a majority at his back, and the six months' vacation before him. They who were entitled to speak to him confidentially as to his position, were almost vehement in declaring his success. Mr. Rattler, about a week ago, had not seen any reason why the Ministry should not endure at least for the next four years. Mr. Roby, from the other side, was equally confident. But, on looking back at what he had done, and indeed on looking forward into his future intentions, he could not see why he, of all men, should be Prime Minister. He had once been Chancellor of the Exchequer, filling that office through two halcyon sessions, and he had known the reason why he had held it. He had ventured to assure himself at the time that he was the best man whom his party could then have found for that office, and he had been satisfied. But he had none of that satisfaction now. There were men under him who were really at work. The Lord Chancellor had legal reforms on foot. Mr. Monk was busy, heart and soul, in regard to income tax and brewers' licences,—making our poor Prime Minister's mouth water. Lord Drummond was active among the colonies. Phineas Finn had at any rate his ideas about Ireland. But with the Prime Minister,—so at least the Duke told himself,—it was all a blank. The policy confided to him and expected at his hands was that of keeping together a Coalition Ministry. That was a task that did not satisfy him. And now, gradually,—very slowly indeed at first, but still with a sure step,—there was creeping upon him the idea that this power of cohesion was sought for, and perhaps found not in his political capacity, but in his rank and wealth. It might, in fact, be the case that it was his wife the Duchess—that Lady Glencora, of whose wild impulses and general impracticability he had always been in dread,—that she with her dinner parties and receptions, with her crowded saloons, her music, her picnics, and social temptations, was Prime Minister rather than he himself. It might be that this had been understood by the coalesced parties;—by everybody, in fact, except himself. It had, perhaps, been found that in the state of things then existing, a ministry could be best kept together, not by parliamentary capacity, but by social arrangements, such as his Duchess, and his Duchess alone, could carry out. She and she only would have the spirit and the money and the sort of cleverness required. In such a state of things he of course, as her husband, must be the nominal Prime Minister.

There was no anger in his bosom as he thought of this. It would be hardly just to say that there was jealousy. His nature was essentially free from jealousy. But there was shame,—and self-accusation at having accepted so great an office with so little fixed purpose as to great work. It might be his duty to subordinate even his pride to the service of his country, and to consent to be a fainéant minister, a gilded Treasury log, because by remaining in that position he would enable the Government to be carried on. But how base the position, how mean, how repugnant to that grand idea of public work which had hitherto been the motive power of all his life! How would he continue to live if this thing were to go on from year to year,—he pretending to govern while others governed,—stalking about from one public hall to another in a blue ribbon, taking the highest place at all tables, receiving mock reverence, and known to all men as fainéant First Lord of the Treasury?

. . . .

But Phineas Finn had read the Duke's character rightly in saying that he was neither gregarious nor communicative, and therefore but little fitted to rule Englishmen. He had thought that it was so himself, and now from day to day he was becoming more assured of his own deficiency. He could not throw himself into cordial relations with the Sir Orlando Droughts, or even with the Mr. Monks. But, though he had never wished to be put into his present high office, now that he was there he dreaded the sense of failure which would follow his descent from it. It is this feeling rather than genuine ambition, rather than the love of power or patronage or pay, which induces men to cling to place. The absence of real work, and the quantity of mock work, both alike made the life wearisome to him; but he could not endure the idea that it should be written in history that he had allowed himself to be made a fainéant Prime Minister, and then had failed even in that. History would forget what he had done as a working Minister in recording the feebleness of the Ministry which would bear his name.

. . . .

And things were not going smooth with him because there had reached him a most troublous dispatch from Sir Orlando Drought only two days before the Cabinet meeting at which the points to be made in the Queen's speech were to be decided. It had been already agreed that a proposition should be made to Parliament by the Government, for an extension of the county suffrage, with some slight redistribution of seats. The towns with less than 20,000 inhabitants were to take in some increased portions of the country parishes around. But there was not enough of a policy in this to satisfy Sir Orlando, nor was the conduct of the bill through the House to be placed in his hands. That was to be intrusted to Mr. Monk, and Mr. Monk would be, if not nominally the leader, yet the chief man of the Government in the House of Commons. This was displeasing to Sir Orlando, and he had, therefore, demanded from the Prime Minister more of a "policy." Sir Orlando's present idea of a policy was the building of four bigger ships of war than had ever been built before,—with larger guns, and more men, and thicker iron plates, and, above all, with a greater expenditure of money. He had even gone so far as to say, though not in his semi-official letter to the Prime Minister, that he thought that "The Salvation of the Empire" should be the cry of the Coalition party. "After all," he said, "what the people care about is the Salvation of the Empire!" Sir Orlando was at the head of the Admiralty; and if glory was to be achieved by the four ships, it would rest first on the head of Sir Orlando.

Now the Duke thought that the Empire was safe, and had been throughout his political life averse to increasing the army and navy estimates. He regarded the four ships as altogether unnecessary,—and when reminded that he might in this way consolidate the Coalition, said that he would rather do without the Coalition and the four ships than have to do with both of them together,—an opinion which was thought by some to be almost traitorous to the party as now organized. The secrets of Cabinets are not to be disclosed lightly, but it came to be understood,—as what is done at Cabinet meetings generally does come to be understood,—that there was something like a disagreement. The Prime Minister, the Duke of St. Bungay, and Mr. Monk were altogether against the four ships. Sir Orlando was supported by Lord Drummond and another of his old friends. At the advice of the elder Duke, a paragraph was hatched, in which it was declared that her Majesty, "having regard to the safety of the nation and the possible, though happily not probable, chances of war, thought that the present strength of the navy should be considered." "It will give him scope for a new gun-boat on an altered principle," said the Duke of St. Bungay. But the Prime Minister, could he have had his own way, would have given Sir Orlando no scope whatever. He would have let the Coalition have gone to the dogs and have fallen himself into infinite political ruin, but that he did not dare that men should hereafter say of him that this attempt at government had failed because he was stubborn, imperious, and self-confident. He had known when he took his present place that he must yield to others; but he had not known how terrible it is to have to yield when a principle is in question,—how great is the suffering when a man finds himself compelled to do that which he thinks should not be done!

. . . .

The Prime Minister had become so moody, so irritable, and so unhappy, that the old Duke was forced to doubt whether things could go on much longer as they were. He was wont to talk of these things to his friend Lord Cantrip, who was not a member of the Government, but who had been a colleague of both the Dukes, and whom the old Duke regarded with peculiar confidence. "I cannot explain it to you," he said to Lord Cantrip. "There is nothing that ought to give him a moment's uneasiness. Since he took office there hasn't once been a majority against him in either House on any question that the Government has made its own. I don't remember such a state of things,—so easy for the Prime Minister,—since the days of Lord Liverpool. He had one thorn in his side, our friend who was at the Admiralty, and that thorn like other thorns has worked itself out. Yet at this moment it is impossible to get him to consent to the nomination of a successor to Sir Orlando." This was said a week before the Session had closed.

"I suppose it is his health," said Lord Cantrip.

"He's well enough as far as I can see;—though he will be ill unless he can relieve himself from the strain on his nerves."

"Do you mean by resigning?"

"Not necessarily. The fault is that he takes things too seriously. If he could be got to believe that he might eat, and sleep, and go to bed, and amuse himself like other men, he might be a very good Prime Minister. He is over troubled by his conscience. I have seen a good many Prime Ministers, Cantrip, and I've taught myself to think that they are not very different from other men. One wants in a Prime Minister a good many things, but not very great things. He should be clever but need not be a genius; he should be conscientious but by no means strait-laced; he should be cautious but never timid, bold but never venturesome; he should have a good digestion, genial manners, and, above all, a thick skin. These are the gifts we want, but we can't always get them, and have to do without them.

. . . .

When the Session began it was understood in the political world that a very strong opposition was to be organized against the Government under the guidance of Sir Orlando Drought, and that the great sin to be imputed to the Cabinet was an utter indifference to the safety and honour of Great Britain, as manifested by their neglect of the navy. All the world knew that Sir Orlando had deserted the Coalition because he was not allowed to build new ships, and of course Sir Orlando would make the most of his grievance. With him was joined Mr. Boffin, the patriotic Conservative who had never listened to the voice of the seducer, and the staunch remainder of the old Tory party. And with them the more violent of the Radicals were prepared to act, not desirous, indeed, that new ships should be built, or that a Conservative Government should be established,—or, indeed, that anything should be done,—but animated by intense disgust that so mild a politician as the Duke of Omnium should be Prime Minister. The fight began at once, Sir Orlando objecting violently to certain passages in the Queen's Speech. It was all very well to say that the country was at present at peace with all the world; but how was peace to be maintained without a fleet? Then Sir Orlando paid a great many compliments to the Duke, and ended his speech by declaring him to be the most absolutely fainéant minister that had disgraced the country since the days of the Duke of Newcastle. Mr. Monk

defended the Coalition, and assured the House that the navy
was not only the most powerful navy existing, but that it was
the most powerful that ever had existed in the possession of
this or any other country, and was probably in absolute effi-
ciency superior to the combined navies of all the world. The
House was not shocked by statements so absolutely at vari-
ance with each other, coming from two gentlemen who had
lately been members of the same Government, and who
must be supposed to know what they were talking about, but
seemed to think that upon the whole Sir Orlando had done
his duty. For though there was complete confidence in the
navy as a navy, and though a very small minority would have
voted for any considerably increased expense, still it was well
that there should be an opposition. And how can there be an
opposition without some subject for grumbling,—some matter on which a minister may be attacked? No one really
thought that the Prussians and French combined would invade our shores and devastate our fields, and plunder London, and carry our daughters away into captivity. The state of
the funds showed very plainly that there was no such fear.
But a good cry is a very good thing,—and it is always well to
rub up the officials of the Admiralty by a little wholesome
abuse. Sir Orlando was thought to have done his business
well. Of course he did not risk a division upon the address.
Had he done so he would have been "nowhere." But, as it
was, he was proud of his achievement.

The ministers generally would have been indifferent to the
very hard words that were said of them, knowing what they
were worth, and feeling aware that a ministry which had

From *The Prime Minister*

everything too easy must lose its interest in the country, had
it not been that their chief was very sore on the subject. The
old Duke's work at this time consisted almost all together in
nursing the younger Duke. It did sometimes occur to his
elder Grace that it might be well to let his brother retire, and
that a Prime Minister, *malgré lui,* could not be a successful
Prime Minister, or a useful one. But if the Duke of Omnium
went the Coalition must go too, and the Coalition had been
the offspring of the old statesman. The country was thriving
under the Coalition, and there was no real reason why it
should not last for the next ten years. He continued, therefore, his system of coddling, and was ready at any moment, or
at every moment, to pour, if not comfort, at any rate consola-
tion into the ears of his unhappy friend. In the present emergency, it was the falsehood and general baseness of Sir
Orlando which nearly broke the heart of the Prime Minister.
"How is one to live," he said, "if one has to do with men of
that kind?"

"But you haven't to do with him any longer," said the Duke
of St. Bungay.

"When I see a man who is supposed to have earned the
name of a statesman, and been high in the councils of his
sovereign, induced by personal jealousy to do as he is doing,
it makes me feel that an honest man should not place himself
where he may have to deal with such persons."

"According to that the honest men are to desert their country in order that the dishonest men may have everything their
own way." Our Duke could not answer this, and therefore for
the moment he yielded. But he was unhappy, saturnine, and

generally silent except when closeted with his ancient mentor. And he knew that he was saturnine and silent, and that it behoved him as a leader of men to be genial and communicative,—listening to counsel even if he did not follow it, and at any rate appearing to have confidence in his colleagues.

. . . .

"I was so proud when they made him Prime Minister; but I think that I am beginning to regret it now." Then there was a pause, and the Duchess went on with her newspapers; but she soon resumed her discourse. Her heart was full, and out of a full heart the mouth speaks. "They should have made me Prime Minister, and have let him be Chancellor of the Exchequer. I begin to see the ways of Government now. I could have done all the dirty work. I could have given away garters and ribbons, and made my bargains while giving them. I could select sleek, easy bishops who wouldn't be troublesome. I could give pensions or withhold them, and make the stupid men peers. I could have the big noblemen at my feet, praying to be Lieutenants of Counties. I could dole out secretaryships and lordships, and never a one without getting something in return. I could brazen out a job and let the *People's Banners* and the Slides make their worst of it. And I think I could make myself popular with my party, and do the high-flowing patriotic talk for the benefit of the Provinces. A man at a regular office has to work. That's what Plantagenet is fit for. He wants always to be doing something that shall be really useful, and a man has to toil at that and really to know

things. But a Prime Minister should never go beyond general-
ities about commerce, agriculture, peace, and general phil-
anthropy. Of course he should have the gift of the gab, and
that Plantagenet hasn't got. He never wants to say anything
unless he has got something to say. I could do a Mansion
House dinner to a marvel!"

LEO TOLSTOY

Leo Tolstoy (1828–1910), recognized as one of the giants of Russian literature, was born in Yasnaya Polyana. Tolstoy, a member of the Russian nobility, felt undeserving of his wealth and was renowned among the peasantry for his generosity. Between 1863 and 1869, Tolstoy published his classic novel *War and Peace*. An epic tale of five families set against the background of Napoléon's invasion of Russia, the novel reflects Tolstoy's view that all in life is predetermined, but that we cannot carry on in our daily lives unless we imagine that we have free will. Tolstoy's other masterpiece, *Anna Karenina* (1873–77), tells a tragic story of a married woman who commits suicide after a ruinous affair with the dashing Count Vronsky.

Tolstoy had a long-running correspondence with Mohandas Gandhi, and is said to have influenced Gandhi's concept of nonviolent resistance. As we see through Tolstoy's work—his stories of who leads whom, and in what manner, with what consequences—political struggle begs for a novelist's narrative passion; politics is yet another instance of human connection, given the larger life of social and cultural expression.

From WAR AND PEACE

From PART ONE

I

Seven years had passed. The storm-tossed sea of European history had sunk to rest upon its shores. The sea appeared to be calm; but the mysterious forces that move humanity (mysterious because the laws that govern their action are unknown to us) were still at work.

Though the surface of the ocean of history seemed motionless, the movement of humanity continued as uninterrupted as the flow of time. Coalitions of men came together and separated again; the causes that would bring about the formation and the dissolution of empires and the displacement of peoples were in course of preparation.

The ocean of history was no longer, as before, swept from shore to shore by squalls: it seethed in its depths. The personages of history were not borne by the waves from coast to coast as before; now they seemed to revolve in stationary eddies. Historical personages who had lately been leading armies and reflecting the movement of the masses by decreeing wars, campaigns and battles now reflected the turbulent flux by political and diplomatic combinations, statutes, treaties, and so on.

This activity of the figures of history the historians call *reaction*.

In dealing with the part played by these historical personages the historians are severe in their criticism, supposing them to be the cause of what they describe as *reaction*. All the famous people of that period, from Alexander and Napoleon to Madame de Staël, Photius, Schelling, Fichte, Chateaubriand, and the rest, are arraigned before their stern tribunal and acquitted or condemned according to whether they conduced to *progress* or *reaction*.

Russia too is described by the historians as the scene at this time of reaction, and for this they throw the chief responsibility on Alexander I—the same Alexander I to whom they also give the credit for the liberal enterprises at the beginning of his reign, and for the saving of Russia.

There is no one in Russian literature today, from schoolboy essay-writer to learned historian, who does not throw his little stone at Alexander I for one or another ill-considered measure at this later period of his sovereignty.

"He ought to have acted in such and such a way. In this case he did well, on that occasion badly. He conducted himself admirably at the beginning of his reign and during 1812; but he erred in granting a constitution to Poland, in establishing the Holy Alliance, in entrusting power to Arakcheyev, in encouraging first Golitsyn and his mysticism and afterwards Shishkov and Photius. He did wrong in interfering with the army on active service, did wrong in disbanding the Semeonovsk regiment, and so on."

It would take a dozen pages to enumerate all the faults the historians find in him on the strength of the knowledge they possess of what is for the good of humanity.

What do these strictures signify?

Do not the very actions for which the historians applaud Alexander I—the attempts at liberalism at the beginning of his reign, his struggle with Napoleon, the firmness he displayed in 1812 and the campaign of 1813—proceed from those very sources—the circumstances of birth, breeding and life that made his personality what it was—from which also flowed the actions for which they censure him, like the Holy Alliance, the restoration of Poland and the reaction of the 1820s?

What is the substance of these strictures?

In this—that an historical character like Alexander I, standing on the highest possible pinnacle of human power with the blinding light of history focused upon him; a character exposed to those most potent of influences—the intrigues, flatteries and self-delusion inseparable from power; a character who at every moment of his life felt a responsibility for all that was being done in Europe; and a character, not from fiction but as much alive as any other man, with his own personal bent, passions, and impulses towards goodness, beauty and truth—that this character, though not lacking in virtue (the historians do not accuse him on that score), living fifty years ago, had not the same conception concerning the welfare of humanity as a present-day professor who from his youth up has been engaged in study, *i.e.* in reading, listening to lectures and making notes on those books and lectures in a note-book.

But if we are going to assume that Alexander I, fifty years ago, was mistaken in his view of what was good for the peoples we can hardly help considering that the historian who criticizes Alexander may, after a certain lapse of time, prove to be equally incorrect in his idea of what is for the good of humanity. This assumption is all the more natural and inevitable because, watching the development of history, we see that every year, with each new writer, opinion as to what constitutes the welfare of humanity changes; so that what once seemed good, ten years later seems bad, and vice versa. That is not all: we even find in history, at one and the same time, quite contradictory views as to what was good and what was bad. Some people place the giving of a constitution to Poland, and the Holy Alliance, to Alexander's credit, while others censure him for them.

The activity of Alexander or of Napoleon cannot be termed beneficial or harmful, since we cannot say for what it was beneficial or harmful. If that activity fails to please someone, this is only because it does not coincide with his restricted conception of what constitutes good. I may regard the preservation of my father's house in Moscow in 1812, or the glory of Russian arms, or the prosperity of Petersburg and other universities, or the independence of Poland, or the might of Russia, or the balance of power in Europe, or a certain kind of European enlightenment called "progress"—I may regard all these as good but I am still bound to admit that, besides these ends and aims, the action of every historic character has other more general purposes beyond my grasp.

But let us suppose that what we call science has the power of reconciling all contradictions and possesses an invariable standard of right and wrong by which to try historical persons and events.

Let us say that Alexander could have done everything differently. Let us assume that he might—in accordance with the prescriptions of those who accuse him and who profess to know the ultimate goal of the movement of humanity—have arranged matters in harmony with the programme of nationalism, freedom, equality and progress (for there would seem to be no other) with which his present-day critics would have provided him. Let us assume that this programme could have been possible and had actually been formulated at the time, and that Alexander could have acted in accordance with it. What then would become of the activity of all those who opposed the tendency of the government of the day—of the activity which in the opinion of the historians was good and beneficial? Their activity would not have existed: there would have been no life, nothing.

Once say that human life can be controlled by reason, and all possibility of life is annihilated.

II

If we assume, as the historians do, that great men lead humanity towards the attainment of certain ends—such as the majesty of Russia or of France, the balance of power in Europe, the propagation of the ideas of the Revolution, progress in general, or anything else you like—it becomes impossible to explain the phenomena of history without intruding the concepts of *chance* and *genius*.

If the object of the European wars of the beginning of this century had been the aggrandizement of Russia, that object might have been attained without any of the preceding wars and without the invasion. If the object was the aggrandizement of France, that might have been attained without either the Revolution or the Empire. If the object was the propagation of ideas, the printing-press could have accomplished that much more effectually than soldiers. If the object was the progress of civilization, one may very readily suppose that there are other more expedient means of diffusing civilization than by slaughtering people and destroying their wealth.

Why then did things happen thus and not otherwise?

Because they did so happen. "*Chance* created the situation; *genius* made use of it," says history.

But what is *chance*? What is *genius*?

The words *chance* and *genius* do not denote anything that actually exists, and therefore they cannot be defined. These two words merely indicate a certain degree of comprehension of phenomena. I do not know why a certain event occurs; I suppose that I cannot know: therefore I do not try to know, and I talk about *chance*. I see a force producing effects beyond the scope of ordinary human agencies; I do not understand why this occurs, and I cry *genius*.

To a flock of sheep, the one the shepherd drives into a separate enclosure every night to feed, and that becomes twice as fat as the others, must seem to be a genius. And the circumstance that every evening this particular sheep, instead of coming into the common fold, chances into a special pen with extra oats, and that this sheep, this particular one, fattens up and is killed for mutton, doubtless impresses the rest of the flock as a remarkable conjunction of genius with a whole series of fortuitous chances.

But the sheep need only rid themselves of the idea that all that is done to them is done solely for the furtherance of their sheepish ends; they have only to concede that what happens to them may also have purposes beyond their ken, and they will immediately perceive a unity and coherence in what happens with their brother that is being fattened. Although it may not be given to them to know to what end he was being fattened, they will at least know that all that happened to him did not occur accidentally, and will no longer need to resort to conceptions of *chance* or *genius*.

It is only by renouncing our claim to discern a purpose immediately intelligible to us, and admitting the ultimate purpose to be beyond our ken, that we shall see a logical connexion in the lives of historical personages, and perceive the why and wherefore of what they do which so transcends the ordinary powers of humanity. We shall then find that the words *chance* and *genius* have become superfluous.

We have only to admit that we do not know the purpose of the convulsions among the European nations, and that we know only the hard facts—the butchery, first in France, then in Italy, in Africa, in Prussia, in Austria, in Spain and in Russia—and that the movements from west to east and from east to west constitute the essence and end of those events, and we shall not only find it no longer necessary to see some exceptional ability—*genius*—in Napoleon and Alexander: we shall be unable to regard them as being anything but men like other men. And far from having to turn to *chance* to explain the little incidents which made those men what they were, it will be clear to us that all those little incidents were inevitable.

If we give up all claim to a knowledge of the ultimate purpose we shall realize that, just as it is impossible to imagine for any given plant other more appropriate blossom or seed than those it produces, so it is impossible to imagine any two persons, with all their antecedents, more completely adapted, down to the smallest detail, to the mission which Napoleon and Alexander were called upon to fulfil.

III

The fundamental and essential point of European events at the beginning of the present century is the militant mass movement of the European peoples from west to east and then from east to west. The first impulse to this flux was given by the movement from west to east. For the peoples of the west to be able to achieve their militant advance as far as Moscow they had to (1) form themselves into a military group of sufficient magnitude to sustain a collision with the military group of the east; (2) renounce all established traditions and customs; and (3) have at their head, during their military movement, a man able to justify to himself and to them the guile, robbery and murder which must be the concomitants of their progress.

So, beginning with the French Revolution, the old group which is not large enough is destroyed; old habits and traditions are abolished; and step by step a group of new dimensions is elaborated, new customs and traditions are developed, and a man is prepared who is to stand at the head of the coming movement and bear the whole responsibility for what has to be done.

A man of no convictions, no habits, no traditions, no name, not even a Frenchman, emerges—by what seems the strangest freak of chance—from among all the seething parties of France, and, without attaching himself to any one of them, is borne forward to a prominent position.

The incompetence of his colleagues, the weakness and inanity of his rivals, the frankness of his falsehoods and his brilliant and self-confident mediocrity raise him to the head of the army. The brilliant quality of the soldiers of the army sent to Italy, his opponents' reluctance to fight and his own childish insolence and conceit secure him military glory. Innumerable so-called *chance* circumstances attend him everywhere. The disfavour into which he falls with the French Directorate turns to his advantage. His attempts to avoid his predestined path are unsuccessful: Russia refused to receive him into her service and the appointment he seeks in Turkey comes to nothing. During the wars in Italy he more than once finds himself on the brink of disaster and each time is saved in some unexpected manner. Owing to various diplomatic considerations the Russian armies—the very armies which have the power to extinguish his glory—do not appear upon the European scene while he is there.

On his return from Italy he finds the government in Paris in the process of dissolution in which all those who are in that government are doomed to erasure and extinction. And by chance an escape from this dangerous situation offers itself to him in the nonsensical, gratuitous expedition to Africa. Again so-called *chance* accompanies him. Malta the impregnable surrenders without a shot; his most reckless schemes are crowned with success. The enemy's fleet, which later on does not let a single row-boat through, now suffers a whole army to elude it. In Africa a whole series of outrages is perpetrated against the practically defenceless inhabitants. And the men committing these atrocities, and their leader most of all, persuade themselves that this is admirable, this is glory, this is like Caesar and Alexander the Great, and is fine.

This ideal of *glory* and *greatness*—which consists not merely in the assurance that nothing one does is to be considered wrong but in glorying in one's every crime and ascribing to it an incomprehensible, supernatural significance—this ideal, destined to guide this man and his associates, is provided with fertile ground for its development in Africa. Whatever he does succeeds. The plague does not touch him. Responsibility for the cruel massacring of prisoners is not laid at his door. His childishly incautious, unreasoning and ignoble departure from Africa, leaving his comrades in distress, is accounted to his credit, and again the enemy's fleet twice lets him slip past. Completely intoxicated by the success of his crimes and ready for his new rôle, though without any plan, he arrives in Paris just when the disintegration of the Republican government, which a year before might have made an end of him, has reached its utmost limit and his presence there now, as a newcomer free from party entanglements, can only lift him to the heights.

He has no plan of any kind; he is afraid of everything; but the parties hold out their hands to him and insist on his participation.

He alone—with the ideal of glory and grandeur built up in

Italy and Egypt, his insane self-adulation, his insolence in crime and frankness in lying—he alone can justify what has to be done.

He is needed for the place that awaits him and so, almost apart from his own volition and in spite of his indecision, his lack of a plan and all the blunders he makes, he is drawn into a conspiracy that aims at seizing power, and the conspiracy is crowned with success.

He is dragged into a meeting of the legislature. In alarm he tries to flee, believing himself in danger; pretends to be falling into a faint; says the most senseless things which should have meant his ruin. But the once proud and discerning rulers of France, feeling their part is over, are even more panic-stricken than he, and fail to pronounce the word they should have spoken to preserve their power and crush him.

Chance, millions of *chances*, invest him with authority, and all men everywhere, as if by agreement together, co-operate to confirm that power. *Chance* forms the characters of the rulers of France who cringe before him; *chance* forms the character of Paul I of Russia who recognizes his power; *chance* contrives a plot against him which not only fails to injure him but strengthens his position. *Chance* throws the duc d'Enghien into his hands and unexpectedly impels him to assassinate him—thereby convincing the mob by the most potent of all arguments that he has right on his side since he has might. *Chance* sees to it that though he strains every nerve to prepare an expedition against England (which would undoubtedly have been his downfall) he never carries this enterprise into execution but abruptly falls upon Mack and the Austrians, who surrender without a battle. *Chance* and *genius* give him the victory at Austerlitz; and by *chance* it comes to pass that all men, not only the French but all Europe—except England, who takes no part in the events about to happen—forget their former horror and detestation of his crimes and now recognize his consequent authority, the title he has bestowed upon himself and his ideal of grandeur and glory, which seems to one and all something excellent and reasonable.

As though measuring and making ready for the movement to come, the forces of the West several times—in 1805, 1806, 1807, 1809—sally eastwards, gaining strength and growing. In 1811 the body of men that had formed in France unites into one enormous body with the peoples of Central Europe. Every increase in the size of this group adds further justification for Napoleon's power. During the ten-year preparatory period before the great push this man forms relations with all the crowned heads of Europe. The discredited rulers of the world have no rational ideal to oppose to the meaningless Napoleonic *mystique* of *glory* and *grandeur*. One after another they rush to display to him their insignificance. The King of Prussia sends his wife to curry favour with the great man; the Emperor of Austria is gratified that this man should take the daughter of the Kaisers to his bed; the Pope, guardian of all that the nations hold sacred, utilizes religion to raise the great man higher. It is less that Napoleon prepares himself for the performance of his rôle than that all about him lead him on to acceptance of entire responsibility for what is happening and has to happen. There is no act, no crime, no petty deceit he might commit, which would not immediately be proclaimed by those about him as a great deed. The most suitable fête the Teutons can think of to observe in his honour is a celebration of Jena and Auerstädt. Not only is he great but so are his forefathers, his brothers, his stepsons and his brothers-in-law. Everything is done to deprive him of the last vestige of his reason and to prepare him for his terrible part. And when he is ready so too are the forces.

The invasion streams eastwards and reaches its final goal—Moscow. The capital is taken: the Russian army suffers heavier losses than the enemy ever suffered in previous wars from Austerlitz to Wagram. But all at once, instead of the *chance* happenings and the *genius* which hitherto had so consistently led him by an uninterrupted series of successes to the predestined goal, an innumerable sequence of reverse *chances* occur—from the cold in his head at Borodino to the frosts and the spark which set Moscow on fire—and, instead of *genius*, folly and baseness without parallel appear.

The invaders run, turn back, run again, and all the *chances* are now not for Napoleon but always against him.

A counter-movement follows, from east to west, bearing a remarkable resemblance to the preceding movement from west to east. There are similar tentative drives westward as had in 1805, 1807 and 1809 preceded the great eastward movement; there is the same coalescence into a group of colossal proportions; the same adhesion of the peoples of Central Europe to the movement; the same hesitation midway and the same increased velocity as the goal is approached.

Paris, the ultimate goal, is reached. The Napoleonic government and army are overthrown. Napoleon himself is no longer of any account; all his actions are manifestly pitiful and mean; but again inexplicable chance steps in: the allies detest Napoleon whom they regard as the cause of their troubles. Stripped of his power and authority, his crimes and his treacheries exposed, he should have appeared to them what he had appeared ten years previously and was to appear a year later—a bandit and an outlaw. But by some strange freak of chance no one perceives this. His rôle is not yet played to a finish. The man who ten years before and a year later was looked on as a miscreant outside the law is sent to an island a couple of days' journey from France, which is given to him as his domain, with guards and millions of money, as though to pay him for some service rendered.

IV

The flood of nations begins to subside into its normal channels. The waves of the great movement abate, leaving a calm surface ruffled by eddies where the diplomatists busy themselves (in the belief that the calm is the result of their work).

But suddenly the smooth sea is convulsed again. The diplomats imagine that their dissensions are the cause of this new upheaval of the elements; they anticipate war between their sovereigns; the position seems to them insoluble. But the wave they feel to be gathering does not come from the quarter expected. It is the same wave as before, and its source the same point as before—Paris. The last backwash of the movement from the west occurs—a backwash which serves to solve the apparently insuperable diplomatic difficulties and put an end to the militant flux of the period.

The man who has devastated France returns to France alone, without any conspiracy and without soldiers. Any gendarme might apprehend him; but by a strange chance not only does no one touch him—they all rapturously acclaim the man they had cursed the day before and will be cursing again within a month.

This man is still needed to justify the final collective act.

The act is performed. The last part is played. The actor is bidden to disrobe and wash off his powder and paint: he will not be wanted any more.

And several years pass during which, in solitude on his island, this man plays his pitiful farce to himself, pettily intriguing and trying to justify his conduct when justification is no longer needed, and revealing to the world at large what it was that people had mistaken for strength so long as an unseen hand directed his actions.

The stage manager, having brought the drama to a close and stripped the puppet of his motley, shows him to us.

"Look—this is what you believed in! Here he stands! Do you see now that it was not he but *I* who moved you?"

But, dazed by the violence of the movement, it was long before people understood this.

A still more striking example of logical sequence and inevitability is to be seen in the life of Alexander I, the figure who stood at the head of the counter-movement from east to west.

What qualities should the man possess if he were to over-

shadow everyone else and head the counter-movement westwards?

He must have a sense of justice and a sympathy with European affairs, but a detached sympathy not obscured by
petty interests; a moral superiority over his peers—the other
sovereigns of the day; a gentle and attractive personality; and
a personal grievance against Napoleon. And all this is found
in Alexander I; all this has been prepared by countless so-
called *chance* circumstances in his life: his upbringing and
early liberalism, the advisers who surrounded him; by Austerlitz and Tilsit and Erfurt.

So long as the war is a national one he remains inactive because he is not needed. But as soon as the necessity for a
general European war becomes apparent, at the given moment he is in his place and, uniting the nations of Europe,
leads them to the goal.

The goal is reached. After the final war of 1815 Alexander
finds himself at the summit of human power. How does he
use it?

Alexander I, the peacemaker of Europe, the man who from
his youth up had striven only for the welfare of his peoples,
the first champion of liberal reforms in his country, now
when it seems that he possesses the utmost power and therefore the possibility of achieving the welfare of his peoples
(while Napoleon in exile is drawing up childish and menda-
cious plans of how he would have made mankind happy had
he retained power)—Alexander I, having fulfilled his mission
and feeling the hand of God upon him, suddenly recognizes
the nothingness of the supposed power that is his, turns away

from it and hands it over to contemptible men whom he despises, saying only:

" 'Not unto us, not unto us, but unto Thy Name!' I too am a man like the rest of you. Let me live like a man, and think of my soul and of God."

Just as the sun and every particle of the ether is a sphere complete in itself and at the same time only a part of a whole too immense for the comprehension of man, so every individual bears within himself his own aims and yet bears them so as to serve a general purpose unfathomable by man.

A bee poised on a flower has stung a child. And so the child is afraid of bees and declares that bees are there to sting people. A poet delights in the bee sipping honey from the calyx of a flower and says the bee exists to suck the nectar of flowers. A bee-keeper, seeing the bee collect pollen and carry it to the hive, says that the object of bees is to gather honey. Another bee-keeper, who has studied the life of the swarm more closely, declares that the bee gathers pollen-dust to feed the young bees and rear a queen, and that it exists for the propagation of its species. The botanist, observing that a bee flying with pollen from one dioecious plant to the pistil of another fertilizes the latter, sees in this the purpose of the bee's existence. Another, remarking the hybridization of plants and seeing that the bee assists in this work, may say that herein lies the purpose of the bee. But the ultimate purpose of the bee is not exhausted by the first or the second or the third of the processes the human mind can discern. The higher the human intellect soars in the discovery of possible purposes, the more obvious it becomes that the ultimate purpose is beyond our comprehension.

Man cannot achieve more than a certain insight into the correlation between the life of the bee and other manifestations of life. And the same is true with regard to the final purpose of historical characters and nations.

From PART TWO

I

History has for its subject the life of nations and of humanity. To catch hold of and encompass in words—to describe exactly—the life of a single people, much less of humanity, would appear impossible.

The ancient historians all employed one and the same method for seizing the seemingly elusive and depicting the life of a people. They wrote of the parts played by the individuals who stood in authority over that people, and regarded their activity as an expression of the activity of the nation as a whole.

To the twofold question of how individuals could oblige nations to act as they wished, and by what the will of those individuals themselves was guided, the historians of old replied by recognizing a Divinity which, in the first case, made the nation subject to the will of one chosen person, and, in the second, guided the will of that chosen person to the accomplishment of predestined ends.

For the old historians the question was thus resolved by belief in the direct participation of the Deity in human affairs.

Neither proposition finds a place in the theory of the new school of history.

It would seem that, having rejected the belief of the ancients in man's subjection to the Deity and in a predetermined aim towards which nations are led, the new school ought to be studying not the manifestations of power but the causes which create power. But modern history has not done this. Though it has repudiated the theory of the older historians it still follows their practice.

In place of men endowed with divine authority and governed directly by the will of God modern history has set up either heroes possessed of extraordinary, superhuman ability, or simply men of any and every degree, from monarchs to journalists, who dominate the masses. Instead of the former divinely appointed purposes of nations—of the Jews, the Greeks, the Romans—which the old historians saw at the back of movements of humanity, the new school postulates aims of its own—such as the welfare of the French, German or English people, or, in its highest flights, the welfare and civilization of humanity in general, by which is usually meant the peoples inhabiting a small, north-western corner of a large continent.

Modern history has rejected the beliefs of the ancients without establishing any new conviction in place of them, and the logic of the situation has obliged the historians, who were under the impression that they had dismissed the hypothesis of the divine authority of kings and the *Fatum* of the ancients, to arrive at the same conclusion by another route— that is, to recognize that (1) nations are guided by individuals, and (2) there exists a certain goal towards which the nations and humanity are moving.

In the works of all the modern historians, from Gibbon to Buckle, in spite of their seeming differences of outlook and the apparent novelty of their opinions, these two time-honoured, unavoidable premisses lie at the basis of the argument.

In the first place the historian describes the activity of separate persons who in his opinion have dictated to humanity (one historian accepts only monarchs, military generals and ministers of state in this category, while another will also include orators, scholars, reformers, philosophers and poets). Secondly, the historians assume that they know the goal towards which humanity is being led: to one this goal is the majesty of the Roman or the Spanish or the French empire; for another it is liberty, equality and the kind of civilization that obtains in the little corner of the globe called Europe.

In 1789 fermentation starts in Paris: it develops and spreads, and finds expression in a movement of peoples from west to east. Several times this movement is directed towards the east and comes into collision with a counter-movement from the east westwards. In the year 1812 it reaches its extreme limit—Moscow—and then, with remarkable symmetry, the counter-movement follows from east to west, attracting to it, as the original movement had done, the peoples of middle Europe. The counter-movement reaches the departure-point in the west of the first movement—Paris—and subsides.

During this period of twenty years an immense number of fields are left untilled; houses are burned; trade changes its orientation; millions of people grow poor, grow rich, move from place to place; and millions of Christian men professing the law of love for their neighbour murder one another.

What does all this mean? Why did it happen? What induced these people to burn houses and kill their fellow-creatures? What were the causes of these events? What force compelled men to act in this fashion? These are the instinctive, guileless and supremely legitimate questions humanity propounds to itself when it encounters the monuments and traditions of that bygone period of turmoil.

For an answer to these questions mankind in common-sense looks to the science of history, whose purpose is to teach nations and humanity to know themselves.

Had history adhered to the ideas of the ancients it would have said that the Deity, to reward or punish His people, gave Napoleon power and guided his will for the attainment of His own divine ends. And this reply would have been complete and lucid. One might or might not believe in the divine significance of Napoleon; but for anyone who believed in it all the history of that period would be intelligible and free from contradictions.

But modern history cannot answer in that way. Science does not admit the conception of the ancients as to the direct participation of the Deity in human affairs, and must therefore give other answers.

Replying to these questions the new school of history says: "You want to know what this movement means, what caused it, and what force produced these events? Listen:

"Louis XIV was a very proud and self-confident man; he had such and such mistresses and such and such ministers,

and he ruled France vilely. Louis' successors, too, were weak
men and they, too, ruled France vilely. And they had such and
such favourites and such and such mistresses. Furthermore,
certain people were at this time writing books. At the end of
the eighteenth century there had gathered in Paris a couple
of dozen persons who began talking about all men being
equal and free. Because of this, over the length and breadth
of France men fell to slaughtering and destroying one another. They killed the king and a good many others. At this
time there was in France a man of genius—Napoleon. He got
the upper hand of everybody everywhere—that is to say, he
killed numbers of his fellows because he was a great genius.
And for some reason he went to kill Africans, and killed them
so well and was so cunning and clever that when he returned
to France he ordered everyone to obey him. And they all did.
Having made himself an Emperor he again went off to kill
people in Italy, Austria and Prussia. There, too, he killed a
great many. Now in Russia there was an Emperor, Alexander,
who decided to restore order in Europe, and so he fought
wars against Napoleon. But in '07 he suddenly made friends
with him, until in 1811 they quarrelled again, and again
began killing a lot of people. And Napoleon brought six hundred thousand men to Russia and captured Moscow; but afterwards he suddenly ran away from Moscow, and then the
Emperor Alexander, aided by the counsels of Stein and others, united Europe into a coalition to march against the dis-
turber of her peace. All Napoleon's allies suddenly turned
into enemies; and their forces advanced against the fresh
forces which he raised. The allies defeated Napoleon, en-

tered Paris, forced Napoleon to abdicate, and exiled him to the island of Elba, not depriving him of the dignity of Emperor or failing to show him every respect, though five years before and one year later they all regarded him as a bandit and an outlaw. Thereupon Louis XVIII, who till then had been a laughing-stock both to the French and the allies, began to reign. As for Napoleon, after shedding tears before the Old Guard he renounced his throne and went into exile. Next, astute statesmen and diplomats (in particular Talleyrand, who had managed to sit down before anyone else in the famous arm-chair and thereby to extend the frontiers of France) proceeded to hold conversations in Vienna, and by this means make the nations happy or unhappy. All at once the diplomats and monarchs almost came to blows: they were on the point of ordering their armies to massacre one another again; but at this point Napoleon arrived in France with a battalion, and the French, who had been abhorring him, immediately all submitted to him. But the allied monarchs got very annoyed at this and again went to war with the French. And they defeated the genius Napoleon and, suddenly confirming that he was a bandit, removed him to St. Helena. And there the exile, parted from his dear ones and his beloved France, died a lingering death on the rocky island, and bequeathed his great deeds to posterity. As for Europe, reaction set in, and the sovereigns all took to outraging their subjects again."

It would be a mistake to think this mere irony—a caricature of historical descriptions. On the contrary, it is a very mild expression of the incongruous answers which fail to answer given by *all* historians, from the compilers of memoirs and of histories of individual countries to the "universal histories" and the new sort of histories of the *culture* of that period.

The grotesqueness of these answers arises from the fact that modern history is like a deaf man answering questions no one has put to him.

If the purpose of history is the description of the flux of humanity and of peoples, the first question to be answered, unless all the rest is to remain unintelligible, will be: What is the power that moves nations? To this the new school laboriously replies either that Napoleon was a great genius or that Louis XIV was very arrogant, or else that certain writers wrote certain books.

All that may well be so, and mankind is quite ready to say Amen; but it is not what was asked. All that might be very interesting if we recognized a divine power, self-subsisting and consistent, governing the nations by means of Napoleons, Louises and philosophical writers; but we acknowledge no such power, and therefore, before any talk of Napoleons, Louises and philosophical writers, we ought to be shown the relation obtaining between these persons and the movement of nations.

If divine power is to be replaced by some other force, then it should be explained what this new force consists of, in which the whole interest of history is contained.

History seems to take it for granted that this force is self-evident and known to everyone. But in spite of every desire to regard it as known the frequent reader of historical works will find himself doubting whether this new force, so variously understood by the historians themselves, is really quite so familiar to all and sundry.

I I

What is the force that moves nations?

Biographical historians and historians of individual peoples understand this force as a power inherent in heroes and rulers. According to their chronicles events occur solely at the will of a Napoleon, an Alexander or in general the personages of whom they treat. The answers which historians of this *genre* return to the question of what force causes events to happen are satisfactory only so long as there is but one historian to each event. But as soon as historians of different nationalities and views begin describing one and the same event, the replies they give immediately lose all meaning, since this force is understood by them not only differently but often in absolutely opposite ways. One historian will maintain that a given event owed its origin to Napoleon's power; another that it was Alexander's power; while a third ascribes the event to the influence of some other person. Moreover, historians of this type contradict one another even in their interpretation of the force on which the authority of one and the same figure was based. Thiers, a Bonapartist, says that Napoleon's power was based on his virtue and his genius; Lanfrey, a Republican, declares that it rested on his rascality and skill in deceiving the people. So that the historians of this class, by mutually destroying one another's position, destroy the conception of the force which produces events, and furnish no reply to history's essential question.

Universal historians, who deal with all the nations, appear to recognize the erroneousness of the specialist historians' view of the force that produces events. They do not recognize it as a power pertaining to heroes and rulers but regard it as the resultant of a multiplicity of variously directed forces. In describing a war, or the subjugation of a people, the general historian looks for the cause of the event not in the power of any one individual but in the interaction of many persons connected with the event.

According to this view, the power of historical personages conceived as the product of several different forces can hardly, it would seem, be regarded as the force which in itself produces events. Yet general historians do almost invariably make use of the concept of power as a force which itself produces events and stands to events in the relation of cause to effect. We find them (the historians) saying at one minute that an historical personage is the product of his time and his power only the outcome of various forces; and at the next that his power is itself a force producing events. Gervinus, Schlosser and others, for instance, in one place argue that Napoleon was the product of the Revolution, of the ideas of 1789 and so forth, and in another plainly state that the campaign of 1812 and other incidents not to their liking were simply the outcome of Napoleon's misdirected will, and that the very ideas of 1789 were arrested in their development by Napoleon's caprice. The ideas of the Revolution and the general temper of the age produced Napoleon's power. But Napoleon's power stifled the ideas of the Revolution and the general temper of the age.

This curious contradiction is no chance occurrence. It not only confronts us at every turn but volume upon volume of universal history is made up of a chain of such contradictions—which spring from the fact that after taking a few steps along the road of analysis the universal historians stop short half-way.

For component forces to give rise to a certain composite or resultant force the sum of the components must equal the resultant. This condition is never observed by the universal historians. Hence, to explain the resultant force they are obliged to admit, in addition to inadequate components, a further, unexplained, force affecting the resultant.

The specialist historian describing the campaign of 1813, or the restoration of the Bourbons, asserts in so many words that these events were brought about by the will of Alexander. But the general historian, Gervinus, refuting this opinion of the specialist historian, seeks to prove that the campaign of 1813 and the restoration of the Bourbons were due not only to Alexander but to the activity of Stein, Metternich, Madame de Staël, Talleyrand, Fichte, Chateaubriand and others. He evidently decomposes Alexander's power into its component factors—Talleyrand, Chateaubriand and the rest—but the sum of these components, that is, the interaction of Chateaubriand, Talleyrand, Madame de Staël and the others, obviously does not equal the resultant, namely, the phenomenon of millions of Frenchmen submitting to the Bourbons. And therefore to explain how the submission of millions resulted from these components—that is, how component forces equal to a given quantity A gave a resultant equal to a thousand times *A*—he is obliged to fall back on the same force—power—which he has been denying inasmuch as he was regarding it as the resultant of the given forces; that is, he has to concede an unexplained force acting on the resultant. And this is just what the universal historians do. And consequently contradict not only the sectional historian but themselves too.

Country people having no clear idea of the cause of rain say, "The wind has blown away the rain," or "The wind is blowing up for rain," according to whether they want rain or fine weather. In the same way the universal historians at times when they want it to be so, when it fits in with their theory, say that power is the result of events; and at others, when it is necessary to prove the opposite, say that power produces the events.

A third class of historians—the so-called historians of *culture,* following on the lines laid down by the writers of universal history who sometimes accept *littérateurs* and *grandes dames* as forces producing events—interpret this force still differently. They see it in what is termed *culture,* in intellectual activity.

The historians of culture from first to last take after their progenitors, the writers of universal histories, for if historical events may be explained by the fact that certain persons treated one another in certain ways, why not explain them by the fact that certain people wrote certain books? Out of all the immense number of tokens that accompany every vital phenomenon these historians select the manifestation of intellectual activity, and declare that this manifestation is the cause.

But, despite their endeavours to prove that the cause of events lies in intellectual activity, only by a great stretch can one agree that there is any connexion between intellectual activity and the movement of peoples, and it is altogether impossible to agree that intellectual activity has controlled the actions of mankind, for such phenomena as the brutal murders of the French Revolution, which were the outcome of the doctrine of the equality of man, and the most wicked wars and executions resulting from the Gospel of Love belie this hypothesis.

But even admitting that all the cunningly devised arguments with which these histories abound are correct: admitting that nations are governed by some undefined force called an *idea,* the essential question of history either still remains unanswered or else to the power of monarchs and the influence of counsellors and other persons introduced by the universal historians we must add another, new force—the *idea,* the relation of which to the masses requires explanation. One can understand that Napoleon had power and so an event came to pass; with some effort one may even grant that Napoleon together with other influences was the cause of an event; but how a book, *Le Contrat social,* had the effect of making Frenchmen destroy one another is unintelligible without some explanation of the causal nexus of this new force with the event.

There undoubtedly exists a connexion between all the people alive at one time, and so it is possible to discover some sort of connexion between the intellectual activity of men and their historical movements, just as such a connexion may be discovered between the movements of humanity and commerce, handicrafts, horticulture, or anything else you please. But why intellectual activity should appear to the historians of culture to be the cause or expression of the whole historical movement is hard to understand. Only the following considerations can have led the historians to such a conclusion: (1) that history is written by learned men and so it is natural and agreeable for them to believe that the pursuit of their calling supplies the ruling element in the movement of all humanity, just as a similar belief is natural and agreeable to merchants, agriculturists or soldiers (only it does not find expression because merchants and soldiers do not write history); and (2) that spiritual activity, enlightenment, civilization, culture, ideas are all vague, indefinite conceptions under whose banner they can very conveniently employ words having a still less definite meaning and which can therefore be readily adapted to any theory.

But leaving aside the question of the intrinsic worth of histories of this kind (which may possibly even be of use to someone for something), the histories of culture, to which all general histories tend more and more to approximate, are remarkable for the fact that after examining seriously and in detail various religious, philosophic and political doctrines as causes of events, so soon as they have to describe an actual historical event, such as the campaign of 1812 for instance, they involuntarily describe it as resulting from an exercise of power—roundly declaring that that campaign was the result of Napoleon's will. In saying this, the historians of culture unconsciously contradict themselves; they show that the new force they have invented does not account for what happens in history, and that history can only be explained by introducing the power which they apparently do not recognize.

III

A locomotive is moving. Someone asks: "What makes it move?" The peasant answers, "'Tis the devil moves it." Another man says the locomotive moves because its wheels are going round. A third maintains that the cause of the motion lies in the smoke being carried away by the wind.

The peasant's contention is irrefutable: he has devised a complete explanation. To refute him someone would have to prove to him that there is no devil, or another peasant would have to tell him that it is not a devil but a German who makes the locomotive go. Only then, because of the contradiction, will they see that they are both wrong. But the man who argues that the movement of the wheels is the cause confounds himself, for having once started on analysis he ought to proceed further and explain why the wheels go round. And until he has reached the ultimate cause of the movement of the locomotive in the pressure of steam in the boiler he has no right to stop in his search for the cause. Finally, the man who explained the movement of the locomotive by the smoke that is borne back has noticed that the theory about the wheels does not furnish a satisfactory explanation, and has seized upon the first feature to attract his attention, and in his turn produces that as an explanation.

The only conception capable of explaining the movement of the locomotive is that of a force commensurate with the movement observed.

The only conception capable of explaining the movement of peoples is that of some force commensurate with the whole movement of the peoples.

Yet to supply this conception various historians assume forces of entirely different kinds, all of which are incommensurate with the movement observed. Some see it as a force directly inherent in heroes, as the peasant sees the devil in the steam-engine; others, as a force resulting from several other forces, like the movement of the wheels; others again, as an intellectual influence, like the smoke that is blown away.

So long as histories are written of separate individuals, whether Caesars, Alexanders, Luthers or Voltaires, and not the histories of *all*—absolutely *all*—those who take part in an event, it is impossible not to ascribe to individual men a force which can compel other men to direct their activity towards a certain end. And the only conception of such a kind known to historians is the idea of power.

This conception is the sole handle by means of which the material of history, as at present expounded, can be dealt with; and anyone who breaks that handle off, as Buckle did, without finding some other method of treating historical material, merely deprives himself of the last possible way of dealing with it. The necessity for the conception of power as an explanation of the phenomena of history is most strikingly illustrated by the universal historians and historians of culture themselves, who, after professedly rejecting the conception of power, inevitably have recourse to it at every step.

Up to now historical science in its relation to humanity's

inquiry is like money in circulation—bank-notes and coin. The biographies and national histories are the paper money. They may pass and circulate and fulfil their function without mischief to anyone, and even to advantage, so long as no question arises as to the security behind them. One has only to forget to ask how the will of heroes produces events, and the histories of Thiers and his fellows will be interesting, instructive and not without their touch of poetry. But in exactly the same way as doubts of the real value of bank-notes arise either because, being easy to manufacture, too many of them get made, or because people try to exchange them for gold, so doubts concerning the real value of histories of this kind arise either because too many of them are written or because someone in the simplicity of his heart inquires: What force enabled Napoleon to do that?—that is, wants to exchange the current paper money for the pure gold of true understanding.

The writers of universal histories and the history of culture are like people who, recognizing the defects of paper money, decide to substitute for it coin of some metal inferior to gold. Their money will be "hard coin," no doubt; but while paper money may deceive, the ignorant coin of inferior metal will deceive no one. Just as gold is gold only where it is employable not merely for barter but also for the real use of gold, so too the universal historians will only rank as gold when they are able to answer the cardinal question of history: What constitutes power? The universal historians give contradictory replies to this question, while the historians of culture thrust it aside altogether and answer something quite different. And as imitation gold counters can only be used among a community of persons who agree to accept them for gold or who are ignorant of the nature of gold, so the universal historians and historians of culture who fail to answer the essential questions of humanity only serve as currency for sundry purposes of their own—in the universities and among the legions who go in for "serious" reading, as they are pleased to call it.

IV

Having dismissed the conviction of the ancients as to the divinely ordained subjection of the will of a nation to the one chosen vessel and the subjection of the will of that chosen vessel to the Deity, history cannot take a single step without being involved in contradictions. It must choose one of two alternatives: either to return to its old belief in the direct intervention of the Deity in human affairs, or to find a definite explanation of the meaning of the force producing historical events which is termed "power."

A return to the first is impossible: the old belief has been shattered, and so an explanation must be found of what is meant by power.

"Napoleon commanded an army to be raised and to march forth to war." Such a statement is so familiar, we are so entirely at home with such a point of view, that the question why six hundred thousand men go out to fight when Napoleon utters certain words seems to us foolish. He had the power and so what he ordered was done.

This solution is perfectly satisfactory if we believe that the power was given him by God. But, as soon as we discountenance that, it becomes essential to determine what this power is that one man has over others.

It cannot be the direct physical ascendancy of a strong creature over a weak one—an ascendancy based on the application or threat of physical force, like the power of Hercules; nor can it be founded on the possession of moral force, as in the innocence of their hearts some historians suppose, who say that the leading figures in history are cast in heroic mould, that is, are endowed with an extra-ordinary strength of soul and mind called genius. This power cannot be based on any preponderance of moral strength seeing that, not to mention heroes such as Napoleon concerning whose moral qualities opinions differ widely, history shows us that neither a Louis XI nor a Metternich, who ruled over millions of their fellows, had any particular moral qualities but on the contrary in most respects were morally weaker than any of the millions they ruled over.

If the source of power lies neither in the physical nor the moral qualities of the individual who possesses it, it is obvious that it must be looked for elsewhere—in the relation to the masses of the man who wields the power.

And that is how power is understood by the science of jurisprudence, that *bureau d'échange* of history, which undertakes to exchange history's concept of power for true gold.

Power is the collective will of the masses, transferred by their expressed or tacit consent to their chosen rulers.

In the domain of jurisprudence, deliberating as it does on how the State and its power ought to be constructed were it possible to do so *a priori,* all this is very clear; but when applied to actual history this definition of power calls for elucidation.

The science of jurisprudence regards the State and its power much as the ancients regarded fire—namely, as something existing absolutely. For history the State and its power are merely phenomena, in the same way as for modern physics fire is not an element but a phenomenon.

From this fundamental difference in the points of view of history and jurisprudence it follows that jurisprudence can discuss in detail how, in its opinion, power should be constituted and what power is in its immutable essence, outside the conditions of time; but to history's questions about the meaning of the mutations of power in time it can return no answer.

If power is the collective will of the masses transferred to their ruler, was Pugachov a representative of the will of the people? If not, then why was Napoleon I? Why was Napoleon III a criminal when he was apprehended at Boulogne, and why were those whom he afterwards apprehended criminals?

Do palace revolutions—in which sometimes only two or three people take part—transfer the will of the people to a new ruler? In international relations is the will of the people also transferred to their conqueror? Was the will of the Confederation of the Rhine transferred to Napoleon in 1808? Was the will of the Russian people transferred to Napoleon in 1809 when our army in alliance with the French made war upon Austria?

These questions may be answered in three different ways:

(1) by maintaining that the will of the people is always unconditionally transferred to the ruler or rulers whom they have chosen, and that therefore every emergence of a new power, every struggle against the power once delegated, must be regarded as a contravention of the real power; or

(2) by maintaining that the will of the masses is delegated to the rulers on certain definite and known conditions, and by showing that all restrictions on, conflicts with and even abolitions of power proceed from non-observance by the rulers of the conditions upon which their power was entrusted to them; or

(3) by maintaining that the will of the masses is delegated to the rulers conditionally but that the conditions are uncertain and undefined, and that the appearance of several authorities, their struggles and their falls result solely from the greater or lesser fulfilment by the rulers of the uncertain conditions upon which the will of the people is transferred from one set of persons to another.

These are the three ways in which the historians explain the relation of the masses to their rulers.

Some historians, failing in their simplicity to understand the question of the meaning of power—those sectional and biographical historians already referred to—seem to believe that the collective will of the people is delegated to historical leaders unconditionally, and therefore in writing about some particular State they assume that Power to be the one absolute and real power, and that any other force opposing it is not a power but a violation of power—mere violence.

This theory of theirs, though convenient for covering primitive and peaceful periods of history, has the disadvantage when applied to complex and stormy periods in the life of nations, during which various powers arise simultaneously and come into collision, that the legitimist historian will try to prove that the Convention, the Directory and Bonaparte were only infringers of the true power, while the Republican and Bonapartist will argue, the one that the Convention and the other that the Empire was the true authority and all the rest a violation of authority. It is evident that the interpretations furnished by these historians, being mutually contradictory, can satisfy none but children of the tenderest age.

Recognizing the falsity of this view of history, another class of historians assert that power rests on a conditional delegation of the collective will of the people to their rulers, and that historical leaders possess power only conditionally on their carrying out the programme which the will of the people has by tacit agreement prescribed to them. But what this programme consists of, these historians do not tell us, or if they do they continually contradict one another.

Each historian, according to his view of what constitutes the goal of a nation's progress, conceives of this programme as, for instance, the greatness, the wealth, the freedom or the enlightenment of the citizens of France or some other country. But ignoring the mutual contradictions of the historians as to the nature of this programme—even granted the existence of some one general programme—we find that the facts of history almost always gainsay this theory. If the conditions on which power is vested in rulers consist in the wealth, freedom and enlightenment of the people, how is it that Louis XIV and Ivan the Terrible live out their reigns in peace, while Louis XVI and Charles I are put to death by their peoples? To this question such historians reply that the actions of Louis XIV, which ran counter to the programme, were visited on Louis XVI. But why did they not react on Louis XIV or Louis XV?—why expressly on Louis XVI? And what is the term for such reactions? To these questions there is and can be no reply. Equally little does this view explain why for several centuries the collective will remains vested in certain rulers and their heirs, and then suddenly in the course of fifty years is transferred to a Convention, to a Directory, to a Napoleon, to an Alexander, to a Louis XVIII, to a Napoleon again, to a Charles X, to a Louis Philippe, to a Republican government and to a Napoleon III. To explain these swift transferences of the people's will from one individual to another, especially when complicated by international relations, conquests and alliances, the historians are reluctantly obliged to allow that a proportion of these phenomena are not normal delegations of the popular will but accidents proceeding from the cunning or the craft, the blundering or the weakness, of a diplomatist, a monarch or a party leader. So that most of the phenomena of history—civil wars, revolutions, conquests—are presented by these historians not as the results of free transferences of the people's will but as the products of the ill-directed will of one or more individuals, that is, once again, as usurpations of power. And so these historians too see historical events as exceptions to their theory.

These historians are like a botanist who, having observed

that some plants germinate with two cotyledons, should insist that every growing thing grows by dividing into a pair of leaflets; and that the palm-tree, therefore, and the mushroom, nay, even the oak—which in its full-grown ramification loses all resemblance to the twin-leaflet, dicotyledonous form—are departures from theory.

Historians of the third class assume that the will of the people is vested in historical personages conditionally, but that the conditions are not known to us. They say that historical leaders have powers only because they are carrying out the will of the people which has been delegated to them.

But in that case, if the force that moves nations lies not in their historical leaders but in the peoples themselves, where is the significance of those leaders?

Historical personages, so these historians tell us, are the expression of the will of the masses: the activity of the historical leader represents the activity of the people.

But in that case the question arises, Does all the activity of the leaders serve as an expression of the people's will, or only a certain side of it? If the whole activity of the leaders serves as the expression of the people's will, as some historians suppose, then all the *minutiae* of court scandal contained in the biographies of the Napoleons and the Catherines serve to express the life of the nation, which is obvious nonsense; but if it is only one side of the activity of an historical leader which serves to express the life of a people, as other so-called "philosophical" historians believe, then in order to determine what side of the activity of the historical personage expresses the nation's life we have first of all to know in what the nation's life consists.

Confronted by this difficulty, historians of the kind I am speaking of will invent some most obscure and impalpable, generalized abstraction to cover the greatest possible number of occurrences, and then declare this abstraction to be the aim of mankind's movement. The most usual generalizations adopted by almost all historians are: freedom, equality, enlightenment, progress, civilization and culture. Having postulated some such generalization as the goal of the movements of humanity, the historians go on to study those personages in history who have left the greatest number of memorials behind them: kings, ministers, generals, authors, reformers, popes and journalists—according as these personages, in their judgement, have contributed to or hindered the abstraction in question. But as it is nowhere proven that the aim of humanity does consist in freedom, equality, enlightenment or civilization, and as the connexion of the masses with the rulers and enlighteners of humanity only rests on the arbitrary assumption that the collective will of the masses is always vested in these figures which attract our attention, it happens that the activity of the millions who migrate, burn their houses, abandon tilling the soil, and butcher one another, never does find expression in descriptions of the activity of some dozen persons who do not burn houses, have nothing to do with agriculture or killing their fellow-creatures.

History proves this at every turn. Is the ferment of the peoples of the west at the end of the last century and their drive eastwards explained by the activity of Louis XIV, XV and XVI, their mistresses and ministers, or by the lives of Napoleon, Rousseau, Diderot, Beaumarchais and others?

Is the movement of the Russian people eastwards to Kazan and Siberia expressed in the details of the morbid character of Ivan the Terrible and his correspondence with Kurbsky?

Is the movement of the peoples at the time of the Crusades explained by the life and activity of the Godfreys and the Louises and their ladies? For us that movement of the peoples from west to east, without any object, without leadership—a crowd of vagrants following Peter the Hermit—remains incomprehensible. And still more incomprehensible is the cessation of that movement when a rational and sacred aim for the Crusades—the deliverance of Jerusalem—had been clearly proclaimed by historical leaders. Popes, kings and knights urged the people to free the Holy Land; but the people did not move, for the unknown cause which had previously impelled them existed no longer. The history of the Godfreys and the Minnesingers evidently cannot be taken as an epitome of the life of the people. And the history of the Godfreys and Minnesingers has remained the history of Godfreys and Minnesingers, while the history of the life of the people and their incentives has remained unknown.

Even less explanatory of the life of the people is the history of writers and reformers.

The history of culture will explain to us the impelling motives and circumstances of the life and thoughts of a writer or a reformer. We may learn that Luther had a hasty temper and delivered such and such orations; we may learn that Rousseau was of a suspicious nature and wrote such and such books; but we shall not learn why the nations flew at one another's throats after the Reformation, or why men guillotined one another during the French Revolution.

If we unite both these kinds of history, as is done by the most modern historians, we shall get histories of monarchs and writers but not history of the lives of nations.

V

The life of nations cannot be summarized in the lives of a few men, for the connexion between those men and the nations has not been discovered. The theory that this connexion is based on the transference of the collective will of a people to certain historical personages is a hypothesis not supported by the experience of history.

The theory of the transference of the collective will of the people to historical personages may perhaps explain much in the domain of jurisprudence and be essential for its purposes, but in its application to history, as soon as revolutions, conquests or civil wars make their appearance—as soon as history begins, in fact—this theory explains nothing.

The theory seems to be irrefutable just because the act of transference of the people's will cannot be verified.

No matter what event takes place, nor who directs it, the theory can always claim that such and such a person took the lead because the collective will was vested in him.

The replies this theory gives to historical questions are like the replies of a man who, watching the movements of a herd of cattle, and paying no attention to the varying quality of the pasturage in different parts of the field, or to the drover's stick, should attribute the direction the herd takes to what animal happens to be at its head.

"The herd goes in that direction because the animal in front leads it there and the collective will of all the other cattle is vested in that leader." That is what historians in our first category say—those who assume an unconditional transference of power.

"If the animals leading the herd change, this happens because the collective will of all the cattle is transferred from one leader to another, according to whether the leader leads them in the direction selected by the whole herd." Such is the reply of the historians who assume that the collective will of the masses is delegated to rulers on terms which they regard as known. (With this method of observation it very often happens that the observer, influenced by the direction he himself prefers, reckons as leaders those who, owing to the people's change of direction, are no longer in front but on one side or even in the rear.)

"If the beasts in front are continually changing and the direction of the whole herd constantly alters, this is because, in order to follow a given direction, the cattle transfer their will to those beasts which attract our attention, and to study the movements of the herd we must watch the movements of all the prominent animals moving on all sides of the herd." So say the third class of historians who accept all historical characters, from monarchs to journalists, as the expression of their age.

The theory of the transference of the will of the masses to historical persons is merely a paraphrase—a re-statement of the question in other words.

What causes historical events? Power.

What is power? Power is the collective will of the masses vested in one person.

On what condition is the will of the people delegated to one person? On condition that that person expresses the will of the whole people.

That is, power is power. That is, power is a word the meaning of which we do not understand.

If the domain of human knowledge were confined to abstract thinking, then humanity, having subjected to criticism the explanation of power that *juridical science* gives us, would conclude that power is merely a word and has no existence in reality. But for the knowledge of phenomena man has, besides abstract reasoning, another instrument—experience—by which he verifies the results of his reasoning. And experience tells him that power is not merely a word but an actually existing phenomenon.

Not to speak of the fact that no description of the collective activity of men can dispense with the concept of power, the existence of power is proved both by history and by observation of contemporary events.

Whenever an event occurs one man or several men make their appearance, by whose will the event seems to take place. Napoleon III issues a decree and the French go to Mexico. The King of Prussia and Bismarck issue decrees and an army enters Bohemia. Napoleon I gives a command and soldiers march into Russia. Alexander I gives a command and the

French submit to the Bourbons. Experience shows us that whatever event occurs it is always related to the will of one or of several men who decreed it should be so.

The historians, from the old habit of recognizing divine intervention in human affairs, are inclined to look for the cause of events in the exercise of the will of the person endowed with power, but this supposition is not confirmed either by reason or by experience.

On the one hand reflection shows that the expression of man's will—his words—are only part of the general activity expressed in an event, as for instance, in a war or a revolution; and so without assuming an incomprehensible, supernatural force—a miracle—it is impossible to admit that words can be the immediate cause of the movements of millions of men. On the other hand, even if we admitted that words could be the cause of events, history shows that the expression of the will of historical personages in the majority of cases does not produce any effect—that is, their commands are often not executed and sometimes the very opposite of what they order is done.

Without admitting divine intervention in the affairs of humanity we cannot accept "power" as the cause of events.

Power, from the standpoint of experience, is merely the relation that exists between the expression of the will of a person and the execution of that will by others.

To explain the conditions of that relationship we must first of all establish a concept of the expression of will, referring it to man and not to the Deity.

If it were the Deity giving commands and expressing His

will (as history written by the older school assures us), the expression of that will could never be dependent upon time nor evoked by temporal things, seeing that the Deity is in no way bound to the event. But when we speak of commands that are the expression of the will of men, functioning in time and having a relation to one another, we must, if we are to understand the connexion of commands with events, restore two conditions: (1) the uninterrupted connexion in the time process both of the events themselves and of the person issuing commands—a condition to which all that occurs is subject; and (2) the indispensable connexion between the person issuing commands and those who execute them.

VI

Only the expression of the will of the Deity, not affected by time, can relate to a whole series of events that have to take place over a period of years or centuries; and only the Deity, who is stirred to action by no temporal agency, can by His sole will determine the direction of humanity's movement. Man is subject to time and himself takes part in the event.

Reinstating the first condition neglected—that of time—we perceive that no single command can be executed without some preceding command making the execution of the last command possible.

No command ever appears spontaneously (i.e. without any external stimulus), or itself covers a whole series of occurrences; but each command follows from another, and never refers to a whole series of events but always to one moment only of an event.

When we say, for instance, that Napoleon ordered armies to go to war we combine in one single expression a series of consecutive commands dependent one on another. Napoleon could not have commanded an invasion of Russia and never did so. One day he ordered certain documents to be dispatched to Vienna, to Berlin and to Petersburg; the following day saw such and such decrees and orders issued to the army, the fleet, the commissariat, and so on and so on—millions of separate commands making up a series of commands corresponding to a series of events which brought the French armies into Russia.

If throughout his reign Napoleon continues to issue commands concerning an invasion of England and expends on no other undertaking so much time and effort, and yet during his whole reign never once attempts to execute his design but undertakes an expedition into Russia, with which country, according to his repeatedly expressed conviction, he considers it to his advantage to be in alliance—then this results from the fact that his commands did not correspond to the course of events in the first case but did so in the latter.

For a command to be carried out to the letter it must be a command actually capable of fulfilment. But to know what can and what cannot be carried out is impossible, not only in the case of Napoleon's invasion of Russia, in which millions participated, but even in the case of the simplest event, seeing that both the one and the other are liable at any moment to find themselves confronted by millions of obstacles. Every command executed is always one of an immense number unexecuted. All the impossible commands are inconsistent with the course of events and do not get carried out. Only the possible ones link up into a consecutive series of commands corresponding to a series of events, and are carried out.

Our erroneous idea that the command which precedes the event causes the event is due to the fact that when the event has taken place and out of thousands of commands those few which were consistent with that event have been executed we forget about the others that were not executed because they could not be. Apart from that, the chief source of our error in this regard arises from the fact that in the historical account a whole series of innumerable, diverse and petty events, such, for example, as all those which led the French soldiers into Russia, is generalized into a single event in accord with the result produced by that series of events; and by a corresponding generalization a whole series of commands is also summed up into a single expression of will.

We say: Napoleon chose to invade Russia and he did so. In reality we never find in all Napoleon's career anything resembling an expression of that design. What we do find is a series of commands or expressions of his will of the most varied and indefinite tenor possible. Out of a countless series of unexecuted commands of Napoleon's one series, for the campaign of 1812, was carried out—not because they differed in any way from other commands that were *not* executed but because they coincided with the course of events which brought the French army into Russia; just as in stencil-work a certain figure comes out, not because the colour was laid on from this side or in a particular way but because colour was smeared all over the figure cut out in the stencil.

So that examining the relation in time of commands to events we find that a command can never in any case be the cause of the event but that a definite interdependence none the less exists between the two.

To understand what this interdependence is, it is necessary to reinstate the second of our two conditions governing every command which emanates from man and not from the Deity—the condition that the man who issues the command must also be a participator in the event.

It is this relation of commander to commanded which is called "power." This relation may be analysed as follows:

For the purpose of common action men always unite in certain combinations in which, regardless of the difference of the aims set for their common action, the relation between those taking part in it always remains the same.

Men uniting in these combinations always assume among themselves such a relationship that the larger number take a more direct part, and the smaller number a less direct part, in the collective action for which they have combined.

Of all such combinations in which men unite for joint action one of the most striking and precise is an army.

Every army is composed of men of the lowest service grades—the rank and file—who always form the majority; then of those of a slightly higher military standing—corporals and non-commissioned officers, fewer in number than the privates; and of still higher officers, of whom there are still fewer, and so on up to the highest military command, which is concentrated in one person.

A military organization may very truly be likened to a cone, the base of which, with the largest diameter, consists of the rank and file; the next higher and smaller section of the cone consists of the next higher grades of the army, and so on to the apex, the point of which will represent the commander-in-chief.

The soldiers forming the majority constitute the lower section of the cone and its base. The soldier himself does the stabbing and hacking, the burning and pillaging, and always receives orders for these actions from the men above him: he himself never gives an order. The non-commissioned officer (there are not so many of him) does less of the immediate work of war than the private, but he gives commands. An officer takes an active part more rarely still but issues commands the more frequently. A general does nothing but command the army, indicates the objective and hardly ever uses a weapon himself. Finally the commander-in-chief: he never takes a direct part in the actual work of war but only makes general dispositions for the movement of the masses under him. A similar mutual relationship of individuals obtains in every combination of men for joint activity—in agriculture, commerce and every administrative department.

Thus, without exaggeratedly separating all the contiguous sections of the cone—all the ranks of an army, or the ranks and positions in any administrative or public body, from lowest to highest—we discern a law by which men concerned to take common action combine in such relations that the more directly they participate in performing the action the less they can command and the more numerous they are, while the less they take any direct part in the work itself the more they command and the fewer they are in number; rising in this way from the lowest strata to a single man at the top, who takes the least direct share in the action and devotes his energy to a greater extent than all the others to the giving of commands.

It is this relationship between commander and commanded which constitutes the essence of the concept called power.

Having restored the conditions of time under which all events take place, we find that a command is executed only when it is related to a corresponding course of events. Likewise restoring the essential condition of connexion between those who command and those who execute, we have seen that by the very nature of the case those who command take the smallest part in the action itself, and that their activity is exclusively directed to commanding.

VII

When some event takes place people express their various opinions and hopes in regard to it, and inasmuch as the event proceeds from the collective activity of many some one of the opinions or hopes expressed is sure to be fulfilled, if only approximately. When one of the opinions expressed is fulfilled that opinion gets connected with the event as the command preceding it.

Men are hauling a log. Each of them may be expressing opinion as to how and where it should be hauled. They haul the log to its destination, and it turns out that it has been done in accordance with what one of them said. He gave the command. This is commanding and power in their primary form. The man who laboured hardest with his arms was the least able to think what he was doing, or reflect on what would be the result of the common activity, or give a command; while the man who was doing the most commanding was obviously the least able of the party, by reason of his greater verbal activity, to perform direct manual labour. In a larger aggregate of men directing their efforts to a common end the category of those who, because their activity is devoted to giving commands, take less part in the joint enterprise stands out still more prominently.

When a man is acting alone he always keeps before him a certain set of considerations which, so he believes, have regulated his action in the past, justify his action in the present and guide him in planning future activity.

In exactly the same way amalgamations of people leave those who do not take a direct part in the activity to devise considerations, justifications and projects concerning their collective activity.

For reasons known or unknown to us the French began to shipwreck and butcher each other. And corresponding to and accompanying this phenomenon we have the justification of the people's expressed determination that this was necessary for the welfare of France, for liberty and for equality. The French cease to murder one another, and justify that on the ground of the necessity of a centralization of power, of resistance to Europe, and so on. Men march from west to east, slaying their fellow-men, and this proceeding is accompanied by figures of speech about the glory of France, the baseness of England, and so on. History shows us that these justifications of events have no general sense and are self-contradictory—like, for instance, killing a man pursuant to recognition of his rights, or the slaughter of millions in Russia for the humiliation of England. But these justifications have a very necessary significance in their own day.

These justifications relieve those who produce the events from moral responsibility. At the time they do the work of the brooms that are fixed in front of a locomotive to clear the snow from the rails ahead: they clear men's moral responsibilities from their path. Without such justifications there would be no reply to the exceedingly simple question which presents itself when we examine any historical event: How do millions of men come to combine to commit crimes, wars, massacres and so forth?

Under the present complex forms of political and social life in Europe can any event be imagined that is not prescribed, decreed or ordered by monarchs, ministers, parliaments or newspapers? Is there any collective action which cannot find its justification in political unity, in patriotism, in the balance of power or in civilization? So that every event that occurs inevitably coincides with some expressed desire and, having found justification for itself, appears as the product of the will of one or more persons.

In whatever direction a ship is moving the surge where the prow cuts the waves will always be noticeable ahead. To those on board the ship the movement of this wave-form will be the only movement they see.

Only by watching closely, moment by moment, the movement of this wave-form and comparing it with that of the ship shall we convince ourselves that it is entirely conditioned by the forward movement of the ship and that we were deluded by the fact that we ourselves are imperceptibly moving.

We see the same thing if we observe, moment by moment, the movement of historical personages (that is, restoring the inevitable condition of all that occurs—continuity in the flow of time) and do not lose sight of the essential connexion of historical figures with the masses.

When the ship keeps on in one direction the surge ahead of her stays constant; if she tacks about, it too will change. But wherever the ship may turn there will always be the surge ahead, anticipating her movement.

Whatever happens it will always appear that precisely this had been foreseen and decreed. Whichever way the ship turns, the surge which neither directs nor accelerates her movement will always foam ahead of her and at a distance seem to us not merely to be moving on its own account but to be governing the ship's movement also.

Examining only those expressions of the will of historical personages which may be considered to have borne to events the relation of commands, historians have assumed that events depend on commands. But examining the events themselves and the connexion in which the historical characters stand to the masses, we have found that historical characters and their commands are dependent on the event. An incontestable proof of this deduction lies in the fact that, however many commands may be given, the event does not take place unless there are other causes for it; but as soon as an event does take place—whatever it may be—then out of all the incessantly expressed wishes of different people some will always be found which in meaning and time of utterance will bear to the event the relation of commands.

Arriving at this conclusion, we are able to give a direct and positive reply to those two essential questions of history:

(1) What is power?

(2) What force produces the movement of nations?

(1) Power is the relation of a given person to other persons, in which the more this person expresses opinions, theories and justifications of the collective action the less is his participation in that action.

(2) The movement of nations is caused not by power, nor by intellectual activity, nor even by a combination of the two, as historians have supposed, but by the activity of *all* the people who participate in the event, and who always combine in such a way that those who take the largest direct share in the event assume the least responsibility, and *vice versa*.

Morally, power appears to cause the event; physically, it is those who are subordinate to that power. But, inasmuch as moral activity is inconceivable without physical activity, the cause of the event is found neither in the one nor the other but in the conjunction of the two.

Or, in other words, the concept of a cause is not applicable to the phenomenon we are examining.

In the last analysis we reach an endless circle—that uttermost limit to which in every domain of thought the human intellect must come if it is not playing with its subject. Electricity produces heat; heat produces electricity. Atoms attract and atoms repel one another.

Speaking of the interaction of heat and electricity and of atoms we cannot say why this occurs, and we say that such is the nature of these phenomena, such is their law. The same applies to historical phenomena. Why do wars or revolutions happen? We do not know. We only know that to produce the one or the other men form themselves into a certain combination in which all take part; and we say that this is the nature of men, that this is a law.

SOPHOCLES

Sophocles, the literary, philosophical, and psychological giant of ancient Greece, and the playwright who explored our mind's life, was born in Colonus, outside Athens, around 496 B.C., and died in 406 B.C. To this day he inspires us to understand how we think—with what stirrings of affection, lust, disagreement, anger, hate. Sophocles reflected on the workings of the individual passions, and dared to show how they affected political life. He portrayed individuals taking stands against unjust political leaders, and defending their own values, lives, homes, and states.

In *Oedipus Rex, Electra,* and *Antigone,* Sophocles uses character, memory, and experience to carry the drama; and in so doing, he depicts the complexities of human relatedness, including the political loyalties we develop, or sometimes, the political defiance we choose to express.

In *Antigone,* Creon, the king of Thebes, has forbidden the proper burial of all those who have rebelled against his rule. Antigone, a young girl soon to marry Creon's son, disobeys this edict to bury her brother, Polyneices. In this play, we see the themes of obedience and trust emerging. Here, a poet of long ago says enough in a few lines to inspire the work of today's psychologists and political scientists.

From ANTIGONE

SCENE: *Courtyard of the royal palace at Thebes. Daybreak.*

Enter ANTIGONE *and* ISMENE

ANTIGONE:

Dear sister! Dear Ismene! How many evils
Our father, Oedipus, bequeathed to us!
And is there one of them—do you know of one
That Zeus has not showered down upon our heads?
I have seen pain, dishonor, shame, and ruin,
I have seen them all, in what we have endured.
And now comes this new edict by the King
Proclaimed throughout the city. Have you heard?
Do you not know, even yet, our friends are threatened?
They are to meet the fate of enemies.

ISMENE:

Our friends, Antigone? No, I have heard
Nothing about them either good or bad.
I have no news except that we two sisters
Lost our two brothers when they killed each other.
I know the Argive army fled last night,
But what that means, or whether it makes my life
Harder or easier, I cannot tell.

ANTIGONE:

This I was sure of. So I brought you here
Beyond the palace gates to talk alone.

ISMENE:

What is the matter? I know you are deeply troubled.

ANTIGONE:

Yes, for our brothers' fate. Creon has given
An honored burial to one, to the other
Only unburied shame. Eteocles
Is laid in the earth with all the rites observed
That give him his due honor with the dead.
But the decree concerning Polyneices
Published through Thebes is that his wretched body
Shall lie unmourned, unwept, unsepulchered.
Sweet will he seem to the vultures when they find him,
A welcome feast that they are eager for.
This is the edict the good Creon uttered
For your observance and for mine—yes, mine.
He is coming here himself to make it plain
To those who have not heard.

. . . .

Now glorious Victory smiles upon jubilant Thebes rich in
        chariots.
    Let us give free rein to our joy, forgetting our late-felt war;
Let us visit in night-long chorus the temples of all the
        immortals,
    With Bacchus, who shakes the land in the dances, going
        before.
    But behold! The son of Monoeceus approaches,
        Creon, the new-crowned King of the land,
    Made King by new fortunes the gods have allotted.

What step has he pondered? What has he planned
To lay before us, his council of elders,
    Who have gathered together at his command?

Enter CREON

CREON:

Elders of Thebes, our city has been tossed
By a tempestuous ocean, but the gods
Have steadied it once more and made it safe.
You, out of all the citizens, I have summoned,
Because I knew that you once reverenced
The sovereignty of Laius, and that later,
When Oedipus was King and when he perished,
Your steadfast loyalty upheld his children.
And now his sons have fallen, each one stained
By his brother's blood, killed by his brother's hand,
So that the sovereignty devolves on me,
Since I by birth am nearest to the dead.
Certainly no man can be fully known,
Known in his soul, his will, his intellect,
Until he is tested and has proved himself
In statesmanship. Because a city's ruler,
Instead of following the wisest counsel,
May through some fear keep silent. Such a man
I think contemptible. And one whose friend
Has stronger claims upon him than his country,
Him I consider worthless. As for me,
I swear by Zeus, forever all-beholding,
That I would not keep silence, if I saw

Ruin instead of safety drawing near us;
Nor would I think an enemy of the state
Could be my friend. For I remember this:
Our country bears us all securely onward,
And only while it sails a steady course
Is friendship possible. Such are the laws
By which I guard the greatness of the city.
And kindred to them is the proclamation
That I have made to all the citizens
Concerning the two sons of Oedipus:
Eteocles, who has fallen in our defence,
Bravest of warriors, shall be entombed
With every honor, every offering given
That may accompany the noble dead
Down to their rest. But as for Polyneices,
He came from exile eager to consume
The city of his fathers with his fire
And all the temples of his fathers' gods,
Eager to drink deep of his kindred's blood,
Eager to drag us off to slavery.
To this man, therefore, nothing shall be given.
None shall lament him, none shall do him honor.
He shall be left without a grave, his corpse
Devoured by birds and dogs, a loathsome sight.

. . . .

CREON:

All of these Thebans disagree with you.

ANTIGONE:

No. They agree, but they control their tongues.

CREON:

You feel no shame in acting without their help?

ANTIGONE:

I feel no shame in honoring a brother.

CREON:

Another brother died who fought against him.

ANTIGONE:

Two brothers. The two sons of the same parents.

CREON:

Honor to one is outrage to the other.

ANTIGONE:

Eteocles will not feel himself dishonored.

. . . .

HAEMON:

The gods have given men the gift of reason,
Greatest of all things that we call our own.
I have no skill, nor do I wish to have it,
To show where you have spoken wrongly. Yet
Some other's thought, beside your own, might prove
To be of value. Therefore it is my duty,
My natural duty as your son, to notice,
On your behalf, all that men say, or do,
Or find to blame. For your frown frightens them,
So that the citizen dares not say a word
That would offend you. I can hear, however,

Murmurs in darkness and laments for her.
They say: "No woman ever less deserved
Her doom, no woman ever was to die
So shamefully for deeds so glorious.
For when her brother fell in bloody battle,
She would not let his body lie unburied
To be devoured by carrion dogs or birds.
Does such a woman not deserve reward,
Reward of golden honor?" This I hear,
A rumor spread in secrecy and darkness.
Father, I prize nothing in life so highly
As your well-being. How can children have
A nobler honor than their father's fame
Or father than his son's? Then do not think
Your mood must never alter; do not feel
Your word, and yours alone, must be correct.
For if a man believes that he is right
And only he, that no one equals him
In what he says or thinks, he will be found
Empty when searched and tested. Because a man
Even if he be wise, feels no disgrace
In learning many things, in taking care
Not to be over-rigid. You have seen
Trees on the margin of a stream in winter:
Those yielding to the flood save every twig,
And those resisting perish root and branch.
So, too, the mariner who never slackens
His taut sheet overturns his craft and spends
Keel uppermost the last part of his voyage.

Let your resentment die. Let yourself change.
For I believe—if I, a younger man,
May have a sound opinion—it is best
That men by nature should be wise in all things.
But most men find they cannot reach that goal;
And when this happens, it is also good
To learn to listen to wise counselors.

CHORUS:

Sir, when his words are timely, you should heed them.
And Haemon, you should profit by his words.
Each one of you has spoken reasonably.

CREON:

Are men as old as I am to be taught
How to behave by men as young as he?

HAEMON:

Not to do wrong. If I am young, ignore
My youth. Consider only what I do.

CREON:

Have you done well in honoring the rebellious?

HAEMON:

Those who do wrong should not command respect.

CREON:

Then that disease has not infected her?

HAEMON:

All of our city with one voice denies it.

CREON:

Does Thebes give orders for the way I rule?

HAEMON:

How young you are! How young in saying that!

CREON:

Am I to govern by another's judgment?

HAEMON:

A city that is one man's is no city.

CREON:

A city is the king's. That much is sure.

HAEMON:

You would rule well in a deserted country.

CREON:

This boy defends a woman, it appears.

HAEMON:

If you are one. I am concerned for you.

CREON:

To quarrel with your father does not shame you?

HAEMON:

Not when I see you failing to do justice.

CREON:

Am I unjust when I respect my crown?

HAEMON:

Respect it! When you trample down religion?

CREON:

Infamous! Giving first place to a woman!

HAEMON:

But never to anything that would disgrace me.

CREON:

Each word you utter is a plea for her.

HAEMON:

For you, too, and for me, and for the gods.

. . . .

From *Antigone*

TIRESIAS:

Elders of Thebes, we have come to you with one
Finding for both the pathway that we followed,
For in this fashion must the blind be guided.

CREON:

What tidings, old Tiresias, are you bringing?

TIRESIAS:

I will inform you, I the seer. Give heed.

CREON:

To ignore your counsel has not been my custom.

TIRESIAS:

Therefore you kept Thebes on a steady course.

CREON:

I can bear witness to the help you gave.

TIRESIAS:

Mark this. You stand upon the brink of ruin.

CREON:

What terrible words are those? What do you mean?

TIRESIAS:

My meaning is made manifest by my art
And my art's omens. As I took my station
Upon my ancient seat of augury,
Where round me birds of every sort come flocking,
I could no longer understand their language.
It was drowned out in a strange, savage clamor,
Shrill, evil, frenzied, inarticulate.
The whirr of wings told me their murderous talons
Tore at each other. Filled with dread, I then
Made trial of burnt sacrifice. The altar

Was fully kindled, but no clear, bright flame
Leaped from the offering; only fatty moisture
Oozed from the flesh and trickled on the embers,
Smoking and sputtering. The bladder burst,
And scattered in the air. The folds of fat
Wrapping the thigh-bones melted and left them bare.
Such was the failure of the sacrifice,
That did not yield the sign that I was seeking.
I learned these things from this boy's observation;
He is my guide as I am guide to others.
Your edict brings this suffering to the city,
For every hearth of ours has been defiled
And every altar. There the birds and dogs
Have brought their carrion, torn from the corpse
Of ill-starred Polyneices. Hence, the gods
Refuse our prayers, refuse our sacrifice,
Refuse the flame of our burnt-offerings.
No birds cry clearly and auspiciously,
For they are glutted with a slain man's blood.
Therefore, my son, consider what has happened.
All men are liable to grievous error;
But he who, having erred, does not remain
Inflexible, but rather makes amends
For ill, is not unwise or unrewarded.
Stubborn self-will incurs the charge of folly.
Give to the fallen the honors he deserves
And do not stab him. Are you being brave
When you inflict new death upon the dead?
Your good I think of; for your good I speak,

From *Antigone*

And a wise counselor is sweet to hear
When the advice he offers proves of value.

. . . .

CREON:

O, how may my sin be told?
The stubborn, death-fraught sin of a darkened brain!
Behold us here, behold
Father and son, the slayer and the slain!
Pain, only pain
Has come of my design.
Fate struck too soon; too soon your spirit fled.
My son, my young son, you are lying dead
Not for your folly, but for mine, for mine.

CHORUS:

Sir, you have come to learn the right too late.

CREON:

My lesson has been bitter and complete.
Some god has struck me down with crushing weight,
Filling my heart with cruelty and hate,
Trampling my happiness beneath his feet.
Grief, bitter grief, is man's fate.

Enter MESSENGER

MESSENGER (*indicating* HAEMON):

Your load is heavy, Sir, but there is more.
That is the burden you are bearing now.
Soon you must bear new woe within your house.

CREON:

And what worse misery can follow this?

MESSENGER:

    Your wife is dead, a mother like her son.

    Poor woman, by her own hand she has died.

CREON:

      By her own hand she died.

    Death, spare me! Can you never have your fill?

      Never be satisfied?

    Herald of evil, messenger of ill,

      Your harsh words kill,

    They smite me now anew.

      My wife is dead—You tell me my wife is dead.

      Death after death is heaped upon my head.

    Speak to me, boy. Is what you tell me true?

    It is no longer hidden. Sir, look there.

(The body of EURYDICE *is disclosed through the palace doors)*

CREON:

      Another horror that makes blind mine eyes!

    What further agony has fate in store?

    My dead son's body in my arms I bore,

      And now beside him his dead mother lies.

      I can endure no more.

MESSENGER:

    There at the altar with a keen-edged knife

    She stabbed herself; and as her eyes were darkened,

    She wailed the death of Megareus, her son,

    Who earlier had met a noble fate;

    She wailed for Haemon; then, with her last breath,

    You, as the slayer of your sons, she cursed.

CREON:

    I am shaken with terror, with terror past belief.

Is there none here to end my anguish? None?

    No sword to pierce me? Broken with my grief,

So steeped in agony that we are one.

MESSENGER:

    Sir, as she died, she burdened you with guilt,

Charging you with the death of both your sons.

CREON:

    And by what act of violence did she die?

MESSENGER:

    Hearing the shrill lament for Haemon's fate,

Deep in her heart she drove the bright blade home.

CREON (*to* HAEMON):

    I am your slayer, I alone.

I am guilty, only I.

    I, and none other, must atone.

Lead me away. The truth I own.

    Nothing is left, except to die.

CHORUS:

    If anything can be good, those words are good.

For when calamity has come upon us,

The thing that is the briefest is the best.

CREON:

    Draw near me, death! O longed for death, draw near!

Most welcome destiny, make no delay.

    Tell me my last hour, my last breath, is here.

I have no wish to see another day.

From OEDIPUS THE KING

OEDIPUS:

How great is the envy roused by wealth, by kingship,
By the subtle skill that triumphs over others
In life's hard struggle! Creon, who has been
For years my trusted friend, has stealthily
Crept in upon me anxious to seize my power,
The unsought gift the city freely gave me.
Anxious to overthrow me, he has bribed
This scheming mountebank, this fraud, this trickster,
Blind in his art and in everything but money!
Your art of prophecy! When have you shown it?
Not when the watch-dog of the gods was here,
Chanting her riddle. Why did you say nothing,
When you might have saved the city? Yet her puzzle
Could not be solved by the first passer-by.
A prophet's skill was needed, and you proved
That you had no such skill, either in birds
Or any other means the gods have given.
But I came, I, the ignorant Oedipus,
And silenced her. I had no birds to help me.
I used my brains. And it is I you now
Are trying to destroy in the hope of standing
Close beside Creon's throne. You will regret
This zeal of yours to purify the land,

You and your fellow-plotter. You seem old;
Otherwise you would pay for your presumption.

. . . .

CREON:

No. You would see, if you thought the matter through
As I have done. Consider. Who would choose
Kingship and all the terrors that go with it,
If, with the same power, he could sleep in peace?
I have no longing for a royal title
Rather than royal freedom. No, not I,
Nor any moderate man. Now I fear nothing.
Every request I make of you is granted,
And yet as king I should have many duties
That went against the grain. Then how could rule
Be sweeter than untroubled influence?
I have not lost my mind. I want no honors
Except the ones that bring me solid good.
Now all men welcome me and wish me joy.
Now all your suitors ask to speak with me,
Knowing they cannot otherwise succeed.
Why should I throw away a life like this
For a king's life? No one is treacherous
Who knows his own best interests. To conspire
With other men, or to be false myself,
Is not my nature. Put me to the test.
First, go to Delphi. Ask if I told the truth
About the oracle. Then if you find
I have had dealings with Tiresias, kill me.

My voice will echo yours in passing sentence.
But base your verdict upon something more
Than mere suspicion. Great injustice comes
From random judgments that bad men are good
And good men bad. To throw away a friend
Is, in effect, to throw away your life,
The prize you treasure most. All this, in time,
Will become clear to you, for time alone
Proves a man's honesty, but wickedness
Can be discovered in a single day.

CHORUS:

Sir, that is good advice, if one is prudent.
Hasty decisions always lead to danger.

OEDIPUS:

When a conspiracy is quick in forming,
I must move quickly to retaliate.
If I sat still and let my enemy act,
I would lose everything that he would gain.

CREON:

So then, my banishment is what you want?

OEDIPUS:

No, not your banishment. Your execution.

CREON:

I think you are mad. OE.: I can protect myself.

CREON:

You should protect me also. OE.: You? A traitor?

CREON:

Suppose you are wrong? OE.: I am the King. I rule.

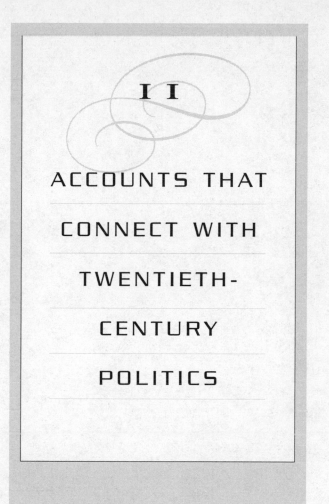

II

ACCOUNTS THAT

CONNECT WITH

TWENTIETH-

CENTURY

POLITICS

THE BITTER AND deadly serious (and sometimes tragic) political circumstances that came to bear on people of the twentieth century—who had to endure the totalitarianism of Germany and the Soviet Union, and the South Africa of apartheid, with its fiercely implacable racism—prompted certain writers to bear witness from afar, as did Orwell, or from near at hand, as Nadine Gordimer dared to do. In our own, more favored America, leaders have asserted themselves in the name of race, privilege, and power; but also decency and moral courage—as Robert Penn Warren and Carl Sandburg remind us.

"Red" Warren, as his friends called him, took on in his novel *All The King's Men* a racially divided and economically vulnerable region he knew well—its vulnerability a potential breeding ground for demagogues, adept at playing on the hopes and hatred of those whose votes can become, alas, instruments of blind assent. For Sandburg, the people, with a leader such as Lincoln, become an important historical *yes,* whereas Warren has us shuddering at the darker side of an electorate who become fodder for a leader's self-promotion, promises, and canniness.

NADINE GORDIMER

Born in Springs, South Africa, in 1923, Nadine Gordimer has lived all her life in South Africa. Author of twelve novels and ten collections of short stories and essays, Gordimer, in the majority of her work, deals with the moral and psychological tensions of her racially divided country. Her novels include *A Guest of Honour, The Conservationist, July's People, A Sport of Nature, My Son's Story,* and most recently, *None to Accompany Me.* Three of her books were banned in South Africa, including *The Late Bourgeois World* in 1966, and *Burger's Daughter* in 1979. Gordimer, also known as a screenwriter, political activist, and champion of the disenfranchised, won the Nobel Prize for Literature in 1991.

In 1990, I wrote the following essay about Gordimer's writing life, I was prompted to do so by the publication of *My Son's Story,* but also by memories of working firsthand in South Africa in an effort to understand how young people lived there under apartheid.

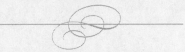

"A DIFFERENT SET OF RULES":
Robert Coles on *My Son's Story*

Throughout her career, the South African novelist Nadine Gordimer has wanted to explore the terrain where personal interests, desires and ambitions encounter (and, not rarely, contend with) the demands and trials of a politically active life. She has had a keen eye for the exceedingly precarious moral situation of her own kind—the privileged white intelligentsia that abhors apartheid, detests the exploitation of twenty-five million unfranchised, economically vulnerable citizens at the hands of five million people who, so far, have had a powerful modern army at their disposal, not to mention the wealth of a vigorous, advanced capitalist society.

To oppose the assumptions and everyday reality of a particular world, yet be among the men and women who enjoy its benefits—those accorded to the substantial upper bourgeoisie of, say, Johannesburg and Cape Town—is at the very least to know and live uneasily, maybe at times shamefacedly, with irony as a central aspect of one's introspective world. At what point is one's thoroughly comfortable, highly rewarded life as it is lived from year to year the issue—no matter the hoped-for extenuation that goes with a progressive voting record, an espousal of liberal pieties? Put differently, when ought one to break decisively with a social and political order, put on the line one's way of living (one's job, the welfare of one's family)?

In past novels, notably *Burger's Daughter*, Ms. Gordimer has asked such questions relentlessly of her own kind and, by extension, of all those readers who share her color and status in other countries less dramatically split and conflicted. Now, in *My Son's Story*, a bold, unnerving tour de force, she offers a story centered around the other side of both the racial line and the railroad tracks—yet the dilemmas that confront her characters are at heart very much like those that plague affluent whites, insofar as they allow themselves to oppose the entrenched authority of the South African government: how to measure up in one's daily, personal life to one's avowed ethical and political principles, one's activist sentiments and commitments.

The father who figures as the central character in this "son's story" is Sonny, a once obscure, humble schoolteacher whose political radicalization and prominence have been achieved at the start of the novel, which is told by the traditional, anonymous narrative voice of the author and by another, equally significant interpretive voice, that of Sonny's son, Will. Right off, the major psychological themes of disenchantment and betrayal are struck. The adolescent Will, telling a lie ("I would say I was going to work with a friend at a friend's house, and then I'd slip off to a cinema"), encounters his father in that very movie theater living a lie—there with a white woman, his lover. This is contemporary urban, cosmopolitan South Africa—movies desegregated, interracial sex no longer outlawed, but the heart of apartheid (its economic and political basis) still very much alive. The son's surprise, anger, disappointment, are expressed with great passion and vehemence—he, in fact, becomes the novelist's alter ego, an interesting split and one that enables a complex, many-sided, even contrapuntal presentation of what is at once a story of domestic manners (those all too familiar triangles of two women and a man, or of father, mother and son) and a tough-minded, fearlessly candid political novel in which any number of psychological and racial clichés are subject to a novelist's searching scrutiny.

In the early sections of *My Son's Story* we learn about the transformation of a "coloured" schoolteacher, his father, an upholsterer, into a revolutionary leader and orator. An autodidact, he had read Shakespeare and Kafka over and over, obtained from them the ultimate secular wisdom of Western letters—a wry, stoic sense of life's tragic and comic (sometimes absurdly comic) aspects. From his people, family and neighbors alike, and out of his own soul's decency and kindness, he found the daily strength needed by anyone who wants to be an honorable, loving husband and father. For Aila, his wife, for Baby, their daughter and first child, for Will, named after Shakespeare (how do some of us jaded folk, schooled for years, ever recapture the innocence and heartfelt sincerity of such a parental decision?), Sonny, the low-paid, earnest, hardworking civil servant and educator, once had an almost infinite supply of concern and affection. He attended them in every way—a sturdy householder, no matter the constant, terrible shadow of apartheid. But gradually Sonny got connected to his people's political struggle, an exceedingly dangerous one in a country whose ruling class for decades ruthlessly punished any and all activist dissent: a democracy for a white minority, a harsh totalitarian regime for a black majority. Gradually, too, he found less and less time for his family. He shows up now and then, but hurriedly leaves. To call upon a well-known biblical polarity, he is trying to gain a whole new world for others, yet his own family's world, maybe his soul, too, are in grave jeopardy.

Sonny's political ascent is a major topic for the novel's one narrator (who is obviously horrified by apartheid and anxious to see it ended, and is struggling to find the self-respect that goes with a principled observer's persistent dissent). It is this narrator who gives us a rather conventional, well-told account of a family's ups and downs, its transition from social and emotional ordinariness to a life of both marginality and prominence. Sonny goes to jail, and with that experience comes a spiritual transfiguration of sorts—the emergence of the political leader whose worth and integrity have been tested in the oppressor's bestial dungeons. Soon enough, he is privy to the exceptional life of the freedom-fighter—the hardship during and after imprisonment of relentless state surveillance, but also the respect and even worship that come his way from certain whites as well as his own people. One of the former, Hannah Plowman (she has a last name, none of the "coloured" people do), visits Sonny (talk about names!) in prison as a representative of an international human rights organization, and upon his release they become intimate.

This love affair is treated by Ms. Gordimer in her regular authorial presence with great tenderness, compassion, good will. Indeed, much of the novel's power and interest derive from her almost uncanny ability to portray each of the novel's characters with sympathy and subtlety. Sonny's gentle goodness, his immense personal dignity, his courage, are emblematic of the best we have come to know over the past decades in Nelson Mandela and Martin Luther King Jr., and in those lesser known but no less brave, resourceful, idealistic men and women who have worked alongside them. Aila's endurance, her carefully maintained emotional stability, her generosity of spirit bring to mind any number of wives who have tried with all their might to hold things together at home while their husbands took on social and racial evils in the public arena.

Hannah Plowman is no fatuous or self-indulgent or arrogantly patronizing white liberal activist, a stereotype the author obviously wants strenuously to avoid giving to the legions waiting for just such satisfactions from her. Hannah's good will and intelligence are obvious, and so is her essential uprightness and honesty. She is the proverbial Other Woman, without the protection that racial victimization and political heroism afford. Yet the author who tells us of her wants us to understand, sympathize with, admire her; and in similar fashion, we are nudged toward a compassionate understanding of Baby, who is, however, the least satisfactorily examined of the major characters. Her youthful, rebellious self-centeredness is all too readily redeemed by an abrupt marriage, exile, and a turn toward her own kind of radical activism against South Africa, though from the relative safety of Tanzania.

There is, however, another way of looking at Sonny and, more broadly, at those who in public exhort others with respect to all sorts of virtues, even fight gallantly on behalf of them, yet who abandon their families for the heavy demand of political activism, though also for personal pleasures—not only sex, the easiest one for many of today's novelists to describe, but arguably more problematic (if not perverse) thrills and addictions such as celebrity and power. This alternative view is given expression by Will; the story, as the title tells us, is his take on yet another of our great men, our heroic figures whose courage and values we gladly applaud.

A novelist's brilliant decision works wonders, ever so slowly yet decisively. A boy stumbles into his august father's secret life, is stunned by the casual, relaxed manner in which the father is living that life, is confused at the seeming expectation that he, too, an adolescent belonging in a once tight-knit family, will take in stride such circumstances. His perplexity and frustration give way to a sustained, withering scorn—a sardonic voice that keeps at the reader, reminds us that this is a novel meant to look closely and with nuanced force at moral complexity, moral ambiguity, but most pointedly at moral hypocrisy, which is in no short supply among many of us, no matter our nation, our race, our class and, not least, our educational attainment. One more leader, a larger-than-life figure, is found to have clay feet—by his son, who has occasions aplenty to witness the human consequences of such a disparity between a public and a private person.

To the end, Will won't let up—his sharp, unsentimental vision contrasts tellingly with the lofty aspirations of the others. Even Aila gets drawn into revolutionary politics and, eventually, a trial that threatens to end in her imprisonment, too. (Like her daughter, she chooses exile.) Only Will stands apart—saddened, hurt, alarmed, disgusted. A fearful, cynical youth, he slowly becomes a discerning, thoughtful observer of his own family, not to mention, by implication, all those who talk up a good storm (in their books and articles, their lectures, their graduation talks, their political speeches) but live by rules other than those they choose to enunciate for their readers, listeners. In a stunning conclusion, a mix of prose and poetry, Ms. Gordimer tells us that her Will has lived up to his name: "What he did—my father—made me a writer. Do I have to thank him for that? Why couldn't I have been something else? I am a writer and this is my first book— that I can never publish."

She is suggesting that with respect to our moral and political leaders many important biographical facts may go unmentioned, even by those who know exactly the nature and significance of those facts. The sons of our idols (or the husbands, the wives, the daughters) keep quiet; friends and colleagues, even journalists and historians, speak tactfully, if at all, about certain matters, and justify their silence, their discretion, their apologies, with clever rationalizations.

The idol must not fall—consequently, a public deception

persists, and with it a kind of public blindness. It is left to playwrights and novelists, our Shakespeares and Tolstoys and their descendants today (they who have no claim upon factuality or realpolitik), to render the many and often disparate truths of human experience, the inconsistencies and contradictions, the troubling paradoxes. The heart and soul of this brilliantly suggestive and knowing novel is its courageous exploration of such matters, of the conceits and deceits that inform the lives not only of ordinary people but those whom the rest of us invest with such majesty and awe.

An Excerpt from MY SON'S STORY

Who is Hannah Plowman?

Not only his father's blonde. Not the woman cast by the adolescent son as an excuse for sulky defensiveness, disdain—and jealousy. Not the fancy-woman fellow-traveller of a coloured with a subversive record, known to the Security Police. The dossier of an individual's conscious origins is really all that is sure, and it goes back only so far as the individual's own living memory. Hers begins with her maternal grandfather, and she knew, at least, that she was named for his Quaker mother although he was an Anglican—a missionary in one of the British Protectorates on the borders of the country. After some minor members of British royalty had come to see the Union Jack lowered and the flag of independence raised, the missionary stayed on in his retirement among the old black *baputi** whose souls he was convinced he had saved and whose language had become the one he most used. He did a little translating of religious works for the local Sunday schools and he reminisced with old Chiefs. His brother had gone to South Africa and become chairman of a finance corporation, with directorships in mining, maize products and the packaging industry. The brother paid for Hannah's education in England when she outgrew the village mission school she attended with the local black children; for her mother had studied nursing in what was then Rhodesia, and come back to the mission pregnant with what turned out to be a girl child. Hannah was told her father had been a soldier, and since she knew soldiers got killed in wars, presumed he was dead. Later she found out he was a Bulawayo policeman who already had a wife. Hannah's mother married a Jewish doctor she met when she was theatre sister at the mission hospital taken over by the independent government, and went to live in Cape Town. Until her mother emigrated with him to Australia, Hannah spent part of her school holidays in the grandfather's mud-brick and thatch house at the mission, and part in the Cape Town suburb among her step-father's collection of modern paintings.

An individual life, Hannah's, but one that has followed the shifts in power of the communities into which she was born. So that what she really is, is a matter of "at that time" and "then"; qualifications and uncertainties. Her step-father would have paid to send her to the Michaelis School of Art,

*Clergymen.

since she showed such intelligent ignorance when studying his pictures, but she hankered after her late-afternoon wanderings in the mission village that had become the outskirts of a town, talking with the young men she had always known, now wearing T-shirts distributed by the brewery, the girls she had played with, now coming back from shift as cleaners at the Holiday Inn. And when she was with her grandfather and he suggested she would be happy qualifying to teach at what had been her old school, founded by him, the idea settled over her in dismay. In Cape Town she had met young people, university students, sons and daughters of comfortable, cultivated white households like her step-father's, who were working with trade unions, legal aid bureaux, community arts programmes, human rights projects in squatter camps— while she would be teaching children just enough to fit them to bottle beer and clean the dirt rims off tourists' bath-tubs. She was not a dilettante but not socially programmed, so to speak; had to choose where to place herself more realistically than in her childish broad sense that all Southern Africa was home: there were boundaries, treaties, barbed wire, heavily-armed border posts.

South Africa is a centripetal force that draws people, in the region, not only out of economic necessity, but also out of the fascination of commitment to political struggle. The fascination came to her in the mud-brick and thatch of the mission, the dust that had reddened her Nordic hair and pink ears: from her grandfather's commitment to struggle against evil in men, for God. For her the drive was to struggle against it for man—for humans. (She was a feminist, careful of genders.

But she wouldn't have thought of it as "evil"—too pretentious, too sanctimonious for her, though not in her grandfather.) She worked to that end in a number of organizations around South Africa. Some were banned, and she would have to move on to a similar socially-committed job elsewhere. She was married for a while to a young lawyer who became clinically depressed by the government's abrogations of the rule of law and persuaded her to emigrate; he went ahead to London but there recovered and fell in love with someone else, she never joined him. The hi-fi equipment, records and books were shipped to him. She took only the mattress from the king-size bed (because with that you could live anywhere) and a painting by a follower of Jackson Pollock her step-father had given her when he packed up for Australia. The trusts and foundations that employed her paid very little, out of a dependency on charitable grants from abroad. Yet you cannot be called poor if you are poor by choice—if she had wanted to, she could have been set up in a boutique or public relations career by the branch of her grandfather's family who had "made good" not in the way he had shown her.

The nature of work she did develops high emotions. It arises from crises. It deals only with disruption, disjunction—circumstances in people's lives that cannot be met with the responses that serve for continuity. To monitor trials is to 'monitor' the soaring and plunging graph of feelings that move men and women to act, endangering themselves; the curves and drops of bravery, loss of nerve, betrayal; cunning learnt by courage, courage learnt by discipline—and others which exceed the competence of any graph to record, would melt its needle in the heat of intensity: the record of people who, receiving a long jail sentence, tell the court they regret nothing; of those who, offered amnesty on condition that they accept this as "freedom" in place of the concept for which they went to prison, choose to live out their lives there. Such inconceivable decisions are beyond the capacity of anyone who does not make one. The spirit's shouldering of the world, as Atlas's muscles took on the physical weight of the world. Such people cannot be monitored. But knowing them and their families, who have this abnormal—Hannah, speaking of it once with Sonny, corrects herself—no, not abnormal, can't use that word for it—that divine strength expands the emotional resources of an ordinary individual (like Hannah) even in grasping that it *does exist*.

Association with prisoners of conscience is a special climate in which this heightening infloresces. Listening in courts while the sacrifice of their individual lives for man against evil slowly is distorted by the law in volumes of recorded words, police videos, in the mouths of State witnesses, into an indictment for having committed evil; touching the hands of the accused across the barrier while they joke about their jailers; visiting the wives, husbands, parents, children, the partners in many kinds of alliances broken by imprisonment— all this extended Hannah's feelings in a way she would not have known possible for anyone. In love. She was in love. Not as the term is understood, as she had been in love, at twenty-three, with her lawyer, and they had ceased to love. *In* love, a temperature and atmospheric pressure of shared tension, response, the glancing contact of trust in place of caresses, and the important, proud responsibility of doing anything asked, even the humblest tasks, in place of passionate private avowals. A loving state of being.

It was in this state that she developed the persistence, the bold lies, the lack of scruple in threatening international action to pressure prison authorities to allow her to see detainees. And it was in this state she understood her mission to visit their families.

She drove a Volkswagen Beetle through the battleground streets of Soweto to find old people who didn't know whether to trust her, she was received in the neat segregated suburbia of Bosmont and Lenasia by women who didn't know how they were going to keep up payments on the glossy furniture, she lost herself in the squatter camps where addresses didn't exist and the only routes marked in the summer muck of mud and rot were those rutted by the wheelbarrows of people fetching their supplies of beer from the liquor store on the main road. The house in the lower-class white suburb into which one of the detainees had moved his family illegally had a twirly wrought-iron gate and a plaster pelican, no doubt left behind by the white owners as the shed cast of any creature exactly reveals itself. The wife was beautiful and correct, composed, stockings and high heels—it had the effect of making Hannah feel not intrusive but unnecessary, and talking away to cover this up. The wife kept listening sympathetically, making Hannah's confusion worse. This quiet woman apparently was accustomed to being obeyed. There was tea ordered to be brought in by a daughter in whom the mother's beauty was reproduced as pert prettiness. A schoolgirl who worked at weekends; and the wife had a good job, she politely made it perfectly clear they wanted no-one to enter the arrangements they themselves had made to manage without the father of the family. The mother, with her fine, slow smile (what perfect teeth for a middle-aged woman; Hannah's were much repaired at only thirty) put a hand on the shoulder of an overgrown-looking boy who had kept Hannah standing a moment, in suspicion, before letting her in. —My son's the man of the house now.—

A house that smelled of stale spiced cooking. On the wall a travelling salesman's Kahlil Gibran texts. But in the glass-fronted bookcase a surprising little library, not only the imitation-leather-bound mail-order classics usually to be found as a sign of hunger for knowledge, and not only the Marx, Lenin, Fanon, Gandhi and Nkrumah, Mandela and Biko always to be found as a sign of political self-education, but Kafka and D. H. Lawrence, she noticed in glimpses aside, while talking, talking, talking like that.

She had been there once again. But that was after. It was when the house was invaded by laughter and music, all that it had been the first time thrust aside, as the furniture was for dancing. The loving state of being in which she had sat with the beautiful wife, the daughter, the son, was also thrust away, terrifyingly transformed into something else: passionate awareness of the ex-prisoner host. The first time he and she made love she had felt a strange threat of loss in the midst of joy, and had tried to explain it to herself by attempting to put it, in another way, to him. He didn't really understand; but sexual love has the matchless advantage of the flesh as reassurance for anything, everything, for the moment. The body speaks and all is silenced.

So everything in that house she remembered from that first day was cherished because it was part of him. It was all she had of that part of him she could not really know, which she had transformed into a lover. It was what both he and she discounted between them, in her room.

She would have liked to be the older confidante of the girl (looked as if she needed someone) and the adult-who-is-not-a-parent, so useful to an adolescent, in the life of the boy, his son. Even the pseudo-philosophy of the cheap framed texts became tender evidence of the qualities of the man who had left behind him fake consolations of uplift taken by the powerless and poor. She put away for safe-keeping her first day's vision of his house like a lock of hair from the head of the child that has become the man.

It's part of the commonplace strategy of adultery to appear in company where both wife and mistress are present. It's accepted as merely a way of hiding, by displaying there's nothing to hide. But Sonny was so inexperienced, he did not know how to suppress, in himself, the real urge discovered to underlie such confrontations. He learned they were not brought about by any social inevitability it would look suspicious to avoid; they were not arranged to reassure and protect Aila or to ensure that if he and Hannah were by chance to be seen in public together it would appear an innocent encounter within a mutual political circle. Giving his view on how to get the boycotting youth back into school without compromising their political clout, he had the attention of a lawyer and two educationists, comrades on the National Education Crisis Committee, when somewhere behind him he heard mingled in group conversation the two voices he knew best in the world. Two birds singing in his emotion: he did not hear the chatter of the other women, the cheeping of sparrows. He became eloquent, his nostrils round with conviction, he had never expressed himself more forcefully than while, the first time, instead of keeping the two women fastidiously apart within him, he possessed both at once. The exaltation was the reverse of his fear of Aila finding out.

Later, alone, desolated, shamed, he understood. He sought, even contrived, ways of appearing with his wife in houses where his other woman would be a guest.

The sexual excitement of bringing the two women together entered him as a tincture, curling cloudy in a glass of water.

She reminds me of pig. Out ancestors didn't eat pig.

A few bright hairs look like filaments of glass embedded in the pink flesh round her mouth.

I have terrible thoughts. About her. About my father with her. I imagine them . . . could I ever think of my mother like that! I'm sick with myself. What he's made me think about.

What'd he send me there for? I keep going over the place. What I saw, what he made me see. Her pants and bras on the radiator. The bed, right there where you walk in. Don't they know about privacy? People like her, so dedicated to our freedom, worming their way to get to see our prisoners, standing on our doorsteps. I should never have let her pass. Stupid kid that I was. The man of the house. They bring you up to be polite and then put you in situations they didn't tell you could ever happen.

What did he send me there for? I keep thinking about it and as I change, get older—every month makes a difference when you're young and finding out about yourself—my answers change. Forbidden pig. Pink pig. I've thought what he wanted was to mix me up in it. What men feel. It suits him, now, to think of me as a man like himself. Who wants to fuck. Who feels guilty about it; he *counts* on me, a kid like me, being guilty of having these mad wild feelings. When I was really a kid he told me just the opposite: I tried to hide the signs of masturbation on my underpants and he told me, son, there's nothing to feel guilty about—what I did to myself was natural. Now he wants me to see her, see what he enjoys and be guilty with him of what he feels because I understand it in myself. A bond. *Tied.* Father and son more like good buddies.

That's what I've thought.

And then again—I've come to understand something else. I think I have. It's come to me from my body, yes. (If he believed I'd learn from my own body, he's right, there.) I think what he wants is to show off his virility. To me. The proof of his virility. That clumsy blonde. The bed where *he* does it, the highbrow music *he's* doing it to, the show-off picture on the wall *he* sees while he's doing it, the underwear she takes off those places where *he* can touch her—he, not me, not me. (Not I—he would correct me.) He sent me to her to show me it's not my turn yet. He's not moving aside, off women's bodies, for me. I needn't think, because I'm tall as he is and I've got the same things between my legs he's got, and (the *tan-nies* don't let me forget it) I'm growing up "handsome as he is," I haven't even been let off those bloody thick eyebrows that make his eyes so sexy—I shouldn't think he needs to give over to me. The old bull still owns the cows, he's still capable of serving his harem, my mother and his blonde.

I don't think my father knows any of these things about himself. Only I know, only I.

When the schoolteacher led the children across the veld he did so on his own impulse and responsibility. That naïvety was no longer possible.   —There's no freedom in working for freedom.—   He could say it to Hannah, and they both laughed. There was pride and scepticism in the laughter. You couldn't say such things to Aila; between Aila and him was the old habit of simple reverence for living useful lives. He had to keep it up, as other things had to be kept up, before her. Why, when he was in prison she evidently had not disturbed her habits, somehow carried on as if nothing had happened; now she treated his way of life—its structures clandestine, its activities directed by Committees and Desks, its dangers constant—as if he had been still the schoolmaster and received a posting to a new school. An enemy of the State: and when he told her the few things about his work he could tell her (he had to talk to her about something, had to find something to drive away the silence between Aila and him) she listened consideringly as she had to the tales of those petty problems he used to have teaching school, when they lived in the ghetto outside Benoni-son-of-sorrow, first married.

He took part in policy decisions somewhere below the highest level and thereafter, in a group where he himself participated in allocation of the activities of others, was in turn given his orders. How much any one should be exposed was always a worried calculation based on the current number of comrades detained or serving prison sentences—how many, outside, could be spared. There were agonized decisions about who should appear where, when public occasions demanded a presence if the movement were to retain its popular power. He was no Tutu or Boesak or Chikane, and he could have been blacker, but as one of the best speakers, bloodied by prison, he had to be used only where he would be most effective with least risk. But who could calculate risk? Something to smile over, again, with Hannah. The black ghettos were army encampments and police dogs with their gun-carrying handlers replaced white ladies with poodles in the shopping malls. The headquarters of trade unions and militant church organizations were tramped through regularly by raiding police. Some were mysteriously blown up or burned. At road-blocks around the city armoured cars stood and every black driver was flagged down and searched. As the schools boycott combined with rent boycotts proved exceptionally effective, taking whole communities out of government control, Sonny was used mostly on occasions when someone from the blacks' National Education Crisis Committee was needed to attack the State education system. At university campuses and ghetto congresses his endearing middle name no longer appeared on posters—he was billed anonymously as "a prominent educationist." At least the police would not have previous knowledge of his arrival on a public platform, if they were planning to pick him up.

But there were times when an event often—and best—cohered hastily, before the proposed gathering could be banned. The call for a speaker would come when there was no choice but to send whoever was available in the area.

Sonny told them both. Aila and Hannah.

He mentioned the black township graveyard ceremony at home, and when he told his wife, his daughter was there—she didn't appear for weeks and then suddenly would come in through the kitchen door at some odd hour. She sat eating her cornflakes, the good little girl. The boy avoided meals with him; Sunday breakfast was one of them.

He was confusedly distracted at the sight of his Baby, where she used to be, in her place. As if in sudden disjuncture everything was back where once it was. But his girl was wearing a black satin blouse creased under the arms and the unnecessary paint round her eyes (they were striking enough already) darkened sleep-crumbs at the corners—she had more likely been out all night rather than have got up early to drop in for breakfast at her old home. A bile of distress rose and was swallowed. No time to deal with that; no right time ever, now.

—Where's that place, Daddy?—

Before he could say, Aila turned her head from the gush of water filling the kettle.   —The other side of Pretoria. North.—

—Oh there. But you'll never get in. The army's all round.—

He saw that Aila was making fresh tea. She always filled the kettle with cold water when making tea, she would never boil up what was already hot.   —I'll have what's in the pot. I've no time.—

—Since when are you a priest, my dear pa-pa.—   Coquetry was inborn, for his Baby, even—and since she *was* a baby—when addressing her father.   —Anyway, you're unique, they'll recognize you in your disguise of cassock and whatnot. Your eyebrows! Shall I pluck your eyebrows? Daddy? Yes!—   She jumped up and rushed over to him with fingers extended like pincers.

—Don't be silly, I'm not going to be disguised as anything.—

The girl's playful threat turned into an embrace, her arm hooked round her father's neck. They were laughing, protesting to each other, and then abruptly stopped; she kissed him fiercely on his cheek. He felt her jaw jar against the bone.

—It's the "cleansing of the graves" of the nine youngsters who were shot by the police last week outside Jubilee Hall. They were buried yesterday. The street committees have asked for some kind of oration. The kids were comrades.—

As he said "oration" the boy came in, after all. In the glance of greeting he gave his son he felt a tic of embarrassment, as if he had been caught out quoting Shakespeare as he used to do to give the boy the freedom, at least, of great art.

They sat together round the table in the breakfast nook Sonny had built with Will's help, as they had made things together back in Benoni; Saturday shopping, the love of a schoolteacher for a virgin, the happiness of the first Baby and then the son named for genius—all this was pressing hard against their thighs. Aila rose and slid into her place again with the grace that did not brush against cup or cloth, fetching yogurt and replenishing margarine. Baby was recounting the highly embellished story of the driving test she had just taken, and tried to rile her brother into the old exchange of sibling insults.   —Oh I'm perfectly confident. I even drove a truck while I was still on my learner's. You know that? The only thing that bugs me is the behaviour of you barbarians on your souped-up bikes, rushing out of nowhere. You think just by keeping your lights on everyone's got to pull out of your way as if you were the fire engine—I don't know why Dad ever gave in to your nagging for one of these things, honestly, Will.—

He hesitated, choosing an apple.   —I never asked for it.—

There was warning in her big, kohl-smeared eyes as he looked up fully at her, though she quickly laughed: .—Oh no, I'll bet you never! Never dreamt of asking! Never entered your curly head, brother of mine!—

Jars and cups passed warm from hand to hand, a headline was read out by someone, the mother arranged with the son to do an errand for her, the chitter of china, crunch of knives through toast and splutter of poured tea linked the ellipses of breakfast remarks. All had been rehearsed countless times. It was not really happening; an echo, a formula being followed. The inconsequential talk was contained in the silence between them that all gathered there heard.

Sonny had said he was in a hurry, in order to get away before the boy appeared. He had to bear out the lie. He rose from the table but Aila got up when he did and left the kitchen before him.

—Ciao, Will.—

Goodbye, he said. The boy always took care to make Sonny feel his son wanted him to be imprisoned again: something to put a stop to him. Farewell. Never come back.

The lovely girl had wiped her eyes clean with her mother's dishcloth, and now was quite unblemished by whatever her night had been. —Be careful, Daddy. Here—put this down for me.— She took a rose, grown in Aila's garden, out of the vase on the breakfast table.

He had Baby's flower in his hand when Aila met him in the passage with a zipped carryall. He knew what was in it. Toothbrush and paste, towel, soap, pyjamas, change of socks and underpants, sweater. The essentials you were allowed to pack up if you were lucky enough to be taken into detention from home and not while speaking at the cleansing of the graves. She had been gone from the kitchen less than a minute. —How did you do that?—

—I keep it ready.— She was smiling. She shrugged as if to discount herself, excuse some interference.

—It's not necessary. I'll be all right.—

She stood there. She licked her lips. Stood there.

He picked up the bag in the hand in which he held the flower. —Baby's, to put on the graves.— He looked about, out of habit, for the briefcase, took it in the other hand, and she opened the front door for him.

Not *ciao*, no *goodbye*. —Don't worry, Aila.—

—I'll be there. I'll hear you. I was going with DPSC* and Black Sash,† anyway.—

He had time for breakfast, with Hannah. A cup of coffee and half a slice of her toast spread with fish-paste—Because I taste of it already.— She was still in the outsize T-shirt in which she slept, and the slight hollow that trembled along the underside of her soft-fleshed arm from armpit to elbow, as she lifted it about the objects on the table, drew his eye and made him lean over and taste her mouth for himself. Her breasts and belly were so near under the cotton rag that the flesh warmed his hand as if it were held before a sleepy fire.

—Couldn't you come with me?—

She took deep, smiling breaths to regain control of herself. —Better not, don't you think?—

—Of course. Maybe I can give you a lift back. You'll find some excuse.—

The treat of spending the short journey together was tempting; she smiled and played with his hand, which recently she had swabbed with cerise water-colour and imprinted on a sheet of paper now pinned to the wall. No. Unless I get them to drop me off in Pretoria, that I could do—and we'd meet somewhere?—

—Outside the Palace of Justice?— It was at that rendezvous that he had stood trial. His dark, cocky grin that came from prison, happy for battle, delighted her. —Unfortunately

---

*Detainees' Parents Support Committee.

†A women's anti-apartheid organization.

I'm going to have to hurry back. There's a meeting around five—
I imagine the ceremony should be over by four-thirty . . . if the
police don't shut it down long before. Hadn't you better get
dressed? What time's your bus leaving?—

—Oh it doesn't take me ten minutes . . . is that for me?—
He had thrown the carryall in the boot but absently brought
in the rose with his briefcase.

—For the graves.—

—What a lovely thing to do.—

He could not lie to her.   —My daughter gave it. She came
in this morning.—

—Good for her. I must pick up some flowers, too, on the
way.—

The face of a woman who uses no make-up has unity with
her body. Seeing Hannah's fair eyelashes catching the morning sun and the shine of the few little cat's whiskers that were
revealed, in this innocent early clarity, at the upper corners of
her mouth, he was seeing the whole of her; he understood
why, in the reproductions of paintings he had puzzled over in
the days of his self-education, Picasso represented frontally
all the features of a woman—head, breasts, eyes, vagina, nose,
buttocks, mouth—as if all were always present even to the casual glance. What would he have known, without Hannah!

She had picked up his hand and buried her big soft face in
it, kissing the palm. When she lifted her head her cheeks
were stinging pink, slapped with pride.   —I'm so glad you're
the one chosen to speak.—

Sunday peace.

The combis that, sending gusts of taped reggae and *mba-qanga* into the traffic, transport blacks back and forth between township and city, now carry a strange cargo of whites. The street committees in the township have advised that this is the way to bring them in, the nature of the vehicles in themselves giving the signal to the people that these envoys from outside the siege are approved.

Through the white suburbs. Past bowling greens where figures like aged schoolboys and girls in banded hats genuflect over balls; past the Robin Hood fantasy of an archery club, the whoops of regular Sunday tennis partners in private gardens, the nylon frills and black suits of the congregation leaving a Nederduitse Gereformeerde Kerk, and the young girls with cupboards full of clothes who choose to stroll barefoot in jeans slashed off at the thigh. Past electronically-operated gates pinnacled with plaster eagles, spike- and razorwire-topped walls behind which peacock-tails of water open over flowers and birds sing. Sunday peace. If it were not for the combi owners' township names and addresses painted on the vehicles, the convoy might be some sort of charity outing on its way to a picnic. Now and then it is paced by joggers who drop back without noticing it.

GEORGE ORWELL

The British author Eric Arthur Blair (1903–50), whose pen name was George Orwell, achieved prominence for his novels *Animal Farm* (1945) and *Nineteen Eighty-four* (1949), brilliant satires that attacked totalitarianism. In the 1930s, Orwell traveled to Spain to report on the Spanish Civil War. He was wounded while fighting for the United Workers Marxist Party, an experience that spawned his disdain for communism and inspired the two novels. *Animal Farm,* a modern beast-fable attacking Stalinism, and *Nineteen Eighty-four,* a dystopian vision of an intrusively bureaucratized future state, articulate quite poignantly his views and fears about power and social control.

In these excerpts from *Animal Farm,* Orwell attends to the vanity—the manipulative ambitions—that informs political life. As humans, all animals of a certain kind, we struggle with one another for dominance. Orwell's fable, aimed at the dictatorships of the 1930s, was also meant to give readers pause about all forms of politics—the effort to obtain authority, and the temptation to abuse it for one's own personal satisfaction.

From ANIMAL FARM

The animals had their breakfast, and then Snowball and Napoleon called them together again.

"Comrades," said Snowball, "it is half-past six and we have a long day before us. Today we begin the hay harvest. But there is another matter that must be attended to first."

The pigs now revealed that during the past three months they had taught themselves to read and write from an old spelling book which had belonged to Mr. Jones's children and which had been thrown on the rubbish heap. Napoleon sent for pots of black and white paint and led the way down to the five-barred gate that gave on to the main road. Then Snowball (for it was Snowball who was best at writing) took a brush between the two knuckles of his trotter, painted out MANOR FARM from the top bar of the gate and in its place painted ANIMAL FARM. This was to be the name of the farm from now onwards. After this they went back to the farm buildings, where Snowball and Napoleon sent for a ladder which they caused to be set against the end wall of the big barn. They explained that by their studies of the past three months the pigs had succeeded in reducing the principles of Animalism to Seven Commandments. These Seven Commandments would now be inscribed on the wall; they would form an unalterable law by which all the animals on Animal Farm must live for ever after. With some difficulty (for it is not easy for a pig to balance himself on a ladder) Snowball climbed up and set to work, with Squealer a few rungs below him holding the paint-pot. The Commandments were written on the tarred wall in great white letters that could be read thirty yards away. They ran thus:

THE SEVEN COMMANDMENTS

1. *Whatever goes upon two legs is an enemy.*
2. *Whatever goes upon four legs, or has wings, is a friend.*
3. *No animal shall wear clothes.*
4. *No animal shall sleep in a bed.*
5. *No animal shall drink alcohol.*
6. *No animal shall kill any other animal.*
7. *All animals are equal.*

It was very neatly written, and except that "friend" was written "freind" and one of the "S's" was the wrong way round, the spelling was correct all the way through. Snowball read it aloud for the benefit of the others. All the animals nodded in complete agreement, and the cleverer ones at once began to learn the Commandments by heart.

. . . .

It was also found that the stupider animals, such as the sheep, hens, and ducks, were unable to learn the Seven Commandments by heart. After much thought Snowball declared that the Seven Commandments could in effect be reduced to a single maxim, namely: "Four legs good, two legs bad." This, he said, contained the essential principle of Animalism. Whoever had thoroughly grasped it would be safe from human influences. The birds at first objected, since it seemed to them that they also had two legs, but Snowball proved to them that this was not so.

"A bird's wing, comrades," he said, "is an organ of propulsion and not of manipulation. It should therefore be regarded as a leg. The distinguishing mark of man is the *hand*, the instrument with which he does all his mischief."

The birds did not understand Snowball's long words, but they accepted his explanation, and all the humbler animals set to work to learn the new maxim by heart. FOUR LEGS GOOD, TWO LEGS BAD, was inscribed on the end wall of the barn, above the Seven Commandments and in bigger letters. When they had once got it by heart, the sheep developed a great liking for this maxim, and often as they lay in the field they would all start bleating "Four legs good, two legs bad! Four legs good, two legs bad!" and keep it up for hours on end, never growing tired of it.

Napoleon took no interest in Snowball's committees. He said that the education of the young was more important than anything that could be done for those who were already grown up. It happened that Jessie and Bluebell had both whelped soon after the hay harvest, giving birth between them to nine sturdy puppies. As soon as they were weaned, Napoleon took them away from their mothers, saying that he would make himself responsible for their education. He took

GEORGE ORWELL

them up into a loft which could only be reached by a ladder from the harness-room, and there kept them in such seclusion that the rest of the farm soon forgot their existence.

The mystery of where the milk went to was soon cleared up. It was mixed every day into the pigs' mash. The early apples were now ripening, and the grass of the orchard was littered with windfalls. The animals had assumed as a matter of course that these would be shared out equally; one day, however, the order went forth that all the windfalls were to be collected and brought to the harness-room for the use of the pigs. At this some of the other animals murmured, but it was no use. All the pigs were in full agreement on this point, even Snowball and Napoleon. Squealer was sent to make the necessary explanations to the others.

"Comrades!" he cried. "You do not imagine, I hope, that we pigs are doing this in a spirit of selfishness and privilege? Many of us actually dislike milk and apples. I dislike them myself. Our sole object in taking these things is to preserve our health. Milk and apples (this has been proved by Science, comrades) contain substances absolutely necessary to the well-being of a pig. We pigs are brainworkers. The whole management and organisation of this farm depend on us. Day and night we are watching over your welfare. It is for *your* sake that we drink that milk and eat those apples. Do you know what would happen if we pigs failed in our duty? Jones would come back! Yes, Jones would come back! Surely, comrades," cried Squealer almost pleadingly, skipping from side to side and whisking his tail, "surely there is no one among you who wants to see Jones come back?"

From ***Animal Farm***

Now if there was one thing that the animals were completely certain of, it was that they did not want Jones back. When it was put to them in this light, they had no more to say. The importance of keeping the pigs in good health was all too obvious. So it was agreed without further argument that the milk and the windfall apples (and also the main crop of apples when they ripened) should be reserved for the pigs alone.

. . . .

In January there came bitterly hard weather. The earth was like iron, and nothing could be done in the fields. Many meetings were held in the big barn, and the pigs occupied themselves with planning out the work of the coming season. It had come to be accepted that the pigs, who were manifestly cleverer than the other animals, should decide all questions of farm policy, though their decisions had to be ratified by a majority vote. This arrangement would have worked well enough if it had not been for the disputes between Snowball and Napoleon. These two disagreed at every point where disagreement was possible. If one of them suggested sowing a bigger acreage with barley, the other was certain to demand a bigger acreage of oats, and if one of them said that such and such a field was just right for cabbages, the other would declare that it was useless for anything except roots. Each had his own following, and there were some violent debates. At the Meetings Snowball often won over the majority by his brilliant speeches, but Napoleon was better at canvassing support for himself in between times. He was especially successful with the sheep. Of late the sheep had taken to bleating "Four legs good, two legs bad" both in and out of season, and they often interrupted the Meeting with this. It was noticed that they were especially liable to break into "Four legs good, two legs bad" at crucial moments in Snowball's speeches. Snowball had made a close study of some back numbers of the *Farmer and Stockbreeder* which he had found in the farmhouse, and was full of plans for innovations and improvements. He talked learnedly about field-drains, silage, and basic slag, and had worked out a complicated scheme for all the animals to drop their dung directly in the fields, at a different spot every day, to save the labour of cartage. Napoleon produced no schemes of his own, but said quietly that Snowball's would come to nothing, and seemed to be biding his time. But of all their controversies, none was so bitter as the one that took place over the windmill.

In the long pasture, not far from the farm buildings, there was a small knoll which was the highest point on the farm. After surveying the ground, Snowball declared that this was just the place for a windmill, which could be made to operate a dynamo and supply the farm with electrical power. This would light the stalls and warm them in winter, and would also run a circular saw, a chaff-cutter, a mangel-slicer, and an electric milking machine. The animals had never heard of anything of this kind before (for the farm was an old-fashioned one and had only the most primitive machinery), and they listened in astonishment while Snowball conjured up pictures of fantastic machines which would do their work for them while they grazed at their ease in the fields or improved their minds with reading and conversation.

Within a few weeks Snowball's plans for the windmill were fully worked out. The mechanical details came mostly from three books which had belonged to Mr. Jones—*One Thousand Useful Things to Do About the House, Every Man His Own Bricklayer,* and *Electricity for Beginners.* Snowball used as his study a shed which had once been used for incubators and had a smooth wooden floor, suitable for drawing on. He was closeted there for hours at a time. With his books held open by a stone, and with a piece of chalk gripped between the knuckles of his trotter, he would move rapidly to and fro, drawing in line after line and uttering little whimpers of excitement. Gradually the plans grew into a complicated mass of cranks and cog-wheels, covering more than half the floor, which the other animals found completely unintelligible but very impressive. All of them came to look at Snowball's drawings at least once a day. Even the hens and ducks came, and were at pains not to tread on the chalk marks. Only Napoleon held aloof. He had declared himself against the windmill from the start. One day, however, he arrived unexpectedly to examine the plans. He walked heavily round the shed, looked closely at every detail of the plans and snuffed at them once or twice, then stood for a little while contemplating them out of the corner of his eye; then suddenly he lifted his leg, urinated over the plans, and walked out without uttering a word.

The whole farm was deeply divided on the subject of the windmill. Snowball did not deny that to build it would be a difficult business. Stone would have to be carried and built up into walls, then the sails would have to be made and after that there would be need for dynamos and cables. (How these were to be procured, Snowball did not say.) But he maintained that it could all be done in a year. And thereafter, he declared, so much labour would be saved that the animals would only need to work three days a week. Napoleon, on the other hand, argued that the great need of the moment was to increase food production, and that if they wasted time on the windmill they would all starve to death. The animals formed themselves into two factions under the slogan, "Vote for Snowball and the three-day week" and "Vote for Napoleon and the full manger." Benjamin was the only animal who did not side with either faction. He refused to believe either that food would become more plentiful or that the windmill would save work. Windmill or no windmill, he said, life would go on as it had always gone on—that is, badly.

Apart from the disputes over the windmill, there was the question of the defence of the farm. It was fully realised that though the human beings had been defeated in the Battle of the Cowshed they might make another and more determined attempt to recapture the farm and reinstate Mr. Jones. They had all the more reason for doing so because the news of their defeat had spread across the countryside and made the animals on the neighbouring farms more restive than ever. As usual, Snowball and Napoleon were in disagreement. According to Napoleon, what the animals must do was to procure firearms and train themselves in the use of them. According to Snowball, they must send out more and more pigeons and stir up rebellion among the animals on the other farms. The one argued that if they could not defend themselves they were bound to be conquered, the other argued that if rebellions happened everywhere they would have no need to defend themselves. The animals listened first to Napoleon, then to Snowball, and could not make up their minds which was right; indeed, they always found themselves in agreement with the one who was speaking at the moment.

At last the day came when Snowball's plans were completed. At the Meeting on the following Sunday the question of whether or not to begin work on the windmill was to be put to the vote. When the animals had assembled in the big barn, Snowball stood up and, though occasionally interrupted by bleating from the sheep, set forth his reasons for advocating the building of the windmill. Then Napoleon stood up to reply. He said very quietly that the windmill was nonsense and that he advised nobody to vote for it, and promptly sat down again; he had spoken for barely thirty seconds, and seemed almost indifferent as to the effect he produced. At this Snowball sprang to his feet, and shouting down the sheep, who had begun bleating again, broke into a passionate appeal in favour of the windmill. Until now the animals had been about equally divided in their sympathies, but in a moment Snowball's eloquence had carried them away. In glowing sentences he painted a picture of Animal Farm as it might be when sordid labour was lifted from the animals' backs. His imagination had now run far beyond chaff-cutters and turnip-slicers. Electricity, he said, could operate threshing machines, ploughs, harrows, rollers, and reapers and binders, besides supplying every stall with its own electric light, hot and cold water, and an electric heater. By the time he had finished speaking, there was no doubt as to which way the vote would go. But just at this moment Napoleon stood up and, casting a peculiar sidelong look at Snowball, uttered a high-pitched whimper of a kind no one had ever heard him utter before.

At this there was a terrible baying sound outside, and nine enormous dogs wearing brass-studded collars came bounding into the barn. They dashed straight for Snowball, who only sprang from his place just in time to escape their snapping jaws. In a moment he was out of the door and they were after him. Too amazed and frightened to speak, all the animals crowded through the door to watch the chase. Snowball was racing across the long pasture that led to the road. He was running as only a pig can run, but the dogs were close on his heels. Suddenly he slipped and it seemed certain that they had him. Then he was up again, running faster than ever, then the dogs were gaining on him again. One of them all but closed his jaws on Snowball's tail, but Snowball whisked it free just in time. Then he put on an extra spurt and, with a few inches to spare, slipped through a hole in the hedge and was seen no more.

Silent and terrified, the animals crept back into the barn. In a moment the dogs came bounding back. At first no one had been able to imagine where these creatures came from, but the problem was soon solved: they were the puppies whom Napoleon had taken away from their mothers and reared privately. Though not yet full-grown, they were huge dogs, and as fierce-looking as wolves. They kept close to Napoleon. It was noticed that they wagged their tails to him in the same way as the other dogs had been used to do to Mr. Jones.

Napoleon, with the dogs following him, now mounted on to the raised portion of the floor where Major had previously stood to deliver his speech. He announced that from now on the Sunday-morning Meetings would come to an end. They were unnecessary, he said, and wasted time. In future all questions relating to the working of the farm would be settled by a special committee of pigs, presided over by himself. These would meet in private and afterwards communicate their decisions to the others. The animals would still assemble on Sunday mornings to salute the flag, sing *Beasts of England,* and receive their orders for the week; but there would be no more debates.

In spite of the shock that Snowball's expulsion had given them, the animals were dismayed by this announcement. Several of them would have protested if they could have found the right arguments. Even Boxer was vaguely troubled. He set his ears back, shook his forelock several times, and tried hard to marshal his thoughts; but in the end he could not think of anything to say. Some of the pigs themselves, however, were more articulate. Four young porkers in the front row uttered shrill squeals of disapproval, and all four of them sprang to their feet and began speaking at once. But suddenly the dogs sitting round Napoleon let out deep, menacing growls, and the pigs fell silent and sat down again.

Then the sheep broke out into a tremendous bleating of "Four legs good, two legs bad!" which went on for nearly a quarter of an hour and put an end to any chance of discussion.

Afterwards Squealer was sent round the farm to explain the new arrangement to the others.

"Comrades," he said, "I trust that every animal here appreciates the sacrifice that Comrade Napoleon has made in taking this extra labour upon himself. Do not imagine, comrades, that leadership is a pleasure! On the contrary, it is a deep and heavy responsibility. No one believes more firmly than Comrade Napoleon that all animals are equal. He would be only too happy to let you make your decisions for yourselves. But sometimes you might make the wrong decisions, comrades, and then where should we be? Suppose you had decided to follow Snowball, with his moonshine of windmills—Snowball, who, as we now know, was no better than a criminal?"

"He fought bravely at the Battle of the Cowshed," said somebody.

"Bravery is not enough," said Squealer. "Loyalty and obedience are more important. And as to the Battle of the Cowshed, I believe the time will come when we shall find that Snowball's part in it was much exaggerated. Discipline, comrades, iron discipline! That is the watchword for today. One false step, and our enemies would be upon us. Surely, comrades, you do not want Jones back?"

Once again this argument was unanswerable. Certainly the animals did not want Jones back; if the holding of debates on Sunday mornings was liable to bring him back, then the debates must stop. Boxer, who had now had time to think things over, voiced the general feeling by saying: "If Comrade Napoleon says it, it must be right." And from then on he adopted the maxim, "Napoleon is always right," in addition to his private motto of "I will work harder."

By this time the weather had broken and the spring ploughing had begun. The shed where Snowball had drawn his plans of the windmill had been shut up and it was assumed that the plans had been rubbed off the floor. Every Sunday morning at ten o'clock the animals assembled in the big barn to receive their orders for the week. The skull of old Major, now clean of flesh, had been disinterred from the orchard and set up on a stump at the foot of the flagstaff, beside the gun. After the hoisting of the flag, the animals were required to file past the skull in a reverent manner before entering the barn. Nowadays they did not sit all together as they had done in the past. Napoleon, with Squealer and another pig named Minimus, who had a remarkable gift for composing songs and poems, sat on the front of the raised platform, with the nine young dogs forming a semicircle round them, and the other pigs sitting behind. The rest of the animals sat facing them in the main body of the barn. Napoleon read out the orders for the week in a gruff soldierly style, and after a single singing of *Beasts of England,* all the animals dispersed.

On the third Sunday after Snowball's expulsion, the animals were somewhat surprised to hear Napoleon announce that the windmill was to be built after all. He did not give any reason for having changed his mind, but merely warned the animals that this extra task would mean very hard work; it might even be necessary to reduce their rations. The plans, however, had all been prepared, down to the last detail. A special committee of pigs had been at work upon them for the past three weeks. The building of the windmill, with various other improvements, was expected to take two years.

That evening Squealer explained privately to the other animals that Napoleon had never in reality been opposed to the windmill. On the contrary, it was he who had advocated it in the beginning, and the plan which Snowball had drawn on the floor of the incubator shed had actually been stolen from among Napoleon's papers. The windmill was, in fact, Napoleon's own creation. Why, then, asked somebody, had he spoken so strongly against it? Here Squealer looked very sly. That, he said, was Comrade Napoleon's cunning. He had *seemed* to oppose the windmill, simply as a manoeuvre to get rid of Snowball, who was a dangerous character and a bad influence. Now that Snowball was out of the way, the plan could go forward without his interference. This, said Squealer, was something called tactics. He repeated a number of times, "Tactics, comrades, tactics!" skipping round and whisking his tail with a merry laugh. The animals were not certain what the word meant, but Squealer spoke so persuasively, and the three dogs who happened to be with him growled so threateningly, that they accepted his explanation without further questions.

. . . .

It was about this time that the pigs suddenly moved into the farmhouse and took up their residence there. Again the animals seemed to remember that a resolution against this had been passed in the early days, and again Squealer was able to convince them that this was not the case. It was absolutely necessary, he said, that the pigs, who were the brains of the farm, should have a quiet place to work in. It was also more suited to the dignity of the Leader (for of late he had taken to speaking of Napoleon under the title of "Leader") to live in a house than in a mere sty. Nevertheless, some of the animals were disturbed when they heard that the pigs not only took their meals in the kitchen and used the drawing-room as a recreation room, but also slept in the beds. Boxer passed it off as usual with "Napoleon is always right!," but Clover, who thought she remembered a definite ruling against beds, went to the end of the barn and tried to puzzle out the Seven Commandments which were inscribed there. Finding herself unable to read more than individual letters, she fetched Muriel.

"Muriel," she said, "read me the Fourth Commandment. Does it not say something about never sleeping in a bed?"

With some difficulty Muriel spelt it out.

"It says, 'No animal shall sleep in a bed *with sheets*,' " she announced finally.

Curiously enough, Clover had not remembered that the Fourth Commandment mentioned sheets; but as it was there on the wall, it must have done so. And Squealer, who happened to be passing at this moment, attended by two or three dogs, was able to put the whole matter in its proper perspective.

"You have heard then, comrades," he said, "that we pigs now sleep in the beds of the farmhouse? And why not? You did not suppose, surely, that there was ever a ruling against *beds*? A bed merely means a place to sleep in. A pile of straw in a stall is a bed, properly regarded. The rule was against *sheets,* which are a human invention. We have removed the sheets from the farmhouse beds, and sleep between blankets. And very comfortable beds they are too! But not more comfortable than we need, I can tell you, comrades, with all the brainwork we have to do nowadays. You would not rob us of our repose, would you, comrades? You would not have us too tired to carry out our duties? Surely none of you wishes to see Jones back?"

The animals reassured him on this point immediately, and no more was said about the pigs sleeping in the farmhouse beds. And when, some days afterwards, it was announced that from now on the pigs would get up an hour later in the mornings than the other animals, no complaint was made about that either.

By the autumn the animals were tired but happy. They had had a hard year, and after the sale of part of the hay and corn, the stores of food for the winter were none too plentiful, but the windmill compensated for everything. It was almost half built now. After the harvest there was a stretch of clear dry weather, and the animals toiled harder than ever, thinking it well worth while to plod to and fro all day with blocks of stone if by doing so they could raise the walls another foot. Boxer would even come out at nights and work for an hour or two on his own by the light of the harvest moon. In their spare moments the animals would walk round and round the half-finished mill, admiring the strength and perpendicularity of its walls and marvelling that they should ever have been able to build anything so imposing. Only old Benjamin refused to grow enthusiastic about the windmill, though, as usual, he would utter nothing beyond the cryptic remark that donkeys live a long time.

November came, with raging south-west winds. Building had to stop because it was now too wet to mix the cement. Finally there came a night when the gale was so violent that the farm buildings rocked on their foundations and several tiles were blown off the roof of the barn. The hens woke up squawking with terror because they had all dreamed simultaneously of hearing a gun go off in the distance. In the morning the animals came out of their stalls to find that the flagstaff had been blown down and an elm tree at the foot of the orchard had been plucked up like a radish. They had just noticed this when a cry of despair broke from every animal's throat. A terrible sight had met their eyes. The windmill was in ruins.

With one accord they dashed down to the spot. Napoleon, who seldom moved out of a walk, raced ahead of them all. Yes, there it lay, the fruit of all their struggles, levelled to its foundations, the stones they had broken and carried so laboriously scattered all around. Unable at first to speak, they stood gazing mournfully at the litter of fallen stone. Napoleon paced to and fro in silence, occasionally snuffing at the ground. His tail had grown rigid and twitched sharply from side to side, a sign in him of intense mental activity. Suddenly he halted as though his mind were made up.

"Comrades," he said quietly, "do you know who is responsible for this? Do you know the enemy who has come in the night and overthrown our windmill? SNOWBALL!" he suddenly roared in a voice of thunder. "Snowball has done this thing! In sheer malignity, thinking to set back our plans and avenge himself for his ignominious expulsion, this traitor has crept here under cover of night and destroyed our work of nearly a year. Comrades, here and now I pronounce the death sentence upon Snowball. 'Animal Hero, Second Class,' and half a bushel of apples to any animal who brings him to justice. A full bushel to anyone who captures him alive!"

The animals were shocked beyond measure to learn that even Snowball could be guilty of such an action. There was a cry of indignation, and everyone began thinking out ways of catching Snowball if he should ever come back. Almost immediately the footprints of a pig were discovered in the grass at a little distance from the knoll. They could only be traced for a few yards, but appeared to lead to a hole in the hedge. Napoleon snuffed deeply at them and pronounced them to be Snowball's. He gave it as his opinion that Snowball had probably come from the direction of Foxwood Farm.

"No more delays, comrades!" cried Napoleon when the footprints had been examined. "There is work to be done. This very morning we begin rebuilding the windmill, and we will build all through the winter, rain or shine. We will teach this miserable traitor that he cannot undo our work so easily. Remember, comrades, there must be no alteration in our plans: they shall be carried out to the day. Forward, comrades! Long live the windmill! Long live Animal Farm!"

. . . .

They knew that life nowadays was harsh and bare, that they were often hungry and often cold, and that they were usually working when they were not asleep. But doubtless it had been worse in the old days. They were glad to believe so. Besides, in those days they had been slaves and now they were free, and that made all the difference, as Squealer did not fail to point out.

There were many more mouths to feed now. In the autumn the four sows had all littered about simultaneously, producing thirty-one young pigs between them. The young pigs were piebald, and as Napoleon was the only boar on the farm, it was possible to guess at their parentage. It was announced that later, when bricks and timber had been purchased, a schoolroom would be built in the farmhouse garden. For the time being, the young pigs were given their instruction by Napoleon himself in the farmhouse kitchen. They took their exercise in the garden, and were discouraged from playing with the other young animals. About this time, too, it was laid down as a rule that when a pig and any other animal met on the path, the other animal must stand aside: and also that all pigs, of whatever degree, were to have the privilege of wearing green ribbons on their tails on Sundays.

The farm had had a fairly successful year, but was still short of money. There were the bricks, sand, and lime for the schoolroom to be purchased, and it would also be necessary to begin saving up again for the machinery for the windmill.

Then there were lamp oil and candles for the house, sugar for Napoleon's own table (he forbade this to the other pigs, on the ground that it made them fat), and all the usual replacements such as tools, nails, string, coal, wire, scrap-iron, and dog biscuits. A stump of hay and part of the potato crop were sold off, and the contract for eggs was increased to six hundred a week, so that that year the hens barely hatched enough chicks to keep their numbers at the same level. Rations, reduced in December, were reduced again in February, and lanterns in the stalls were forbidden to save oil. But the pigs seemed comfortable enough, and in fact were putting on weight if anything. One afternoon in late February a warm, rich, appetising scent, such as the animals had never smelt before, wafted itself across the yard from the little brew-house, which had been disused in Jones's time, and which stood beyond the kitchen. Someone said it was the smell of cooking barley. The animals sniffed the air hungrily and wondered whether a warm mash was being prepared for their supper. But no warm mash appeared, and on the following Sunday it was announced that from now onwards all barley would be reserved for the pigs. The field beyond the orchard had already been sown with barley. And the news soon leaked out that every pig was now receiving a ration of a pint of beer daily, with half a gallon for Napoleon himself, which was always served to him in the Crown Derby soup tureen.

But if there were hardships to be borne, they were partly offset by the fact that life nowadays had a greater dignity than it had had before. There were more songs, more speeches, more processions. Napoleon had commanded that once a week there should be held something called a Spontaneous Demonstration, the object of which was to celebrate the struggles and triumphs of Animal Farm. At the appointed time the animals would leave their work and march round the precincts of the farm in military formation, with the pigs leading, then the horses, then the cows, then the sheep, and then the poultry. The dogs flanked the procession and at the head of all marched Napoleon's black cockerel. Boxer and Clover always carried between them a green banner marked with the hoof and the horn and the caption, "Long live Comrade Napoleon!" Afterwards there were recitations of poems composed in Napoleon's honour, and a speech by Squealer giving particulars of the latest increases in the production of foodstuffs, and on occasion a shot was fired from the gun. The sheep were the greatest devotees of the Spontaneous Demonstration, and if anyone complained (as a few animals sometimes did, when no pigs or dogs were near) that they wasted time and meant a lot of standing about in the cold, the sheep were sure to silence him with a tremendous bleating of "Four legs good, two legs bad!" But by and large the animals enjoyed these celebrations. They found it comforting to be reminded that, after all, they were truly their own masters and that the work they did was for their own benefit. So that, what with the songs, the processions, Squealer's lists of figures, the thunder of the gun, the crowing of the cockerel, and the fluttering of the flag, they were able to forget that their bellies were empty, at least part of the time.

In April, Animal Farm was proclaimed a Republic, and it became necessary to elect a President. There was only one candidate, Napoleon, who was elected unanimously. On the same day it was given out that fresh documents had been discovered which revealed further details about Snowball's complicity with Jones. It now appeared that Snowball had not, as the animals had previously imagined, merely attempted to lose the Battle of the Cowshed by means of a stratagem, but had been openly fighting on Jones's side. In fact, it was he who had actually been the leader of the human forces, and had charged into battle with the words "Long live Humanity!" on his lips. The wounds on Snowball's back, which a few of the animals still remembered to have seen, had been inflicted by Napoleon's teeth.

In the middle of the summer Moses the raven suddenly reappeared on the farm, after an absence of several years. He was quite unchanged, still did no work, and talked in the same strain as ever about Sugarcandy Mountain. He would perch on a stump, flap his black wings, and talk by the hour to anyone who would listen. "Up there, comrades," he would say solemnly, pointing to the sky with his large beak—"up there, just on the other side of that dark cloud that you can see—there it lies, Sugarcandy Mountain, that happy country where we poor animals shall rest for ever from our labours!" He even claimed to have been there on one of his higher flights, and to have seen the everlasting fields of clover and the linseed cake and lump sugar growing on the hedges. Many of the animals believed him. Their lives now, they reasoned, were hungry and laborious; was it not right and just that a better world should exist somewhere else?

. . . .

The farm was more prosperous now, and better organised: it had even been enlarged by two fields which had been bought from Mr. Pilkington. The windmill had been successfully completed at last, and the farm possessed a threshing machine and a hay elevator of its own, and various new buildings had been added to it. Whymper had bought himself a dogcart. The windmill, however, had not after all been used for generating electrical power. It was used for milling corn, and brought in a handsome money profit. The animals were hard at work building yet another windmill; when that one was finished, so it was said, the dynamos would be installed. But the luxuries of which Snowball had once taught the animals to dream, the stalls with electric light and hot and cold water, and the three-day week, were no longer talked about. Napoleon had denounced such ideas as contrary to the spirit of Animalism. The truest happiness, he said, lay in working hard and living frugally.

Somehow it seemed as though the farm had grown richer without making the animals themselves any richer—except, of course, for the pigs and the dogs. Perhaps this was partly because there were so many pigs and so many dogs. It was not that these creatures did not work, after their fashion. There was, as Squealer was never tired of explaining, endless work in the supervision and organisation of the farm. Much of this work was of a kind that the other animals were too ignorant to understand. For example, Squealer told them that the pigs had to expend enormous labours every day upon mysterious things called "files," "reports," "minutes," and "memoranda." These were large sheets of paper which had to be closely covered with writing, and as soon as they were so covered, they were burnt in the furnace. This was of the highest importance for the welfare of the farm, Squealer said. But still, neither pigs nor dogs produced any food by their own labour; and there were very many of them, and their appetites were always good.

As for the others, their life, so far as they knew, was as it had always been. They were generally hungry, they slept on straw, they drank from the pool, they laboured in the fields; in winter they were troubled by the cold, and in summer by the flies. Sometimes the older ones among them racked their dim memories and tried to determine whether in the early days of the Rebellion, when Jones's expulsion was still recent, things had been better or worse than now. They could not remember. There was nothing with which they could compare their present lives: they had nothing to go upon except Squealer's lists of figures, which invariably demonstrated that everything was getting better and better. The animals found the problem insoluble; in any case, they had little time for speculating on such things now. Only old Benjamin professed to remember every detail of his long life and to know that things never had been, nor ever could be much better or much worse—hunger, hardship, and disappointment being, so he said, the unalterable law of life.

And yet the animals never gave up hope. More, they never lost, even for an instant, their sense of honour and privilege in being members of Animal Farm. They were still the only farm in the whole county—in all England!—owned and operated by animals. Not one of them, not even the youngest, not even the newcomers who had been brought from farms ten or twenty miles away, ever ceased to marvel at that. And when they heard the gun booming and saw the green flag fluttering at the masthead, their hearts swelled with imperishable pride, and the talk turned always towards the old heroic days, the expulsion of Jones, the writing of the Seven Commandments, the great battles in which the human invaders had been defeated. None of the old dreams had been abandoned. The Republic of the Animals which Major had foretold, when the green fields of England should be untrodden by human feet, was still believed in. Some day it was coming: it might not be soon, it might not be within the lifetime of any animal now living, but still it was coming. Even the tune of *Beasts of England* was perhaps hummed secretly here and there: at any rate, it was a fact that every animal on the farm knew it, though no one would have dared to sing it aloud. It might be that their lives were hard and that not all of their hopes had been fulfilled; but they were conscious that they were not as other animals. If they went hungry, it was not from feeding tyrannical human beings; if they worked hard, at least they worked for themselves. No creature among them went upon two legs. No creature called any other creature "Master." All animals were equal.

ROBERT PENN WARREN

Robert Penn Warren (1905–89), born and raised in Kentucky, was educated at Vanderbilt, the University of California, and at Oxford University as a Rhodes scholar. Warren published ten novels in his career and won three Pulitzer prizes, the first for his most famous novel, *All the King's Men* (1946). Also well-known as a poet, Warren was awarded the Pulitzer prize for his collections *Promises* (1957) and *Now and Then* (1979). In 1986, Robert Penn Warren was named the first U.S. poet laureate.

All the King's Men concerns the rise to power of a political demagogue and is regarded as one of the greatest novels ever written about American politics. Here, Warren examines how power is dangled, sought, and obtained in the American heartland during the twentieth century. We witness episodic acts of beneficence and brutishness as individuals strive for favors or rewards, and as those on the top calculate who is to receive, and who will be refused. This is a stunning portrait of politics as betrayal and denial.

From ALL THE KING'S MEN

The fellow ran up to the Boss, and the Boss took a couple of steps to meet him, and the fellow with the white coat grabbed Willie's hand as though he were drowning. He didn't shake Willie's hand, not by ordinary standards. He just hung on to it and twitched all over and gargled the sacred syllables of *Willie*. Then, when the attack had passed, he turned to the crowd, which was ringing around at a polite distance and staring, and announced, "My God, folks, it's Willie!"

The remark was superfluous. One look at the faces rallied around and you knew that if any citizen over the age of three didn't know that the strong-set man standing there in the Palm Beach suit was Willie Stark, that citizen was a half-wit. In the first place, all he would have to do would be to lift his eyes to the big picture high up there above the soda fountain, a picture about six times life size, which showed the same face, the big eyes, which in the picture had the suggestion of a sleepy and inward look (the eyes of the man in the Palm Beach suit didn't have that look now, but I've seen it), the pouches under the eyes and the jowls beginning to sag off, and the meaty lips, which didn't sag but if you looked close were laid one on top of the other like a couple of bricks, and the tousle of hair hanging down on the not very high squarish forehead. Under the picture was the legend: *My study is the heart of the people.* In quotation marks, and signed, *Willie Stark*. I had seen that picture in a thousand places, pool halls to palaces.

Somebody back in the crowd yelled, "Hi, Willie!" The Boss lifted his right hand and waved in acknowledgment to the unknown admirer. Then the Boss spied a fellow at the far end of the soda fountain, a tall, gaunt-shanked, malarial, leather-faced side of jerked venison, wearing jean pants and a brace of mustaches hanging off the kind of face you see in photographs of General Forrest's cavalrymen, and the Boss started toward him and put out his hand. Old Leather-Face didn't show. Maybe he shuffled one of his broken brogans on the tiles, and his Adam's apple jerked once or twice, and the eyes were watchful out of that face which resembled the seat of an old saddle left out in the weather, but when the Boss got close, his hand came up from the elbow, as though it didn't belong to Old Leather-Face but was operating on its own, and the Boss took it.

"How you making it, Malaciah?" the Boss asked.

The Adam's apple worked a couple of times, and the Boss shook the hand which was hanging out there in the air as if it didn't belong to anybody, and Old Leather-Face said, "We's grabblen."

"How's your boy?" the Boss asked.

"Ain't doen so good," Old Leather-Face allowed.

"Sick?"

"Naw," Old Leather-Face allowed, "jail."

"My God," the Boss said, "what they doing round here, putting good boys in jail?"

"He's a good boy," Old Leather-Face allowed. "Hit wuz a fahr fight, but he had a lettle bad luck."

"Huh?"

"Hit wuz fahr and squahr, but he had a lettle bad luck. He stobbed the feller and he died."

"Tough tiddy," the Boss said. Then: "Tried yet?"

"Not yit."

"Tough tiddy," the Boss said.

"I ain't complainen," Old Leather-Face said. "Hit wuz fit fahr and squahr."

"Glad to seen you," the Boss said. "Tell your boy to keep his tail over the dashboard."

"He ain't complainen," Old Leather-Face said.

The Boss started to turn away to the rest of us who after a hundred miles in the dazzle were looking at that soda fountain as though it were a mirage, but Old Leather-Face said, "Willie."

"Huh?" the Boss answered.

"Yore pitcher," Old Leather-Face allowed, and jerked his head creakily toward the six-times-life-size photograph over the soda fountain. "Yore pitcher," he said, "hit don't do you no credit, Willie."

"Hell, no," the Boss said, studying the picture, cocking his head to one side and squinting at it, "but I was porely when they took it. I was like I'd had the cholera morbus. Get in there busting some sense into that Legislature, and it leaves a man worsen'n the summer complaint."

"Git in thar and bust 'em, Willie!" somebody yelled from back in the crowd, which was thickening out now, for folks were trying to get in from the street.

"I'll bust 'em," Willie said, and turned around to the little man with the white coat. "Give us some cokes, Doc," he said, "for God's sake."

It looked as if Doc would have heart failure getting around to the other side of the soda fountain. The tail of that white coat was flat on the air behind him when he switched the corner and started clawing past the couple of girls in the lettuce-green smocks so he could do the drawing. He got the first one set up, and passed it to the Boss, who handed it to his wife. Then he started drawing the next one, and kept on saying, "It's on the house, Willie, it's on the house." The Boss took that one himself, and Doc kept on drawing them and saying, "It's on the house, Willie, it's on the house." He kept on drawing them till he got about five too many.

By that time folks were packed outside the door solid to the middle of the street. Faces were pressed up against the screen door, the way you do when you try to see through a screen into a dim room. Outside, they kept yelling, "Speech, Willie, speech!"

"My God," the Boss said, in the direction of Doc, who was hanging on to one of the nickel-plated spouts of the fountain and watching every drop of the coke go down the Boss's gullet. "My God," the Boss said, "I didn't come here to make a speech. I came here to go out and see my pappy."

"Speech, Willie, speech!" they were yelling out there.

The Boss set his little glass on the marble.

"It's on the house," Doc uttered croakingly with what strength was left in him after the rapture.

"Thanks, Doc," the Boss said. He turned away to head toward the door, then looked back. "You better get back in here and sell a lot of aspirin, Doc," he said, "to make up for the charity."

Then he plowed out the door, and the crowd fell back, and we tailed after him.

Mr. Duffy stepped up beside the Boss and asked him was he going to make a speech, but the Boss didn't even look at him. He kept walking slow and steady right across the street into the crowd, as though the crowd hadn't been there. The red, long faces with the eyes in them watching like something wary and wild and watchful in a thicket fell back, and there wasn't a sound. The crowd creamed back from his passage, and we followed in his wake, all of us who had been in the Cadillac, and the others who had been in the second car. Then the crowd closed behind.

The Boss kept walking straight ahead, his head bowed a little, the way a man bows his head when he is out walking by himself and has something on his mind. His hair fell down over his forehead, for he was carrying his hat in his hand. I knew his hair was down over his forehead, for I saw him give his head a quick jerk once or twice, the way he always did when he was walking alone and it fell down toward his eyes, the kind of motion a horse gives just after the bit is in and he's full of beans.

He walked straight across the street and across the patch of grass roots and up the steps of the courthouse. Nobody else followed him up the steps. At the top he turned around, slow, to face the crowd. He simply looked at them, blinking his big eyes a little, just as though he had just stepped out of the open doors and the dark hall of the courthouse behind him and was blinking to get his eyes adjusted to the light. He stood up there blinking, the hair down on his forehead, and the dark sweat patch showing under each arm of his Palm Beach coat. Then he gave his head a twitch, and his eyes bulged wide suddenly, even if the light was hitting him full in the face, and you could see the glitter in them.

It's coming, I thought.

You saw the eyes bulge suddenly like that, as though something had happened inside him, and there was that glitter. You knew something had happened inside him, and thought: *It's coming.* It was always that way. There was the bulge and the glitter, and there was the cold grip way down in the stomach as though somebody had laid hold of something in there, in the dark which is you, with a cold hand in a cold rubber glove. It was like the second when you come home late at night and see the yellow envelope of the telegram sticking out from under your door and you lean and pick it up, but don't open it yet, not for a second. While you stand there in the hall, with the envelope in your hand, you feel there's an eye on you, a great big eye looking straight at you from miles and dark and through walls and houses and through your coat and vest and hide and sees you huddled up way inside, in the dark which is you, inside yourself, like a clammy, sad little foetus you carry around inside yourself. The eye knows what's in the envelope, and it is watching you to see you when you open it and know, too. But the clammy, sad little

From *All the King's Men*

foetus which is you way down in the dark which is you too lifts up its sad little face and its eyes are blind, and it shivers cold inside you for it doesn't want to know what is in that envelope. It wants to lie in the dark and not know, and be warm in its not-knowing. The end of man is knowledge, but there is one thing he can't know. He can't know whether knowledge will save him or kill him. He will be killed, all right, but he can't know whether he is killed because of the knowledge which he has got or because of the knowledge which he hasn't got and which if he had it, would save him. There's the cold in your stomach, but you open the envelope, you have to open the envelope, for the end of man is to know.

The Boss stood up there quiet, with the bulge and glitter in the eyes, and there wasn't a sound in the crowd. You could hear one insane and irrelevant July fly sawing away up in one of the catalpa trees in the square. Then that sound stopped, and there wasn't anything but the waiting. Then the Boss lounged a step forward, easy and soft-footed.

"I'm not going to make any speech," the Boss said, and grinned. But the eyes were still big and the glitter was in them. "I didn't come here to make any speech. I came up here to go out and see my pappy, and see if he's got anything left in the smokehouse fit to eat. I'm gonna say: Pappy, now what about all that smoked sausage you wuz bragging about, what about all that ham you wuz bragging about all last winter, what about—" That's what he was saying, but the voice was different, going up in his nose and coming out flat with that little break they've got in the red hills, saying, "Pappy, now what about—"

But the glitter was still there, and I thought: *Maybe it's coming.* Maybe it was not too late. You never could tell. Suddenly, it might be there, he might say it.

But he was saying, "—and so I'm not going to make any speech—" In his old voice, his own voice. Or was that his voice? Which was his true voice, which one of all the voices, you would wonder.

He was saying, "And I didn't come here to ask you to give me anything, not even a vote. The Good Book says, 'There are three things that are never satisfied, yea, four things say not, it is enough—' " and the voice was different now—" 'the grave, and the barren womb, the earth that is not filled with water, and the fire that saith not, it is enough.' But Solomon might have added just one little item. He might have just made his little list complete, and added, the politician who never stops saying, Gimme."

He was lounging back on himself now, and his head was cocked a little to one side, and his eyes blinked. Then he grinned, and said, "If they had politicians back in those days, they said, Gimme, just like all of us politicians do. Gimme, gimme, my name's Jimmie. But I'm not a politician today. I'm taking the day off. I'm not even going to ask you to vote for me. To tell the God's unvarnished and unbuckled truth, I don't have to ask you. Not today. I still got quite a little hitch up there in the big house with the white columns two stories high on the front porch and peach ice cream for breakfast. Not that a passel of those statesmen wouldn't like to throw me out. You know—" and he leaned forward a little now, as if to tell them a secret—"it's funny how I just can't make friends with some folks. No matter how hard I try. I been just as polite. I said, Please. But *please* didn't do any good. But it looks like they got to put up with me a spell longer. And you have. Before you get shet of me. So you better just grin and bear it. It's not any worse'n boils. Now, is it?"

He stopped, and looked all around, right down at them, moving his head slow, so that he seemed to look right in a face here and stop for just a split second, and then to move on to another one a little farther. Then he grinned, and his eyes blinked, and he said, "Huh? What's the matter? Cat got yore tongue?"

"Boils on the tail!" somebody yelled back in the crowd.

"Dammit," Willie yelled right back, "lie on yore stummick and go to sleep!"

Somebody laughed.

"And," yelled Willie, "thank the good Lord who in his everlasting mercy saw fit to make something with a back side and a front side to it out of the skimpy little piece of material provided in your case!"

"You tell 'em, Willie!" somebody yelled back in the crowd. Then they started to laugh.

The Boss lifted up his right hand about as high as his head, out in front of him, palm down, and waited till they stopped laughing and whistling. Then he said: "No, I'm not here to ask you for anything. A vote or anything else. I reckon I'll be back later for that. If I keep on relishing that peach ice cream for breakfast in the big house. But I don't expect all of you to vote for me. My God, if all of you went and voted for Willie, what the hell would you find to argue about? There wouldn't be anything left but the weather, and you can't vote on that.

"No," he said, and it was another voice, quiet and easy and coming slow and from a distance, "I'm not here to ask for anything today. I'm taking the day off, and I've come home. A man goes away from his home and it is in him to do it. He lies in strange beds in the dark, and the wind is different in the trees. He walks in the street and there are the faces in front of his eyes, but there are no names for the faces. The voices he hears are not the voices he carried away in his ears a long time back when he went away. The voices he hears are loud. They are so loud he does not hear for a long time at a stretch those voices he carried away in his ears. But there comes a minute when it is quiet and he can hear those voices he carried away in his ears a long time back. He can make out what they say, and they say: Come back. They say: Come back, boy. So he comes back."

His voice just stopped. It didn't trail off like a voice coming to a stop. One second it was there, going on, word by word, in the stillness which filled the square and the crowd in front of the courthouse and was stiller for the grinding of the July flies in the two catalpas rising above the heads of the people who had crowded up on the patch of grass roots. The voice was going there, word by word, then suddenly it was not there. There was only the sound of the July flies, which seems to be inside your head as though it were the grind and whir of the springs and cogs which are you and which will not stop no matter what you say until they are good and ready.

From *All the King's Men*

He stood there a half minute, not saying a word, and not moving. He didn't even seem to be noticing the crowd down there. Then he seemed, all at once, to discover them, and grinned. "So he comes back," he said, grinning now. "When he gets half a day off. And he says, Hello, folks, how are you making it? And that's what I'm saying."

That's what he said. He looked down, grinning, and his head turned as his eyes went down in the crowd, and seemed to stop on a face there, and then go on to stop on another face.

Then he started walking down the steps, as if he had just come out of that dusky-dark hallway beyond the big open doors behind him and was walking down the steps by himself, with nobody there in front of him and no eyes on him. He came straight down the steps toward where his gang was standing, Lucy Stark and the rest of us, and nodded at us as though he were simply passing us on the street and didn't know us any too well anyway, and kept right on walking, straight into the crowd as though the crowd weren't there. The people fell back a little to make a passage for him, with their eyes looking right at him, and the rest of us in his gang followed behind him, and the crowd closed up behind us.

People were clapping now, and yelling. Somebody kept yelling, "Hi, Willie!"

The Boss walked straight across the street, through the crowd, and got into the Cadillac and sat down. We got in with him and the photographer and the others went back to their car. Sugar-Boy started up and nosed out into the street. People didn't get out of the way very fast. They couldn't, they were so jammed in. When we nosed out into the crowd, the faces were right there outside the car, not more than a foot or so away. The faces looked right in at us. But they were out there and we were inside now. The eyes in the red, slick-skinned long faces, or the brown, crinkled faces, looked in at us.

Sugar-Boy kept pecking at his horn. The words were piling up inside him. His lips started to work. I could see his face in the driver's mirror, and the lips were working. "The b-b-b-b-as-tuds," he said, and the spit flew.

The Boss had sunk in on himself now.

"The b-b-b-b-as-tuds," Sugar-Boy said, and pecked at his horn, but we were easing out of the square now to a side street where there weren't any people. We were doing forty by the time we passed the brick schoolhouse on the outskirts of town. Seeing the schoolhouse made me remember how I had first met Willie, about fourteen years before, back in 1922, when he wasn't anything but the County Treasurer of Mason County and had come down to the city to see about the bond issue to build that schoolhouse. Then I remembered how I had met him, in the back room of Slade's pool hall, where Slade sold the needle beer, and we were sitting at one of those little marble-topped tables with wirework legs, the kind they used to have in drugstores when you were a boy and took your high-school sweetie down on Saturday night to get that chocolate banana split and rub knees under the table and the wirework would always get in the way.

There were four of us. There was Tiny Duffy, who was almost as big back then as he was to get to be. He didn't need any sign to let you know what he was. If the wind was right,

you knew he was a city-hall slob long before you could see
the whites of his eyes. He had the belly and he sweated
through his shirt just above the belt buckle, and he had the
face, which was creamed and curded like a cow patty in a
spring pasture, only it was the color of biscuit dough, and in
the middle was his grin with the gold teeth. He was Tax As-
sessor, and he wore a flat hard straw hat on the back of his
head. There was a striped band on the hat.

Then there was Alex Michel, who was a country boy from
up in Mason County but who was learning fast. He had
learned fast enough to get to be a deputy sheriff. But he
wasn't that long. He wasn't anything, for he got cut in the gut
by a coke-frisky piano player in a cribhouse where he had
gone to take out a little in trade on his protection account.
Alex was, as I have said, from up in Mason County.

Duffy and I had been in the back room of Slade's place
waiting for Alex, with whom I had the hope of transacting a
little business. I was a newspaperman and Alex knew something I wanted to know. Duffy had called him in, for Duffy
was a friend of mine. At least, he knew that I worked for the
Chronicle, which at that time was supporting the Joe Harrison outfit. Joe Harrison was Governor then. And Duffy was
one of Joe Harrison's boys.

So I was sitting in the back room of Slade's place, one hot
morning in June or July, back in 1922, waiting for Alex
Michel to turn up and listening to the silence in the back
room of Slade's place. A funeral parlor at midnight is ear-
splitting compared to the effect you get in the middle of the
morning in the back room of a place like Slade's if you are the

first man there. You sit there and think how cozy it was last night, with the effluvium of brotherly bodies and the haw-haw of camaraderie and you look at the floor where now there are little parallel trails of damp sawdust the old broom left this morning when the unenthusiastic old Negro man cleaned up, and the general impression is that you are alone with the Alone and it is His move. So I sat there in the silence (Duffy was never talkative in the morning before he had worried down two or three drinks), and listened to my tissues break down and the beads of perspiration explode delicately out of the ducts embedded in the ample flesh of my companion.

Alex came in with a fellow with him, and I knew my little conversation was not promising. My mission was of some delicacy, not fit for the ear of a stranger. I figured that might be the reason Alex had his friend in tow. Maybe it was, for Alex was cagey in an amateurish sort of way. In any case, he had the Boss with him.

Only it was not the Boss. Not to the crude eye of the *homme sensuel*. Metaphysically it was the Boss, but how was I to know?

. . . .

Then Willie stood all alone by the table, saying, "My friends," and turning his alabaster face precariously from one side to the other, and fumbling in the right side pocket of his coat to fish out the speech.

While he was fumbling with the sheets, and looking down

at them with a slightly bemused expression as though the stuff before him were in a foreign language, somebody tugged at my sleeve. There was Sadie.

"How was it?" she asked.

"Take a look and guess," I replied.

She gave a good look up to the platform, and then asked, "How'd you do it?"

"Hair of the dog."

She looked up to the platform again. "Hair, hell," she said, "he must have swallowed the dog."

I inspected Willie, who stood up there sweating and swaying and speechless, under the hot sun.

"He's on the ropes," Sadie said.

"Hell, he's been on 'em all morning," I said, "and lucky to have 'em."

She was still looking at him. It was much the way she had looked at him the night before when he lay on the bed in my room, out cold, and she stood by the side of the bed. It wasn't pity and it wasn't contempt. It was an ambiguous, speculative look. Then she said, "Maybe he was born on 'em."

She said it in a tone which seemed to imply that she had settled that subject. But she kept on looking up there at him in the same way.

The candidate could still stand, at least with one thigh propped against the table. He had begun to talk by this time, too. He had called them his friends in two or three ways and had said he was glad to be there. Now he stood there clutching the manuscript in both hands, with his head lowered like a dehorned cow beset by a couple of fierce dogs in the barn-yard, while the sun beat on him and the sweat dropped. Then he took a grip on himself, and lifted his head.

"I have a speech here," he said. "It is a speech about what this state needs. But there's no use telling you what this state needs. You are the state. You know what you need. Look at your pants. Have they got holes in the knee? Listen to your belly. Did it ever rumble for emptiness? Look at your crop. Did it ever rot in the field because the road was so bad you couldn't get it to market? Look at your kids. Are they growing up ignorant as you and dirt because there isn't any school for them?"

Willie paused, and blinked around at the crowd. "No," he said, "I'm not going to read you any speech. You know what you need better'n I could tell you. But I'm going to tell you a story."

And he paused, steadied himself by the table, and took a deep breath while the sweat dripped.

I leaned toward Sadie. "What the hell's the bugger up to?" I asked.

"Shut up," she commanded, watching him.

He began again. "It's a funny story," he said. "Get ready to laugh. Get ready to bust your sides for it is sure a funny story. It's about a hick. It's about a red-neck, like you all, if you please. Yeah, like you. He grew up like any other mother's son on the dirt roads and gully washes of a north-state farm. He knew all about being a hick. He knew what it was to get up before day and get cow dung between his toes and feed and slop and milk before breakfast so he could set off by sunup to walk six miles to a one-room, slab-sided schoolhouse. He knew what it was to pay high taxes for that windy shack of a schoolhouse and those gully-washed red-clay roads to walk over—or to break his wagon axle or string-halt his mules on.

"Oh, he knew what it was to be a hick, summer and winter. He figured if he wanted to do anything he had to do it himself. So he sat up nights and studied books and studied law so maybe he could do something about changing things. He didn't study that law in any man's school or college. He studied it nights after a hard day's work in the field. So he could change things some. For himself and for folks like him. I am not lying to you. He didn't start out thinking about all the other hicks and how he was going to do wonderful things for them. He started out thinking of number one, but something came to him on the way. How he could not do something for himself and not for other folks or for himself without the help of other folks. It was going to be all together or none. That came to him.

"And it came to him with the powerful force of God's own lightning on a tragic time back in his own home county two years ago when the first brick schoolhouse ever built in his county collapsed because it was built of politics-rotten brick, and it killed and mangled a dozen poor little scholars. Oh, you know that story. He had fought the politics back of building that schoolhouse of rotten brick but he lost and it fell. But it started him thinking. Next time would be different.

"People were his friends because he had fought that rotten

brick. And some of the public leaders down in the city knew that and they rode up to his pappy's place in a big fine car and said how they wanted him to run for Governor."

I plucked Sadie's arm. "You think he's going to—"

"Shut up," she said savagely.

I looked toward Duffy up there on the platform back of Willie. Duffy's face was worried. It was red and round and sweating, and it was worried.

"Oh, they told him," Willie was saying, "and that hick swallowed it. He looked in his heart and thought he might try to change things. In all humility he thought how he might try. He was just a human, country boy, who believed like we have always believed back here in the hills that even the plainest, poorest fellow can be Governor if his fellow citizens find he has got the stuff and the character for the job.

"Those fellows in the striped pants saw the hick and they took him in. They said how MacMurfee was a limber-back and a dead-head and how Joe Harrison was the tool of the city machine, and how they wanted that hick to step in and try to give some honest government. They told him that. But—" Willie stopped, and lifted his right hand clutching the manuscript to high heaven—"do you know who they were? They were Joe Harrison's hired hands and lickspittles and they wanted to get a hick to run to split MacMurfee's hick vote. Did I guess this? I did not. No, for I heard their sweet talk. And I wouldn't know the truth this minute if that woman right there—" and he pointed down at Sadie—"if that woman right there—"

I nudged Sadie and said, "Sister, you are out of a job."

"—if that fine woman right there hadn't been honest enough and decent enough to tell the foul truth which stinks in the nostrils of the Most High!"

Duffy was on his feet, edging uncertainly toward the front of the platform. He kept looking desperately toward the band as though he might signal them to burst into music and then at the crowd as though he were trying to think of something to say. Then he edged toward Willie and said something to him.

But the words, whatever they were, were scarcely out of his mouth before Willie had turned on him. "There!" Willie roared. "There!" And he waved his right hand, the hand clutching the manuscript of his speech. "There is the Judas Iscariot, the lickspittle, the nose-wiper!"

And Willie waved his right arm at Duffy, clutching the manuscript which he had not read. Duffy was trying to say something to him, but Willie wasn't hearing it, for he was waving the manuscript under Duffy's retreating nose and shouting, "Look at him! Look at him!"

Duffy, still retreating, looked toward the band and waved his arms at them and shouted, "Play, play! Play the 'Star Spangled Banner'!"

But the band didn't play. And just then as Duffy turned back to Willie, Willie made a more than usually energetic pass of the fluttering manuscript under Duffy's nose and shouted, "Look at him, Joe Harrison's dummy!"

Duffy shouted, "It's a lie!" and stepped back from the accusing arm.

I don't know whether Willie meant to do it. But anyway, he did it. He didn't exactly shove Duffy off the platform. He just

started Duffy doing a dance along the edge, a kind of delicate, feather-toed, bemused, slow-motion adagio accompanied by arms pinwheeling around a face which was like a
surprised custard pie with a hole scooped in the middle of
the meringue, and the hole was Duffy's mouth, but no sound
came out of it. There wasn't a sound over that five-acre tract
of sweating humanity. They just watched Duffy do his dance.

Then he danced right off the platform. He broke his fall
and half lay, half sat, propped against the bottom of the platform with his mouth still open. No sound came out of it now,
for there wasn't any breath to make a sound.

All of that, and me without a camera.

Willie hadn't even bothered to look over the edge. "Let the
hog lie!" he shouted. "Let the hog lie, and listen to me, you
hicks. Yeah, you're hicks, too, and they've fooled you, too, a
thousand times, just like they fooled me. For that's what they
think we're for. To fool. Well, this time I'm going to fool somebody. I'm getting out of this race. You know why?"

He paused and wiped the sweat off his face with his left
hand, a flat scouring motion.

"Not because my little feelings are hurt. They aren't hurt, I
never felt better in my life, because now I know the truth.
What I ought to known long back. Whatever a hick wants
he's got to do for himself. Nobody in a fine automobile and
sweet-talking is going to do it for him. When I come back to
run for Governor again, I'm coming on my own and I'm coming for blood. But I'm getting out now.

"I'm resigning in favor of MacMurfee. By God, everything

I've said about MacMurfee stands and I'll say it again, but I'm going to stump this state for him. Me and the other hicks, we are going to kill Joe Harrison so dead he'll never even run for dogcatcher in this state. Then we'll see what MacMurfee does. This is his last chance. The time has come. The truth is going to be told and I'm going to tell it. I'm going to tell it over this state from one end to the other if I have to ride the rods or steal me a mule to do it, and no man, Joe Harrison or any other man, can stop me. For I got me a gospel and I—"

I leaned to Sadie. "Listen," I said, "I've got to get on a telephone. I'm starting to town or the first telephone I hit. I got to telephone this in. You stay here and for God's sake remember what happens."

"All right," she said, not paying much mind to me.

"And nab Willie when it's over and bring him to town. It's a sure thing Duffy won't ask you to ride with him. You nab the sap, and—"

"Sap, hell," she said. And added, "You go on."

I went. I worked around the edge of the grandstand, through the crowd, with the sound of Willie's voice hammering on the eardrums and shaking dead leaves off the oak trees. As I rounded the end of the grandstand, I looked back and there was Willie flinging the sheets of his manuscript from him so they swirled about his feet and beating on his chest and shouting how the truth was there and didn't need writing down. There he was, with the papers about his feet and one arm up, the coat sleeve jammed elbow high, face red as a bruised beet and the sweat sluicing, hair over his forehead, eyes bugged out and shining, drunk as a hoot owl, and behind him the bunting, red-white-and-blue, and over him God's bright, brassy, incandescent sky.

I walked down the gravel road a piece and hitched a ride on a truck to town.

That night when all was still and the train bearing Duffy back to the city (to report, no doubt, to Joe Harrison) was puffing across the sage country under the stars and Willie had been in bed for hours sleeping off the fumes, I reached for the bottle on the writing table in my room at the hotel in Upton and said to Sadie, "How about a little more of the stuff that let the bars down and kicked the boards loose?"

"What?" she asked.

"You would not understand that to which I so grammatically refer," I said, and poured the drink for her.

"Oh, I forgot," she said, "you're the fellow who went to college."

Yes, I was the fellow who had gone so grammatically to college where I had not learned, I decided, all there was to know.

Willie kept his word. He stumped the state for MacMurfee. He didn't ride the rods or buy him a mule or steal him one. But he drove the pants off his pretty good secondhand car over the washboard and through the hub-deep dust and got mired in the black gumbo when a rain came and sat in his car waiting for the span of mules to come and pull him out. He stood on schoolhouse steps, and on the top of boxes borrowed from the dry-goods store and on the seats of farm wagons and on the porches of crossroads stores, and talked. "Friends, red-necks, suckers, and fellow hicks," he would say, leaning forward, leaning at them, looking at them. And he would pause, letting the words sink in. And in the quiet the crowd would be restless and resentful under these words, the words they knew people called them but the words nobody ever got up and called them to their face. "Yeah," he would say, "yeah," and twist his mouth on the word, "that's what you are, and you needn't get mad at me for telling you. Well, get mad, but I'm telling you. That's what you are. And me—I'm one, too. Oh, I'm a red-neck, for the sun has beat down on me. Oh, I'm a sucker, for I fell for that sweet-talking fellow in the fine automobile. Oh, I took the sugar tit and hushed my crying. Oh, I'm a hick and I am the hick they were going to try to use and split the hick vote. But I'm standing here on my own hind legs, for even a dog can learn to do that, give him time. I learned. It took me a time but I learned, and here I am on my own hind legs." And he would lean at them. And demand, "Are you, are you on your hind legs? Have you learned that much yet? You think you can learn that much?"

He told them things they didn't like. He called them the names they didn't like to be called, but always, almost always, the restlessness and resentment died and he leaned at them with his eyes bugging and his face glistening in the hot sunlight or the red light of a gasoline flare. They listened while he told them to stand on their own hind legs. Go and vote, he told them. Vote for MacMurfee this time, he told them, for he is all you have got to vote for. But vote strong, strong enough to show what you can do. Vote him in and then if he doesn't deliver, nail up his hide. "Yeah," he would say, leaning, "yeah, nail him up if he don't deliver. Hand me the hammer and I'll nail him." Vote, he told them. Put MacMurfee on the spot, he told them.

He leaned at them and said, "Listen to me, you hicks. Listen here and lift up your eyes and look on the God's blessed and unflyblown truth. If you've got the brain of a sapsucker left and can recognize the truth when you see it. This is the truth; you are a hick and nobody ever helped a hick but the hick himself. Up there in town they won't help you. It is up to you and God, and God helps those who help themselves!"

He gave them that, and they stood there in front of him, with a thumb hooked in the overall strap, and the eyes under the pulled down hat brim squinting at him as though he were something spied across a valley or cove, something they weren't quite easy in the mind about, too far away to make out good, or a sudden movement in the brush seen way off yonder across the valley or across the field and something might pop out of the brush, and under the eyes the jaw revolving worked the quid with a slow, punctilious, immitigable motion, like historical process. And Time is nothing to a hog, or to History, either. They watched him, and if you watched close you might be able to see something beginning to happen. They stand so quiet, they don't even shift from one foot to the other— they've got a talent for being quiet, you can see them stand on the street corner when they come to town, not moving or talking, or see one of them squatting on his heels by the road, just looking off where the road drops over the hill—and their squinched eyes don't flicker off the man up there in front of them. They've got a talent for being quiet. But sometimes the quietness stops. It snaps all of a sudden, like a piece of string pulled tight. One of them sits quiet on the bench, at the brush-arbor revival, listening, and all of a sudden he jumps up and lifts up his arms and yells, "Oh, Jesus! I have seen His name!" Or one of them presses his finger on the trigger, and the sound of the gun surprises even him.

Willie is up there. In the sun, or in the red light of the gasoline flare. "You ask me what my program is. Here it is, you hicks. And don't you forget it. Nail 'em up! Nail up Joe Harrison. Nail up anybody who stands in your way. Nail up MacMurfee if he don't deliver. Nail up anybody who stands in your way. You hand me the hammer and I'll do it with my own hand. Nail 'em up on the barn door! And don't fan away the bluebottles with any turkey wing!"

It was Willie, all right. It was the fellow with the same name.

MacMurfee was elected. Willie had something to do with it, for the biggest vote was polled in the sections Willie had worked that they had any record of. But all the time Mac-Murfee didn't quite know what to make of Willie. He shied off him at first, for Willie had said some pretty hard things about him, and then when it did look as though Willie would make an impression, he shilly-shallied. And in the end Willie got up on his hind legs and said how the MacMurfee people were offering to pay his expenses but he was on his own, he wasn't MacMurfee's man, even if he was saying to vote for MacMurfee. He was paying his way, he said, even if he had to put another mortgage on his pappy's farm and the last one it would hold. Yes, and if there was anybody who couldn't afford two dollars to pay his poll tax and came to him and said it straight out, he, Willie Stark, would pay that tax out of money he had got by mortgaging his pappy's farm. That was how much he believed in what he was saying.

MacMurfee was in, and Willie went back to Mason City and practiced law. He must have dragged on for a year or so, handling chicken-stealing cases and stray-hog cases and cutting scrapes (which are part of the entertainment at Saturday-night square dances in Mason County). Then a gang of workmen got hurt when some of the rig collapsed on a bridge the state was building over the Ackamulgee River, and two or three got killed. A lot of the workmen were from Mason County and they got Willie for their lawyer. He got all over the papers for that. And he won the case. Then they struck oil just west of Mason County over in Ackamulgee County, and in that section Willie got mixed up in the litigation between an oil company and some independent leaseholders. Willie's side won, and he saw folding money for the first time in his life. He saw quite a lot of it.

During all that time I didn't see Willie. I didn't see him again until he announced in the Democratic primary in 1930. But it wasn't a primary. It was hell among the yearlings and the Charge of the Light Brigade and Saturday night in the back room of Casey's saloon rolled into one, and when the smoke cleared away not a picture still hung on the walls. And there wasn't any Democratic party. There was just Willie, with his hair in his eyes and his shirt sticking to his stomach with sweat. And he had a meat ax in his hand and was screaming for blood. In the background of the picture, under a purplish tumbled sky flecked with sinister white like driven foam, flanking Willie, one on each side, were two figures, Sadie Burke and a tallish, stooped, slow-spoken man with a sad, tanned face and what they call the eyes of a dreamer. The man was Hugh Miller, Harvard Law School, Lafayette Escadrille, Croix de Guerre, clean hands, pure heart, and no political past. He was a fellow who had sat still for years, and then somebody (Willie Stark) handed him a baseball bat and he felt his fingers close on the tape. He was a man and was Attorney General. And Sadie Burke was just Sadie Burke.

Over the brow of the hill, there were, of course, some other people. There were, for instance, certain gentlemen who had once been devoted to Joe Harrison, but who, when they discovered that there wasn't going to be any more Joe Harrison politically speaking, had had to hunt up a new friend. The new friend happened to be Willie. He was the only place for them to go. They figured they would sign on with Willie and grow up with the country. Willie signed them on, all right, and as a result got quite a few votes not of the wool-hat and cocklebur variety. After a while, Willie even signed on Tiny Duffy, who became Highway Commissioner and, later, Lieutenant Governor in Willie's last term. I used to wonder why Willie kept him around. Sometimes I used to ask the Boss, "What do you keep that lunk-head for?" Sometimes he would just laugh and say nothing. Sometimes he would say, "Hell, somebody's got to be Lieutenant Governor, and they all look alike." But once he said: "I keep him because he reminds me of something."

"What?"

"Something I don't ever want to forget," he said.

"What's that?"

"That when they come to you sweet talking you better not listen to anything they say. I don't aim to forget that."

So that was it. Tiny was the fellow who had come in a big automobile and had talked sweet to Willie back when Willie was a little country lawyer.

. . . .

"Not that it's any of my business," I said, "but what's all the shouting about?"

"Didn't you read the paper?"

"No, I was on vacation."

"And Sadie didn't tell you?"

"Just got here," I said.

"Well, Byram rigged him up a nice little scheme to get rich. Got himself a tie-in with a realty outfit and fixed things up with Hamill in the Tax Lands Bureau. Pretty, only they wanted it all to themselves and somebody got sore at not being cut in, and squawked to the MacMurfee boys in the Legislature. And if I get my hands on who it was—"

"Was what?"

"Squawked to the MacMurfee outfit. Ought to taken it up with Duffy. Everybody knows he's supposed to handle complaints. And now we got this impeachment business."

"Of who?"

"Byram."

"What's happened to Hamill?"

"He's moved to Cuba. You know, better climate. And, from reports, he moved fast. Duffy went around this morning, and Hamill caught a train. But we got to handle this impeachment."

"I don't think they could put it through."

"They ain't even going to try. You let a thing like that get started and no telling what'll happen. The time to stomp 'em is now. I've got boys out picking up soreheads and wobblies and getting 'em to town. Sadie's been on the phone all day taking the news. Some of the birds are hiding out, for the word must have got round by this time, but the boys are running 'em down. Brought in three this afternoon, and we gave 'em what it took. But we had something ready on them all. You ought to've seen Jeff Hopkins's face when he found out I knew about his pappy selling likker out of that little one-horse drugstore he's got over in Talmadge and then forging prescriptions for the record. Or Martten's when he found out I knew how the bank over in Okaloosa holds a mortgage on his place falling due in about five weeks. Well—" and he wriggled his toes comfortably inside of the socks—"I quieted their nerves. It's the old tonic, but it still soothes."

"What am I supposed to do?"

"Get over to Harmonville tomorrow and see if you can beat some sense into Sim Harmon's head."

"That all?"

Before he could answer Sadie popped her head in the door,

and said the boys had brought in Witherspoon, who was a representative from the north tip of the state.

"Put him in the other room," the Boss said, "and let him stew." Then, as Sadie popped out again, he turned to me and answered my question. "All, except get me together all you have on Al Coyle before you leave town. The boys are trying to run him down and I want to be heeled when they book him."

"O.K.," I said, and stood up.

He looked at me as though he were about to say something. For a second I had the notion that he was working himself up to it, and I stood in front of my chair, waiting. But Sadie stuck her head in. "Mr. Miller would like to see you," she said to the Boss, and didn't give the impression of glad tidings.

"Send him in," the Boss ordered, and I could tell that, no matter what he had on his mind to say to me a second before, he had something else on it now. He had Hugh Miller, Harvard Law School, Lafayette Escadrille, Croix de Guerre, clean hands, pure heart, Attorney General, on his mind.

"He won't like it," I said.

"No," he said, "he won't."

And then in the doorway stood the tall, lean, somewhat stooped man, with swarthy face and unkempt dark hair and sad eyes under black brows, and with a Phi Beta Kappa key slung across his untidy blue serge. He stood there for a second, blinking the sad eyes, as though he had come out of darkness into a sudden light, or had stumbled into the wrong room. He looked like the wrong thing to be coming through that door, all right.

The Boss had stood up and padded across in his sock-feet, holding out his hand, saying, "Hello, Hugh."

Hugh Miller shook hands, and stepped into the room, and I started to edge out the door. Then I caught the Boss's eye, and he nodded, quick, toward my chair. So I shook hands with Hugh Miller, too, and sat back down.

"Have a seat," the Boss said to Hugh Miller.

"No, thanks, Willie," Hugh Miller replied in his slow solemn way. "But you sit down, Willie."

The Boss dropped back into his chair, cocked his feet up again, and demanded, "What's on your mind?"

"I reckon you know," Hugh Miller said.

"I reckon I do," the Boss said.

"You are saving White's hide, aren't you?"

"I don't give a damn about White's hide," the Boss said. "I'm saving something else."

"He's guilty."

"As hell," the Boss agreed cheerfully. "If the category of guilt and innocence can be said to have any relevance to something like Byram B. White."

"He's guilty," Hugh Miller said.

"My God, you talk like Byram was human! He's a thing! You don't prosecute an adding machine if a spring goes bust and makes a mistake. You fix it. Well, I fixed Byram. I fixed him so his unborn great-grandchildren will wet their pants on this anniversary and not know why. Boy, it will be the shock in the genes. Hell, Byram is just something you use, and he'll sure be useful from now on."

"That sounds fine, Willie, but it just boils down to the fact you're saving White's hide."

"White's hide be damned," the Boss said, "I'm saving something else. You let that gang of MacMurfee's boys in the Legislature get the notion they can pull something like this and there's no telling where they'd stop. Do you think they like anything that's been done? The extraction tax? Raising the royalty rate on state land? The income tax? The highway program? The Public Health Bill?"

"No, they don't," Hugh Miller admitted. "Or rather, the people behind MacMurfee don't like it."

"Do you like it?"

"Yes," Hugh Miller said, "I like it. But I can't say I like some of the stuff around it."

"Hugh," the Boss said, and grinned, "the trouble with you is you are a lawyer. You are a damned fine lawyer."

"You're a lawyer," Hugh Miller said.

"No," the Boss corrected, "I'm not a lawyer. I know some law. In fact, I know a lot of law. And I made me some money out of law. But I'm not a lawyer. That's why I can see what the law is like. It's like a single-bed blanket on a double bed and three folks in the bed and a cold night. There ain't ever enough blanket to cover the case, no matter how much pulling and hauling, and somebody is always going to nigh catch pneumonia. Hell, the law is like the pants you bought last year for a growing boy, but it is always this year and the seams are popped and the shankbone's to the breeze. The law is always too short and too tight for growing humankind. The best you can do is do something and then make up some law to fit and by the time that law gets on the books you would have done something different. Do you think half the things I've done were clear, distinct, and simple in the constitution of this state?"

"The Supreme Court has ruled—" Hugh Miller began.

"Yeah, and they ruled because I put 'em there to rule it, and they saw what had to be done. Half the things *weren't* in the constitution but they are now, by God. And how did they get there? Simply because somebody did 'em."

The blood began to climb up in Hugh Miller's face, and he shook his head just a little, just barely, the way a slow animal does when a fly skims by. Then he said, "There's nothing in the constitution says that Byram B. White can commit a felony with impunity."

"Hugh," the Boss began, soft, "don't you see that Byram doesn't mean a thing? Not in this situation. What they're after is to break the administration. They don't care about Byram, except so far as it's human nature to hate to think somebody else is getting something when you aren't. What they care about is undoing what this administration has done. And now is the time to stomp 'em. And when you start out to do something—" he sat up straight in the chair now, with his hands on the overstuffed sides, and thrust his head forward at Hugh Miller—"you got to use what you've got. You got to use fellows like Byram, and Tiny Duffy, and that scum down in the Legislature. You can't make bricks without straw, and most of the time all the straw you got is secondhand straw from the cowpen. And if you think you can make it any different, you're crazy as a hoot owl."

Hugh Miller straightened his shoulders a little. He did not look at the Boss but at the wall beyond the Boss. "I am offering my resignation as Attorney General," he said. "You will have it in writing, by messenger, in the morning."

"You took a long time to do it," the Boss said softly. "A long time, Hugh. What made you take such a long time?"

Hugh Miller didn't answer, but he did move his gaze from the wall to the Boss's face.

"I'll tell you, Hugh," the Boss said. "You sat in your law office fifteen years and watched the sons-of-bitches warm chairs in this state and not do a thing, and the rich get richer and the pore get porer. Then I came along and slipped a Louisville Slugger in your hand and whispered low, 'You want to step in there and lay round you a little?' And you did. You had a wonderful time. You made the fur fly and you put nine tin-horn grafters in the pen. But you never touched what was behind 'em. The law isn't made for that. All you can do about that is take the damned government away from the behind guys and keep it away from 'em. Whatever way you can. You know that down in your heart. You want to keep your Harvard hands clean, but way down in your heart you know I'm telling the truth, and you're asking the benefit of somebody getting his little panties potty-black. You know you're welching if you pull out. That," he said, softer than ever, and leaned toward Hugh Miller, peering up at him, "is why it took you so long to do it. To pull out."

Hugh Miller looked down at him a half minute, down into

the beefy upturned face and the steady protruding eyes. There was a shadowed, puzzled expression on Hugh Miller's face, as though he were trying to read something in a bad light, or in a foreign language he didn't know very well. Then he said, "My mind is made up."

"I know your mind's made up," the Boss said. "I know I couldn't change your mind, Hugh." He stood up in front of his chair, hitched his trousers up, the way a fellow has to who is putting it on some around the middle, and sock-footed over to Hugh Miller. "Too bad," he said. "You and me make quite a team. Your brains and my brawn."

Hugh Miller gave something which resembled an incipient smile.

"No hard feelings?" the Boss said, and stuck out his hand.

Hugh Miller took it.

"If you don't give up likker, you might drop in and have a drink with me some time," the Boss said. "I won't talk politics."

"All right," Hugh Miller said, and turned toward the door.

He had just about made the door, when the Boss said, "Hugh." Hugh Miller stopped and looked back.

"You're leaving me all alone," the Boss said, in semicomic woe, "with the sons-of-bitches. Mine and the other fellow's."

Hugh Miller smiled in a stiff, embarrassed way, shook his head, said, "Hell—Willie—" let his voice trail off without ever saying what he had started to say, and then Harvard Law School, Lafayette Escadrille, Croix de Guerre, clean hands and pure heart, was with us no longer.

The Boss sank down on the foot of the bed, heaved his left

ankle up over his right knee; and while he meditatively scratched the left foot, the way a farmer does when he takes off his shoes at night, he stared at the closed door.

"With the sons-of-bitches," he said, and let the foot slip off the knee and plop to the floor, while he still stared at the door.

I stood up again. It was my third try for getting out of the place and getting back to my hotel for some sleep. The Boss could sit up all night, night after night, and never show it, and that fact was sure hell on his associates. I edged toward the door again, but the Boss swung his stare to me and I knew something was coming. So I just stopped and waited for it, while the stare worked over my face and tried to probe around in the gray stuff inside my head, like a pair of forceps.

Then he said, "You think I ought to thrown White to the wolves?"

"It's a hell of a time to be asking that question," I said.

"You think I ought?"

"*Ought* is a funny word," I said. "If you mean, to win, then time will tell. If you mean, to do right, then nobody will ever be able to tell you."

"What do you think?"

"Thinking is not my line," I said, "and I'd advise you to stop thinking about it because you know damned well what you are going to do. You are going to do what you are doing."

"Lucy is figuring on leaving," he said calmly, as though that answered something I had said.

"Well, I'm damned," I said, in genuine surprise, for I had Lucy figured as the long-suffering type on whose bosom repentant tears always eventually fall. Very eventually. Then my glance strayed to the closed door, beyond which Sadie Burke sat in front of the telephone with that pair of black bituminous eyes in the middle of the pocked face and cigarette smoke tangled in that wild black hacked-off Irish hair like morning mist in a pine thicket.

He caught my glance at the door. "No," he said, "it's not that."

"Well, that would be enough by ordinary standards," I said.

"She didn't know. Not that I know of."

"She's a woman," I said, "and they can smell it."

"That wasn't it," he said. "She said if I took care of Byram White she would leave me."

"Looks like everybody is trying to run your business for you."

"God damn it!" he said, and came up off the bed, and paced savagely across the carpet for four paces, and swung, and paced again, and seeing that motion and the heavy sway of the head when he turned, I thought back to the nights when I had heard the pacing in the next room in those jerkwater hotels over the state, back in the days when the Boss had been Willie Stark, and Willie Stark had been the sucker with the high-school-debater speech full of facts and figures and the kick-me sign on his coattails.

Well, I was seeing it now—the lunging, taut motion that had then been on the other side of the wall, in the dry-goods-box little hotel room. Well, it was out of that room now. It was prowling the veldt.

"God damn it!" he said again, "they don't know a thing about it, they don't know how it is, and you can't tell 'em."

He paced back and forth a couple of times more, then said, "They don't know."

He swung again, paced, and stopped, his head thrust out toward me. "You know what I'm going to do? Soon as I bust the tar out of that gang?"

"No," I said, "I don't know."

"I'm going to build me the God-damnedest, biggest, chromium-platedest, formaldehyde-stinkingest free hospital and health center the All-Father ever let live. Boy, I tell you, I'm going to have a cage of canaries in every room that can sing Italian grand opera and there ain't going to be a nurse hasn't won a beauty contest at Atlantic City and every bed-pan will be eighteen-carat gold and by God, every bedpan will have a Swiss music-box attachment to play 'Turkey in the Straw' or 'The Sextet from Lucia,' take your choice."

"That will be swell," I said.

"I'll do it," he said. "You don't believe me, but I'm going to do it."

. . . .

The big black Cadillac, the hood glistening dully under the street lamps—as I could see even from the back seat—eased down the street, making its expensive whisper under the boughs which had new leaves on them, for it was early April now. Then we got to a street where there were not any nice trees arching over.

"Here," I said, "that place on the right, just beyond that grocery."

Sugar-Boy put the Cadillac up to the curb, like a mother

laying Little Precious down with a last kiss. Then he ran
around to open the door for the Boss, but the Boss was already on the curb. I uncoiled myself and stood beside him.
"This is the joint," I remarked, and started in.

For we were going to see Adam Stanton.

When I told the Boss that Adam Stanton would take the
job and that he had sent me a message to arrange things, the
Boss had said, "Well." Then he had looked at me from toe to
crown, and said, "You must be Svengali."

"Yeah," I had said, "I am Svengali."

"I want to see him," the Boss had said.

"I'll try to get him up here."

"Get him up here?" the Boss had said. "I'll go there. Hell,
he's doing me a favor."

"Well, you're the Governor, aren't you?"

"You're damned right I am," the Boss had said, "but he is
Doc Stanton. When do we go?"

I had told him it would have to be at night, that you never
could catch him except at night.

So here we were, at night, entering the door of the crummy
apartment house, climbing the dark stairs, stumbling over
the kiddie car, inhaling the odor of cabbage and diapers. "He
sure picked himself a place to live," the Boss said.

"Yeah," I agreed, "and lots of folks can't figure out why."

"I reckon I can," the Boss said.

And as I wondered whether he could or not, we reached
the door, and I knocked, entered, and confronted the level
eyes of Adam Stanton.

For a half moment, while Sugar-Boy was easing in, and I

was shutting the door, Adam and the Boss simply took each other in, without a word. Then I turned and said, "Governor Stark, this is Dr. Stanton."

The Boss took a step forward and put out his right hand. Perhaps I imagined it, but I thought I noticed a shade of hesitation before Adam took it. And the Boss must have noticed it, too, for when Adam did put out his hand, the Boss, in the middle of the shake, before any other word had been spoken, grinned suddenly, and said, "See, boy, it's not as bad as you thought, it won't kill you."

Then, by God, Adam grinned, too.

Then I said, "And this is Mr. O'Sheean," and Sugar-Boy lurched forward and put out one of his stubby arms with a hand hanging on the end of it like a stuffed glove, and twisted his face and began, "I'm pl-pl-pl-pl—"

"I'm glad to know you," Adam said. Then I saw his glance pick up the bulge under Sugar-Boy's left armpit. He turned to the Boss. "So this is one of your gunmen I've heard about?" he said, definitely not grinning now.

"Hell," the Boss said, "Sugar-Boy just carries that for fun. Sugar-Boy is just a pal. Ain't anybody can drive a car like Sugar-Boy."

Sugar-Boy was looking at him like a dog you've just scratched on the head.

Adam stood there, and didn't reply. For a second I thought the deal was about to blow up. Then Adam said, very formally, "Won't you gentlemen have seats?"

We did.

Sugar-Boy sneaked one of his lumps of sugar out of the

side pocket of his coat, put it into his mouth, and began to suck it, with his fey Irish cheeks drawn in and his eyes blurred with bliss.

Adam waited, sitting straight up in his chair.

The Boss, leaning back in one of the overstuffed wrecks, didn't seem to be in any hurry. But he finally said, "Well, Doc, what do you think of it?"

"Of what?" Adam demanded.

"Of my hospital?"

"I think it will do the people of the state some good," he said. Then added, "And get you some votes."

"You can forget about the vote side of it," the Boss said. "There are lots of ways to get votes, son."

"So I understand," Adam said. Then he handed the Boss another big chunk of silence to admire.

The Boss admired it awhile, then said, "Yeah, it'll do some good. But not too much unless you take over."

"I won't stand any interference," Adam said, and bit the sentence off.

"Don't worry," the Boss laughed. "I might fire you, boy, but I won't interfere."

"If that is a threat," Adam said, and the pale-blue blaze flickered up in his eyes, "you have wasted your time by coming here. You know my opinions of this administration. They have been no secret. And they will be no secret in the future. You understand that?"

"Doc," the Boss said, "Doc, you just don't understand politics. I'll be frank with you. I could run this state and ten more like it with you howling on every street corner like a

ROBERT PENN WARREN

hound with a sore tail. No offense. But you just don't understand."

"I understand some things," Adam said grimly, and the jaw set.

"And some you don't, just like I don't, but one thing I understand and you don't is what makes the mare go. I can make the mare go. And one more thing, now we are taking down our hair—" The Boss suddenly stopped, cocked his head, leered at Adam, then demanded, "Or are we?"

"You said there was one more thing," Adam replied, ignoring the question, sitting straight in his chair.

"Yeah, one more thing. But look here, Doc—you know Hugh Miller?"

"Yes," Adam said, "yes, I know him."

"Well, he was in with me—yeah, Attorney General—and he resigned. And you know why?" But he went on without waiting for the answer. "He resigned because he wanted to keep his little hands clean. He wanted the bricks but he just didn't know somebody has to paddle in the mud to make 'em. He was like somebody that just loves beefsteak but just can't bear to go to a slaughter pen because there are some bad, rough men down there who aren't animal lovers and who ought to be reported to the S.P.C.A. Well, he resigned."

I watched Adam's face. It was white and stony, as though carved out of some slick stone. He was like a man braced to hear what the jury foreman was going to say. Or what the doctor was going to say. Adam must have seen a lot of faces like that in his time. He must have had to look into them and tell them what he had to tell.

238

"Yeah," the Boss said, "he resigned. He was one of those guys wants everything and wants everything two ways at once. You know the kind, Doc?"

He flicked a look over at Adam, like a man flicking a fly over by the willows in the trout stream. But there wasn't any strike.

"Yeah, old Hugh—he never learned that you can't have everything. That you can have mighty little. And you never have anything you don't make. Just because he inherited a little money and the name Miller he thought you could have everything. Yeah, and he wanted the one last damned thing you can't inherit. And you know what it is?" He stared at Adam's face.

"What?" Adam said, after a long pause.

"Goodness. Yeah, just plain, simple goodness. Well you can't inherit that from anybody. You got to make it, Doc. If you want it. And you got to make it out of badness. Badness. And you know why, Doc?" He raised his bulk up in the broken-down wreck of an overstuffed chair he was in, and leaned forward, his hands on his knees, his elbows cocked out, his head outthrust and the hair coming down to his eyes, and stared into Adam's face. "Out of badness," he repeated. "And you know why? Because there isn't anything else to make it out of." Then, sinking back into the wreck, he asked softly, "Did you know that, Doc?"

Adam didn't say a word.

Then the Boss asked, softer still, almost whispering, "Did you know that, Doc?"

Adam wet his lips and said, "There is one question I

should like to ask you. It is this. If, as you say, there is only the bad to start with, and the good must be made from the bad, then how do you ever know what the good is? How do you even recognize the good? Assuming you have made it from the bad. Answer me that."

"Easy, Doc, easy," the Boss said.

"Well, answer it."

"You just make it up as you go along."

"Make up what?"

"The good," the Boss said, "What the hell else are we talking about. Good with a capital G."

"So you make it up as you go along?" Adam repeated gently.

"What the hell else you think folks been doing for a million years, Doc? When your great-great-grandpappy climbed down out of the tree, he didn't have any more notion of good or bad, or right and wrong, than the hoot owl that stayed up in the tree. Well, he climbed down and he began to make Good up as he went along. He made up what he needed to do business, Doc. And what he made up and got everybody to mirate on as good and right was always just a couple of jumps behind what he needed to do business on. That's why things change, Doc. Because what folks claim is right is always just a couple of jumps short of what they need to do business. Now an individual, one fellow, he will stop doing business because he's got a notion of what is right, and he is a hero. But folks in general, which is society, Doc, is never going to stop doing business. Society is just going to cook up a new notion of what is right. Society is sure not ever going to commit suicide. At least, not that way and of a purpose. And that is a fact. Now ain't it?"

"It is?" Adam said.

"You're damned right it is, Doc. And right is a lid you put on something and some of the things under the lid look just like some of the things not under the lid, and there never was any notion of what was right if you put it down on folks in general that a lot of them didn't start squalling because they just couldn't do any human business under that kind of right. Hell, look at when folks couldn't get a divorce. Look at all the good women got beat and the good men got nagged and couldn't do any human damned thing about it. Then, all of a sudden, a divorce got to be right. What next, you don't know. Nor me. But I do know this." He stopped, leaned forward again, the elbows again cocked out.

"What?" Adam demanded.

"This. I'm not denying there's got to be a notion of right to get business done, but by God, any particular notion at any particular time will sooner or later get to be just like a stopper put tight in a bottle of water and thrown in a hot stove the way we kids used to do at school to hear the bang. The steam that blows the bottle and scares the teacher to wet her drawers is just the human business that is going to get done, and it will blow anything you put it in if you seal it tight, but you put it in the right place and let it get out in a certain way and it will run a freight engine." He sank back again into the chair, his eyelids sagging now, but the eyes watchful, and the hair down over his forehead like an ambush.

Adam got up suddenly, and walked across the room. He

stopped in front of the dead fireplace, with old ashes still in it, and some half-burned paper, though spring was on us, and there hadn't been any fire for a time. The window was up, and the night air came into the room, with a smell different from the diaper-and-cabbage smell, a smell of damp grass and the leaves hanging down from the arched trees in the dark, a smell that definitely did not belong there in that room. And all of a sudden I remembered once how into a room where I was sitting one night, a big pale apple-green moth, big as a bullbat and soft and silent as a dream—a Luna moth, the name is, and it is a wonderful name—came flying in. Somebody had left the screen door open, and the moth drifted in over the tables and chairs like a big pale-green, silky, live leaf, drifting and dancing along without any word under the electric light where a Luna moth certainly did not belong. The night air coming into the room now was like that.

Adam leaned an elbow on the wooden mantelpiece where you could write your name in the dust and the books were stacked and the old, dregs-crusted coffee cup sat. He stood there as though he were all by himself.

The Boss was watching him.

"Yeah," the Boss said, watchful, "it will run a freight engine and—"

But Adam broke in, "What are you trying to convince me of? You don't have to convince me of anything. I've told you I'd take the job. That's all!" He glared at the bulky man in the big chair, and said, "That's all! And my reasons are my own."

The Boss gave a slow smile, shifted his weight in the chair, and said, "Yeah, your reasons are your own, Doc. But I just thought you might want to know something about mine. Since we're going to do business together."

"I am going to run the hospital," Adam said, and added with curling lip, "If you call that doing business together."

The Boss laughed out loud. Then he got up from the chair. "Doc," he said, "just don't you worry. I'll keep your little mitts clean. I'll keep you clean all over, Doc. I'll put you in that beautiful, antiseptic, sterile, six-million-dollar hospital, and wrap you in cellophane, untouched by human hands." He stepped to Adam, and slapped him on the shoulder. "Don't you worry, Doc," he said.

"I can take care of myself," Adam affirmed, and looked down at the hand on his shoulder.

"Sure you can, Doc," the Boss said. He removed his hand from the shoulder. Then his tone changed, suddenly businesslike and calm. "You will no doubt want to see all the plans which have been drawn up. They are subject to your revision after you consult with the architects. Mr. Todd, of Todd and Waters, will come to see you about it. And you can start picking your staff. It is all your baby."

He turned away and picked up his hat from the piano top. He swung back toward Adam and gave him a summarizing look, from top to toe and back. "You're a great boy, Doc," he said, "and don't let 'em tell you different."

Then he wheeled to the door, and went out before Adam could say a word. If there was any word he had to say.

Sugar-Boy and I followed. We didn't stop to say good night and thanks for the hospitality. That just didn't seem to be in the cards. At the door, however, I looked back and said, "So long, boy," but Adam didn't answer.

Down in the street, the Boss hesitated on the curb, beside the car. Then he said, "You all go on. I'm walking." He turned up the street, toward town, past the crummy apartment house and the little grocery and the boarding houses and the shotgun bungalows.

Just as I climbed in beside Sugar-Boy, in the place the Boss always took, I heard the burst of music from the apartment house. The window was open and the music was very loud. Adam was beating the hell out of that expensive piano, and filling the night air with racket like Niagara Falls.

We rolled down the street, and passed the Boss, who, walking along with his head down, didn't pay us any mind. We pulled on into one of the good streets with the trees arching overhead and the new leaves looking black against the sky, or pale, almost whitish, where the rays of a street lamp struck them. We were beyond the sound of Adam's music now.

I lay back and closed my eyes and took the sway and dip of the car, which was soft and easy, and thought of the Boss and Adam Stanton facing each other across that room. I had never expected to see that. But it had happened.

I had found the truth, I had dug the truth up out of the ash pile, the garbage heap, the kitchen midden, the bone yard, and had sent that little piece of truth to Adam Stanton. I couldn't cut the truth to match his ideas. Well, he'd have to make his ideas match the truth. That is what all of us historical researchers believe. The truth shall make you free.

So I lay back and thought of Adam and the truth. And of the Boss and what he had said the truth was. The good was. The right was. And lying there, lulled in the Cadillac, I wondered if he believed what he had said. He had said that you have to make the good out of the bad because that is all you have got to make it out of. Well, he had made some good out of some bad. The hospital. The Willie Stark Hospital, which was going to be there when Willie Stark was dead and gone. As Willie Stark had said. Now if Willie Stark believed that you always had to make the good out of the bad, why did he get so excited when Tiny just wanted to make a logical little deal with the hospital contract? Why did he get so heated up just because Tiny's brand of Bad might get mixed in the raw materials from which he was going to make some Good? "Can't you understand?" the Boss had demanded of me, grabbing my lapel. "Can't you understand, either? I'm building that place, the best in the country, the best in the world, and a bugger like Tiny is not going to mess with it, and I'm going to call it the Willie Stark Hospital and it will be there a long time after I'm dead and gone and you are dead and gone and all those sons-of-bitches are dead and gone—" That was scarcely consistent. It was not at all consistent. I would have to ask the Boss about it sometime.

I had asked the Boss about something else once. The night after the impeachment blew up. The night when the great crowd that had poured into town stood on the lawn of the Capitol, trampling the flower beds beneath the great frock-coated and buckskin-clad and sword-bearing bronze statues which were History. When out of the tall dark doorway of the

Capitol, under the blue glares of the spotlights Willie Stark walked out to stand at the top of the high steps, heavy and slow-looking, blinking in the light. He stood there, the only person up there on the wide expanse of stone, seeming to be lonely and lost against the mass of stone which reared behind him, standing there blinking. The long chant of "Willie—Willie—we want Willie," which had swelled up from the crowd, stopped as he came out. For an instant as he waited, there wasn't a sound. Then suddenly there was the great roar from the crowd, without any words. It was a long time before he lifted his hand to stop it. Then the roar died away as though under the pressure of his slowly descending hand.

Then he said, "They tried to ruin me, but they are ruined."

And the roar came again, and died away, under the hand.

He said, "They tried to ruin me because they did not like what I have done. Do you like what I have done?"

The roar came, and died.

He said, "I tell you what I am going to do. I am going to build a hospital. The biggest and the finest money can buy. It will belong to you. Any man or woman or child who is sick or in pain can go in those doors and know that all will be done that man can do. To heal sickness. To ease pain. Free. Not as charity. But as a right. It is your right. Do you hear? It is your right!"

The roar came.

He said, "And it is your right that every child shall have a complete education. That no person aged and infirm shall want or beg for bread. That the man who produces something shall be able to carry it to market without miring to the hub, without toll. That no poor man's house or land shall be taxed. That the rich man and the great companies that draw wealth from this state shall pay this state a fair share. That you shall not be deprived of hope!"

The roar came. As it died away, Anne Stanton, who had her arm through mine and was pressed close by the weight of the crowd, asked, "Does he mean that, Jack? Really?"

"He's done a great deal of it already," I said.

"Yes," Adam Stanton said, and his lips curled back with the words, "yes—that's his bribe."

I didn't answer—and I didn't know what my answer would have been—for Willie Stark, up there on the high steps, was saying, "I will do those things. So help me God. I shall live in your will and your right. And if any man tries to stop me in the fulfilling of that right and that will I'll break him. I'll break him like that!" He spread his arms far apart, shoulder-high, and crashed the right fist into the left palm. "Like that! I'll smite him. Hip and thigh, shinbone and neckbone, kidney punch, rabbit punch, uppercut, and solar plexus. And I don't care what I hit him with. Or how!"

Then, in the midst of the roar, I leaned toward Anne's ear and yelled, "He damned well means that."

I didn't know whether or not Anne heard me. She was watching the man up there on the steps, who was leaning forward toward the crowd, with bulging eyes, saying, "I'll hit him. I'll hit him with that meat ax!"

Then he suddenly stretched his arms above his head, the coat sleeves drawn tight to expose the shirt sleeves, the hands spread and clutching. He screamed, "Gimme that meat ax!"

And the crowd roared.

He brought both hands slowly down, for silence.

Then said, "Your will is my strength."

And after a moment of silence said, "Your need is my Justice."

Then, "That is all."

He turned and walked slowly back into the tall doorway of the Capitol, into the darkness there, and disappeared. The roar was swelling and heaving in the air now, louder than ever, and I felt it inside of me, too, swelling like blood and victory. I stared into the darkness of the great doorway of the Capitol, where he had gone, while the roar kept on.

Anne Stanton was tugging at my arm. She asked me, "Does he mean that, Jack?"

"Hell," I said, and heard the savage tone in my own voice, "hell, how the hell do I know?"

Adam Stanton's lip curled and he said, "Justice! He used that word."

And suddenly, for the flicker of an instant, I hated Adam Stanton.

I told them I had to go, which was true, and worked my way around through the edge of the crowd, to the police cordon. There I went around to the back of the Capitol, where I joined the Boss.

Late that night, back at the Mansion, after he had thrown Tiny and his rabble out of the study, I asked him the question. I asked, "Did you mean what you said?"

Propped back on the big leather couch, he stared at me, and demanded, "What?"

"What you said," I replied, "tonight. You said your strength was their will. You said your justice was their need. All of that."

He kept on staring at me, his eyes bulging, his stare grappling and probing into me.

"You said that," I said.

"God damn it," he exclaimed, violently, still staring at me, "God damn it—" he clenched his right fist and struck himself twice on the chest—"God damn it, there's something inside you—there's something inside you—"

He left the words hanging there. He turned his eyes from me and stared moodily into the fire. I didn't press my question.

Well, that was how it had been when I asked him a question, a long time back. Now I had a new question to ask him: If he believed that you had to make the good out of the bad because there wasn't anything else to make it out of, why did he stir up such a fuss about keeping Tiny's hands off the Willie Stark Hospital?

There was another little question. One I would have to ask Anne Stanton. It had come to me that night down on the pier at the mist-streaked river when Anne said that she had gone up to Adam Stanton's apartment "to talk to him about it"— about the offer of the directorship of the Willie Stark Hospital. She had said that to me, and at the moment, it had disturbed like an itch that comes when your hands are full and you can't scratch. I hadn't, in the press of the moment, defined what was disturbing, what was the question. I had simply pushed the whole pot to the back of the stove and left it to simmer. And there it simmered for weeks. But one day, all at once, it boiled over and I knew what the question was: How had Anne Stanton known about the hospital offer?

One thing was a cinch. I hadn't told her.

Perhaps Adam had told her, and then she had gone up there "to talk to him about it." So I went to see Adam, who was furiously deep in work, his usual practice and teaching, and in addition, the work on the hospital plans, who hadn't been able, he said, to touch the piano in almost a month, whose eyes fixed on me glacially out of a face now thin from sleeplessness, and who treated me with a courtesy too chromium-plated to be given to the friend of your youth. It took some doing, on my part, in the face of that courtesy, to get my nerve up to ask him the question. But I finally asked it. I said, "Adam, that first time Anne came up to talk to you about—about the job—you know, the hospital—had you told—"

And he said, with a voice like a scalpel, "I don't want to discuss it."

But I had to know. So I said, "Had you told her about the proposition?"

"No," he said, "and I said I didn't want to discuss it."

"O.K.," I heard myself saying, in a flat voice which wasn't quite my own. "O.K."

. . . .

I only told her the truth, I said savagely to myself, *and she can't blame me for the truth!*

But was there some fatal appropriateness inherent in the very nature of the world and of me that I should be the one to tell her that truth? I had to ask myself that question, too. And I couldn't be sure of the answer. So I walked on down the street, turning that question over and over in my mind without any answer until the question lost meaning and dropped from my mind as something heavy drops from numb fingers. I would have faced the responsibility and the guilt, I was ready to do that, if I could know. But who is going to tell you?

So I walked on, and after a while I remembered how she had said I had never known him. And the *him* was Willie Stark, whom I had known for the many years since Cousin Willie from the country, the Boy with the Christmas Tie, had walked into the back room of Slade's old place. Sure, I knew him. Like a book. I had known him a long time.

Too long. I thought then, *too long to know him.* For maybe the time had blinded me, or rather I had not been aware of the passing of time and always the round face of Cousin Willie had come between me and the other face so that I had never really seen the other face. Except perhaps in those moments when it had leaned forward to the crowds and the forelock had fallen and the eyes had bulged, and the crowd had roared and I had felt the surge in me and had felt that I was on the verge of the truth. But always the face of Cousin Willie above the Christmas tie had come again.

But it did not come now. I saw the face. Enormous. Bigger than a billboard. The forelock shagged down like a mane.

The big jaw. The heavy lips laid together like masonry. The eyes burning and bulging powerfully.

Funny, I had never seen it before. Not really.

That night I telephoned the Boss, told him what had happened and how Anne had told me, and made my suggestion about getting Adam to swear out a warrant for Coffee. He said to do it. To do anything that would nail Adam. So I went to the hotel, where I lay on my bed under the electric fan until the desk called me to get up at about six o'clock. Then by seven I was on Adam's doorstep, with a single cup of java sloshing about in my insides and a fresh razor cut on my chin and sleep like sand under my eyelids.

I worked it. It was a hard little job I had cut out for me. First, I had to enlist Adam on the side of righteousness by getting him to agree to swear out a warrant for Coffee. My method was to assume, of course, that he was aching for the opportunity to nail Coffee, and to indicate that the Boss was cheering on the glorious exploit. Then I had to lead him to the discovery, which had to be all his own, that this would involve Anne as a witness. Then I had to play the half-wit and imply that this had never occurred to me before. The danger was, with a fellow like Adam, that he would get so set on seeing justice done that he would let Anne testify, hell and high water. He almost did that, but I painted a gory picture of the courtroom scene (but not as gory by half as it would have been in truth), refused to be party to the business, hinted that he was an unnatural brother, and wound up with a vague notion of another way to get Coffee for a similar attempt in another quarter—a vague notion of laying myself open for Coffee to approach me. I could put out a feeler for him, and all that. So Adam dropped the idea of the charge, but retained the implied idea that he and the Boss had teamed up to keep things clean for the hospital.

Just as we were ready to walk out of the apartment, he stepped to the mantelpiece and picked up the stamped letters waiting there to be mailed. I had spotted the top envelope already, the one addressed to the Boss. So as he turned around with the letters in his hand, I simply lifted that one out of his grasp, said with my best smile, "Hell, you haven't got any use for this in the daylight," and tore it across and put the pieces into my pocket.

Then we went out back and got into his car. I rode with him all the way to his office. I would have sat with him all day to keep an eye on him if it had been possible. Anyway, I chatted briskly all the way down-town to keep his mind clear. My chatter was as gay and sprightly as bird song.

So the summer moved on, swelling slowly like a great fruit, and everything was as it had been before. I went to my office. I went back to my hotel and sometimes ate a meal and sometimes did not and lay under the fan and read till late. I saw the same faces, Duffy, the Boss, Sadie Burke, all the faces I had known for a long time and saw so often I didn't notice the changes in them. But I did not see Adam and Anne for a while. And I had not seen Lucy Stark for a long time. She was living out in the country now. The Boss would still go out to see her now and then, to keep up appearances, and have his picture taken among the white leghorns. Sometimes Tom Stark would stand there with him and, perhaps, Lucy, with the white leghorns in the foreground and a wire fence behind. *Governor Willie Stark and Family,* the caption would read.

Yes, those pictures were an asset to the Boss. Half the people in the state knew that the Boss had been tom-catting around for years, but the pictures of the family and the white leghorns gave the voters a nice warm glow, it made them feel solid, substantial, and virtuous, it made them think of gingerbread and nice cold buttermilk, and if somewhere not too far in the wings there was a flicker of a black-lace negligee and a whiff of musky perfume, then, "Well, you cain't blame him a-taken hit, they put hit up to him." It only meant that the Boss was having it both ways, and that seemed a mark of the chosen and superior. It was what the voter did when he shook loose and came up to town to the furniture dealers' convention and gave the bellhop a couple of bucks to get him a girl up to the room. Or if he wasn't doing it classy, he rode into town with his truckload of hogs and for two bucks got the whole works down at a crib. But either way, classy or crib, the voter knew what it meant, and wanted both Mom's gingerbread and the black-lace negligee and didn't hold it against the Boss for having both. What he would have held against the Boss was a divorce. Anne was right about that. It would have hurt even the Boss. That would have been very different, and would have robbed the voter of something he valued, the nice warm glow of complacency, the picture that flattered him and his own fat or thin wife standing in front of the henhouse.

Meanwhile, if the voter knew that the Boss had been tom-catting for years, and could name the names of half of the ladies involved, he didn't know about Anne Stanton. Sadie had found out, but that was no miracle. But as far as I could detect, nobody else knew, not even Duffy with his wheezing, elephantine wit and leer. Maybe Sugar-Boy knew, but he could be depended upon. He knew everything. The Boss didn't mind telling anything in front of Sugar-Boy, or close to it—anything, that is, that he would tell. Which probably left a lot untold, at that. Once Congressman Randall was in the Boss's library with him, Sugar-Boy, and me, pacing up and down the floor, and the Boss was giving him play-by-play instructions on how to conduct himself when the Milton-Broderick Bill was presented to Congress. The instructions were pretty frank, and the Congressman kept looking nervously at Sugar-Boy. The Boss noticed him. "God damn it," the Boss said, "you afraid Sugar-Boy's finding out something? Well, you're right, he's finding out something. Well, Sugar-Boy has found out plenty. He knows more about this state than you do. And I trust him a hell of a lot farther than I'd trust you. You're my pal, ain't you, Sugar-Boy?"

Sugar-Boy's face darkened with the rush of pleasurable, embarrassed blood and his lips began to work and the spit to fly as he prepared to speak.

"Yeah, Sugar's my pal, ain't you, Sugar-Boy?" he said, and slapped Sugar-Boy on the shoulder, and then swung again toward the Congressman while Sugar-Boy finally was managing to say, "I'm—y-y-y-your pal—and—I—ain't ta-ta-ta-talking—none."

Yes, Sugar-Boy probably knew, but he was dependable.

And Sadie was dependable, too. She had told me, but that was in the flush of her first fine rage and I (I thought of this with a certain grim humor) was, you might say, in the family. She wouldn't tell anybody else. Sadie Burke didn't have any confidant, for she didn't trust anybody. She didn't ask any sympathy, for the world she had grown up in didn't have any. So she would keep her mouth shut. And she had plenty of patience. She knew he'd come back. Meanwhile, she could hack him into a rage, or could try to for it was hard to do, and she herself would get into one, and you would think that they would be ready to fly at each other in the frenzy they could build up. By that time, too, you wouldn't be able to tell whether it was a frenzy of love or hate that coiled and tangled them together. And after all the years it had been going on, it probably didn't matter which it was. Her eyes would blaze black out of her chalk-white, pocked face and her wild black hair would seem to lift electrically off her scalp and her hands would flay out in a gesture of rending and tearing. While the flood of her language poured over him, his head would rock massively but almost imperceptibly from side to side and his eyes would follow her every motion, at first drowsily, then raptly, until he would heave himself up, the big veins in his temples pumping and his right fist raised. Then the raised fist would crash into the palm of the other hand, and he would burst out, "God damn, God damn it, Sadie!"

Or for weeks there wouldn't be any shenanigans. Sadie would treat the Boss with an icy decorum, meeting him only and strictly in the course of business, standing quietly before him while he talked. She would stand there before him and study him out of the black eyes, in which the blaze was banked now. Well, despite all the shenanigans, Sadie knew how to wait. She had learned that a long time back. She had had to wait for everything she had ever got out of the world.

So the summer went on, and we all lived in it. It was a way to live, and when you have lived one way for a while you forget that there was ever any other way and that there may be another way again. Even when the change came, it didn't at first seem like a change but like more of the same, an extension and repetition.

CARL SANDBURG

American poet, historian, novelist, and folklorist Carl Sandburg (1878–1967) was born in Galesburg, Illinois, and was virtually unknown to the literary world until a group of his poems appeared in the nationally circulated *Poetry* magazine in 1914. His six-volume masterpiece, *Abraham Lincoln: The Prairie Years,* won the Pulitzer prize in 1940. In *The People, Yes* (1936), Sandburg's most popular single volume, his interest in folk speech and expression becomes clear. Because Sandburg's writing celebrated the American spirit, he was often called the successor to Walt Whitman. Sandburg was a poet who sang of American populism, embodied in a politician's activities—a good leader's manner of being, as well as doing.

From THE PEOPLE, YES

Lincoln?
He was a mystery in smoke and flags
saying yes to the smoke, yes to the flags,
yes to the paradoxes of democracy,
yes to the hopes of government
of the people by the people for the people,
no to debauchery of the public mind,
no to personal malice nursed and fed,
yes to the Constitution when a help,
no to the Constitution when a hindrance,
yes to man as a struggler amid illusions,
each man fated to answer for himself:
Which of the faiths and illusions of mankind
must I choose for my own sustaining light
to bring me beyond the present wilderness?

  Lincoln? was he a poet?
  and did he write verses?
"I have not willingly planted a thorn
  in any man's bosom."
"I shall do nothing through malice; what
  I deal with is too vast for malice."

Death was in the air.
So was birth.

What was dying few could say.
What was being born none could know.

He took the wheel in a lashing roaring
  hurricane.
And by what compass did he steer the course
  of the ship?
"My policy is to have no policy," he said in
  the early months,
And three years later, "I have been controlled
  by events."

He could play with the wayward human mind, saying at Charleston, Illinois, September 18, 1858, it was no answer to an argument to call a man a liar.
"I assert that you [pointing a finger in the face of a man in the crowd] are here today, and you undertake to prove me a liar by showing that you were in Mattoon yesterday.
"I say that you took your hat off your head and you prove me a liar by putting it on your head."

He saw personal liberty across wide horizons.
"Our progress in degeneracy appears to me to be pretty rapid," he wrote Joshua F. Speed, August 24, 1855. "As a nation we began by declaring that 'all men are created equal, except negroes.' When the Know-Nothings get control, it will read 'all men are created equal except negroes and foreigners and Catholics.' When it comes to this, I shall prefer emigrating to some country where they make no pretense of loving liberty."

Did he look deep into a crazy pool
and see the strife and wrangling
with a clear eye, writing the military
head of a stormswept area:
"If both factions, or neither, shall abuse
you, you will probably be about right. Be-
ware of being assailed by one and praised
by the other"?

Lincoln? was he a historian?
did he know mass chaos?
did he have an answer for those
who asked him to organize chaos?

"Actual war coming, blood grows hot, and blood is spilled. Thought is forced from old channels into confusion. Deception breeds and thrives. Confidence dies and universal suspicion reigns.

"Each man feels an impulse to kill his neighbor, lest he be first killed by him. Revenge and retaliation follow. And all this, as before said, may be among honest men only; but this is not all.

"Every foul bird comes abroad and every dirty reptile rises up. These add crime to confusion.

"Strong measures, deemed indispensable, but harsh at best, such men make worse by maladministration. Murders for old grudges, and murders for pelf, proceed under any cloak that will best cover for the occasion. These causes amply account for what has happened in Missouri."

Early in '64 the Committee of the New York Workingman's
 Democratic Republican Association called on him with
 assurances and he meditated aloud for them, recalling
 race and draft riots:
"The most notable feature of a disturbance in your city
 last summer was the hanging of some working people
 by other working people. It should never be so.
"The strongest bond of human sympathy, outside of the family relation, should be one uniting all working people, of
 all nations and tongues and kindreds.
"Let not him who is houseless pull down the house of another, but let him labor diligently and build one for himself, thus by example assuring that his own shall be safe
 from violence when built."

    Lincoln? did he gather
    the feel of the American dream
    and see its kindred over the earth?

"As labor is the common burden of our race,
so the effort of some to shift
their share of the burden
onto the shoulders of others
is the great durable curse of the race."

    "I hold,
if the Almighty had ever made a set of men
that should do all of the eating
and none of the work,

he would have made them
with mouths only, and no hands;
and if he had ever made another class,
that he had intended should do all the work
and none of the eating,
he would have made them
without mouths and all hands."

"—the same spirit that says, 'You toil and
work and earn bread, and I'll eat it.' No
matter in what shape it comes, whether
from the mouth of a king who seeks to
bestride the people of his own nation
and live by the fruit of their labor, or
from one race of men as an apology for
enslaving another race, it is the same
tyrannical principle."

"As I would not be a *slave,* so I would not be a *master.*
This expresses my idea of democracy. Whatever differs
from this, to the extent of the difference, is no democracy."

"I never knew a man who wished to be himself a slave.
Consider if you know any *good* thing that no man desires for himself."

"The sheep and the wolf
are not agreed upon a definition
of the word liberty."

"The whole people of this nation
    will ever do well
    if well done by."

"The plainest print cannot be read
    through a gold eagle."

"How does it feel to be President?" an Illinois friend
    asked.

"Well, I'm like the man they rode out of town on a rail.
    He said if it wasn't for the honor of it he would just as
    soon walk."

    Lincoln? he was a dreamer.
    He saw ships at sea,
    he saw himself living and dead
    in dreams that came.

Into a secretary's diary December 23, 1863, went an
entry: "The President tonight had a dream. He was in a
party of plain people, and, as it became known who he
was, they began to comment on his appearance. One of
them said: 'He is a very common-looking man.' The
President replied: 'The Lord prefers common-looking
people. That is the reason he makes so many of them.' "

He spoke one verse for then and now:
    "If we could first know where we are,
    and whither we are tending,
    we could better judge
    what to do, and how to do it."

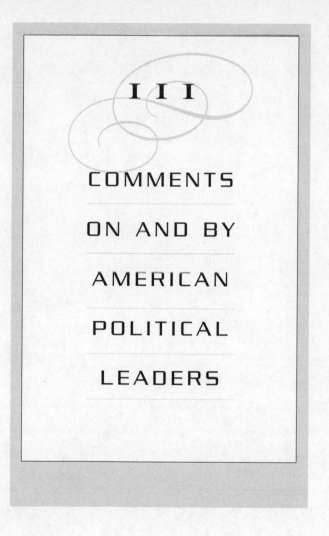

III

COMMENTS

ON AND BY

AMERICAN

POLITICAL

LEADERS

THE FOREGOING EXCERPTS come to us from those who have written novels, plays, poems, which in one way or another shed light on politics as it gets shaped. What follows are essays that draw on the documentary tradition of first-hand observation, followed by an effort to convey through written words the desires and deeds of certain individuals.

Like any of us, our political leaders are not beyond moments of self-reflection. Even as they give voice to the concerns of thousands of their public followers, who are eager to see the world stay as is, or to be changed significantly, politicians like to talk about themselves, and to *be* talked about. It is left to us, their admirers and critics, to formulate opinions about our leaders, and as voters, to have our say.

Sometimes a particular leader, in the course of an interview, will put a lot on the line, or convey to an immediate observer what is usually reserved for a larger political arena, such as a speech or a debate. Here, I'd like to present two American political leaders, heroes to particular segments of the American population during the 1960s: Lester Garfield Maddox, the seventy-fifth governor of Georgia, and Robert Kennedy, whom I had the opportunity to observe among the poor and in the Senate. In the following extracts, each man is witnessed as he goes about his busy day in the eye of the public; in search of a political office to have and to hold, through the endorsements of his fellow citizens. As an observer, I had the opportunity to meet them, talk with them, write about them, and thereby consider them for myself, as well as for others.

From FAREWELL TO THE SOUTH:
Robert Coles on Maddox of Georgia

The term "Southern Demagogue" should be recognized for what it is, a political epithet. It does not contribute anything to our understanding of the men to whom it is applied. I hold no brief for men of this type, nor for Tom Watson in so far as he was representative of them. I do not believe it is accurate to blame Watson for the "sinister forces" already mentioned. To do so would be to assign him far too important a role, a role that belongs to the vastly more impersonal forces of economics and race and historical heritage.

—C. VANN WOODWARD in
Tom Watson: Agrarian Rebel

Lester Garfield Maddox, seventy-fifth governor of Georgia, walks by a statue of Tom Watson every day. Watson stands in front of Georgia's capitol building, his right hand forward, his left hand raised high, the South's Demosthenes in action. Below him one reads of his many achievements—he was an editor, a lawyer, a historian, an author, and in Washington, Georgia's representative and senator—and one also reads these words of his: "Give us the fortune which, through the cloud and gloom and sorrow of apparent failure, can see the instant pinnacles upon which the everlasting sunlight rests."

Governor Maddox knows about those "instant pinnacles," and if thousands of Georgians who live in what they now call "Maddox Country" have any further say, he will know about "the everlasting sunlight" of political power, perhaps one day like Tom Watson as a United States Senator. When I lived in Atlanta a few years ago Maddox was not quite, or not only, the loser and eccentric he is often described as once being. He was, in fact, a successful businessman, and an exceedingly well-known man who in 1961 had shown his strong hold on Atlanta's white vote in a mayoralty race with Ivan Allen, the present incumbent. If a successful politician is among other things a man who knows how to command and keep the attention and sympathy of his potential voters, the Maddox I used to see in the early sixties knew the people he was after, and knew how to reach them and stay in touch with them.

Sometimes I went to his restaurant, the Pickrick. The food was good and inexpensive. The owner was right there, friendly and willing to talk to anyone, as if his store were his home, and his customer his guest. The Pickrick's chicken was always being advertised in the very Atlanta papers Maddox considered so infamous and radical, but did not hesitate to use. He bought space to urge his food on the public, but he also wanted them to know they were victims. Washington, Communists, outsiders, a coalition of sinister and unpatriotic forces were not only at work, but in power; they controlled

Atlanta through its "moderates," who step-by-step were selling out every conceivable principle for the almighty dollar.

"He's honest," I kept hearing from the white students, and even from the Negro students, who found the open, direct outrage that he directed at their cause easier to comprehend and fight against than slogans like "too busy to hate," the more or less official slogan that Atlanta used—and used successfully—to help avoid the riots that had plagued Little Rock and New Orleans when they yielded to the court-ordered desegregation of their schools. When the Civil Rights Law of 1964 was passed, so that Maddox was required to serve Negroes, he consolidated himself in the minds of millions all over the country as the beleaguered idealist, the odd businessman who in the clinch would sacrifice a going concern, an established moneymaking enterprise, for the sake of his strongly held feelings. He would not be evasive, and raise his prices to keep Negroes out, or try to get around the law by calling his restaurant a club. He would not let them in while under scrutiny or "attack," then do everything possible to ignore or insult them later—when, anyway, few of them would want to come. He would stand and defend his turf with a gun and a hatchet, and eventually he would surrender and fold his tent and walk away.

To the white upper-class people of Atlanta—a number of whom in 1961 had sent their children to private schools in order to avoid the "tension" and "disturbance" that school desegregation might bring—he was a fool, a nuisance and an embarrassment. They had no desire to take on once again—a hundred years after Appomattox—the money and power of the North. They wanted their share of what New York or New England have; they were beginning to get it; and they were glad.

"Lester, he's a nut," one heard again and again. Lester went on to open a furniture store, and to sell souvenir axes, reminders of his last stand. Lester also was "crazy" enough, "grandiose" enough to feel that his resentment, his sense of galling defeat, his desire to strike out, strike back, get revenge, was shared by others—others in Georgia's countryside, its backwoods and small towns. He kept talking and running—in 1966 for governor.

The rest now has to be called "history," rather than one man's fate. The campaign was a fascinating one, with a prominent millionaire, Howard ("Bo") Callaway, the owner of textile mills and a graduate of West Point, trying to lead the Republican party to a victory over what seemed like the fatally divided Democrats. Everyone expected the Democrats to nominate Ellis Arnall, a liberal former governor, and everyone expected the segregationist conservative Republican to take after the Democrat as a dangerous radical, who would bring in more "federal controls," that is, further changes in Georgia's racial climate.

All the while Lester Maddox was going about and saying that he would be governor, and those in the know wouldn't even take the trouble to laugh anymore. The real thing to watch was the Republican resurgence. Georgia had gone for Goldwater. The state was prospering, with a lot of new business and a rising middle class. Callaway offered respectability and clear-cut power to the lawyers and doctors and bankers and engineers and managers. At long last they could join company with their counterparts elsewhere. The Southern Democrats could become the Republicans so many of them in essence are. As an avowed opponent of John F. Kennedy and Lyndon Johnson and the Civil Rights Bill of 1964, Callaway was a Republican who could defend the Southern Way of Life, but not at the cost of an economic recession. He was an industrialist, and he would bring in more industrialists; and the nervous poor whites, they'd vote for him too—because it was the Democrats who were the race-mixers, not only in Washington, but Atlanta. With Callaway in office Brooks Brothers might be persuaded to open a store in Atlanta, and there wouldn't be a lot of Negroes wanting to buy—or even sell—the clothes.

Well, Lester kept on visiting what Faulkner called the "hamlets" and the nearby towns, one after another; and down in Waycross, and over in Tallapoosa, and up around Jasper, white people stood around and said: "that man Arnall, he's one of the Atlanta boys, northern-bought, who's trying to slip the nigger over on us, so that they can keep on making their money. And Callaway, he's a rich boy with lots of airs, and a Republican. Hell, what choice have we got?" But then, there was Lester, tacking up his homemade signs and reminding anyone who came near that he was still going strong, despite the laughs and the jeers and the indifference of the wealthy people and the college types and their Negro friends, who are voting all over now. (It had come to that!)

When Primary Day came Lester Maddox became the nominee of the Democratic Party of Georgia. Callaway had to go out and tell people he was better, more stable, more reliable. He kept on pushing his conservative, segregationist views and he had a lot of money to help him do so; but Lester Maddox had some capital that the richest man in America couldn't equal. He had his life, all the words he'd spoken and the deeds he'd done—and let his fellow Georgians know about. No one's credentials as a conservative and a segregationist could possibly equal his; so he was free to take his reputation for granted and indeed build on it in a way that put Callaway on the run. He was Lester the loner, the little man who was self-made, not rich but with some savings from hard work. He had no big eastern money to fall back on, and he didn't have the railroads and the utilities behind him, and he wasn't going to be a front man for the *Atlanta Constitution* and its connections in Washington, D.C., and New York and God knows where else.

Callaway realized he was being boxed in, and grew desperate. The liberals said they weren't going to support him and they never could stomach Maddox. Lester kept pointing to himself as the honest white underdog and convinced a lot of people to vote for him. He didn't get a majority, but neither did Callaway, because thousands of liberals begged the issue by writing in Ellis Arnall's name. The Democratic legislature had to make the choice, and Maddox was a Democrat.

As governor, Maddox has been something of a surprise, so far. He made a temperate inaugural speech, and ever since has rather consistently toned down his language and stopped emphasizing his horror at the course of recent southern history. Since his election was considered first unbelievable and then the worst possible disaster by hundreds of thousands of Negroes and white liberals, his behavior to date puzzles them. "What happened to Lester?" I hear from some whites in Atlanta. When I asked a Negro youth I know to evaluate the governor's few months in office he put it this way: "It's still the same old Maddox underneath; you can feel it, and every once in a while he forgets, and then you *know* it. But I guess they're all sitting on him up there in the capitol and telling him what to say and he listens to them." I asked him *why* Maddox listens: "I don't know. Now that he's governor he sees he has to play ball with people and keep quiet." Then he asked himself and me the same question: "Sometimes I wonder why he *does* seem to be listening to the 'moderates.' Now that he's governor you'd think he'd really let loose; but no. It's as if he's changed—though you can't really believe it."

One hears he is shrewd; that he knows he has won, and cannot succeed himself; that he *has* the rednecks, and need only toss them an occasional word or act, whereas a restrained administration will gain him the skeptical white middle class, many of whom objected more to his manner than the substance of his ideas. Then, there are the "socio-economic" interpretations. He was born poor and worked his way up. Now he is there, and dizzy because of the height. He is insecure, or in some "deep" way troubled, and his past rancor can be attributed to that fact. Since hard work and luck have carried him to the very top, his sensitive, uneasy self is at last appeased, and he no longer "needs" to tremble at the prospect of desegregation. Anyway—say those who dismiss all other explanations as superficial and frivolous—there is just so much a governor can do, and Maddox has found that out. A handful of bankers and corporation presidents and those who carry out their orders really run things, and every governor has to make his peace with them. Somehow "they" have "taken care" of Lester.

A short while ago I went to see Governor Maddox. In one sense things hadn't really changed much. In the Pickrick restaurant he had handed out chicken all day long, and now it is pork—favors, jobs and appointments for "the people." His outside office was full of them, the Flem Snopeses of Georgia who want, want, want. The phone calls come in from all over and without letup. I've had some experience with *need;* in the emergency ward of a hospital there always seems to be someone in trouble, day or night. For a moment I made the comparison: citizens have their troubles, and they take them to their governors. Yet the talk in the governor's anterooms and on his phones gradually weakened my analogy. Greed is a very special kind of need, and deserves its own recognition.

Perhaps we are so surprised or puzzled by the "change" in a man like Lester Maddox because we see all men as consistently and inevitably the "products" of what they *were.* They had a particular kind of childhood; they grew up in this neighborhood or that region; they formerly said or did something; and so there they are, fixed and predictable, easy prey for our categorical minds. Yet, at any moment new possibilities and new demands can come upon a person—and make him different; not different from what he *was*, but different because of what *is*.

I asked the governor why he seemed to strike so many people as a different man, an unexpectedly "moderate" one in the political sense of the word. (Personally he is a devoutly moderate man, a Baptist who prays often and hard and avoids liquor or cigarettes.) Ask his friends, he said; they would tell me he was the same person, "the very same one." So I said that if that were true, he was the same person doing different work. And he said yes, that was the case, and he loved his new job. Then he talked about the job. It was hard and demanding. He was in the middle of things as he never was before, and subject to pressures he'd never known about, and aware for the first time of countless problems and people. Moreover, every day he had to act, or seem to act; say something, or sound as if he was saying something; take sides, or claim himself neutral and from that position use his weight here or there.

Faced with the difficulties and ambiguities of a kind of "power" that is always apparent but not quite as immediate, tangible and unequivocal as its trappings suggest, Maddox is doing what many political leaders always do. In that sense he has not "changed," but come to terms with his position in a particular way. In his own words he is "going to the people" rather than trying to be a lawgiver. ("New legislation isn't as important as being the best example, being for Georgia an honest governor.") He wants to sell the state, "unite the people and stand for sensible government." As if Georgia were a Beauty Queen, he has mastered all of her vital statistics, and he will advertise them and defend them—every day, in every way, and all over. He is up to the job, to the travel, to the begging and coaxing, to the flattery that he must give as well as get, to the reporters and the television cameras, to the various people and groups who want from him the *act* of a statement, the *move* of patronage, rather than any sustained and coherent social policy or initiative. Gestures of course can become so much sham, but here I think Lester Maddox will not fail. He conveys sincerity and he is also tireless. No aura of cynicism or pragmatism will surround his administration.

Polite, methodical, persistent, able to tell every stranger how good it is to see him (and make it sound believable) he has seized upon the Truth of Enterprise; beside it issues of race or reform seem unimportant. Did I know that "tourist expansion" is way up in Georgia? Did I know that he is welcoming more visitors, more business leaders to the state than any of his predecessors? Did I know that for the first time *anyone* can come into his office, on the first and third Wednesday of each month? "They come in, all the people, wealthy or barefoot." He hasn't asked for new taxes from his rich visitors, and I didn't see any shoes around for the barefoot ones, though I spotted a book called *Praying Can Change Your Life*.

In a flash he can surprise his listener with the use of the expression "power structure." He was elected governor "without the help of the power structure." To spell it out, "not one big paper, not one railroad, not one magazine, not one courthouse" supported him. But "the power structure" he once fought at a distance is now nearby, and ready to be of help. He told me that he wants "to prove his critics wrong." He already has. He has learned how to deal with them—and with himself. If you pick him up on the term "power structure" and ask him about "it," he can reply with all the indirection that the rest of us learn: "People in office tend to get isolated. They stick with the power structure too much and they're not close to the people anymore." The literal danger then is guilt by association. Maddox has always worried about the company he keeps, and he realizes that not only Negroes, but well-to-do whites refused to vote for him.

In essence he will avoid a fight and run to the voters. The "power structure" will meet up with no angry populist—at last in power, at last ready to get revenge. A man who has been called every psychiatric epithet emerges as "sane and sensible." What is more, he will use as well as be used, and thus show how "creative" and "adaptive" he is. The poor and the hungry can enter his office. They may not get food or cash from it, but they will see it, and not picture its owner a traitor who spends all his time currying favor with high society.

Maddox is hardly a Tom Watson, but he does manage to take up where Watson left off. The brilliant "agrarian rebel" found turn-of-the-century southern politics so frustrating, so dishonest, and so devious that he just about lost his senses, and surrendered his mind to the region's terrible historical ironies. First he kept his populism, but cut it off from the Negro; and then he became so obsessed with the Negro (and additional "others," like the Jews and the Catholics) that he even lost interest in the poor white man. Having fought "the power structure" and lost to it, he learned to escape noticing it through the rhetoric of blind hate.

I do not know whether "they" in rural Georgia "really" believe Lester can make a difference in their lives, but I think the governor has indicated that he understands their feelings. He knows what in sophisticated Atlanta inspires their awe, and he knows that awe is a mixture of fear and desire. Through them he has "made good," but if he wants to stay in power he'd better not forget that.

It all works out well for "the power structure," too. The governor who says he's for "the little man" has to speak and act like one. All the pieties of America and the South will be his to mix adroitly: the democratic ones with the racist ones, the ones that urge "equality" with those that glorify competition and the lonely winner. The "little man" like everyone needs someone to trust, someone who speaks for him regularly and "naturally." Because he will concentrate his energies on keeping that trust alive, Maddox will threaten no one important, and in fact be a very handy man for many of those who fought him to have in power. He will "keep them happy down on the farm" or in the towns by doing his share to make certain that the real workings of Paris never come to anyone's attention—even his own.

DICK PETTYS ON LESTER MADDOX

"LESTER MADDOX, ONE OF SOUTH'S LAST
SEGREGATIONIST GOVERNORS"
by DICK PETTYS, Associated Press writer

ATLANTA—Lester Maddox, who was elected one of the last of the South's fist-shaking segregationist governors in 1966 after he and his friends used pick handles and a gun to scare blacks away from his fried-chicken restaurant, died Wednesday at 87.

Maddox never backed down from his stance on segregation, even after Alabama's George Wallace and many of the other hard-line Southern governors eventually said they were wrong to fight integration. "I think forced segregation was wrong. I think it was just as wrong to force integration," he told the Associated Press in 1996. And if he had to do it over again, he said, "I'd fight even harder."

"That puts a stain on the legacy," said State Representative Tyrone Brooks, a civil rights veteran.

Maddox served as governor from 1967 to 1971 after being elected as something of a fluke in a disputed contest that had to be decided by the Legislature. Despite his views on integration, he was more moderate as governor than most expected, appointing more blacks to key positions than any of his predecessors.

"In spite of all that, he couldn't shake the yoke of racism and segregation," Brooks said. "If Lester had said, 'I was wrong,' I believe the vast majority of African-Americans would have said, 'OK, we forgive you.' "

Maddox had battled cancer since 1983 and cracked two ribs earlier this month when he fell at an assisted-living home. He later developed pneumonia and died in an Atlanta hospice. The flamboyant restaurant owner often seemed more caricature than flesh. His slick pate and thick glasses were fodder for cartoonists, and he was known for quaint sayings and outrageous gestures like riding a bicycle backward.

"How you, chief?" was one customary greeting. Another: "It's great to be alive. A lot of folks aren't, you know."

A high school dropout born in a working-class section of Atlanta, Maddox gained national attention in 1964 when he brandished a pistol and chased black protesters from his Pickrick restaurant the day after the Civil Rights Act was signed into law. Whites from his restaurant chased the protesters with pick handles. Maddox closed and then sold the Pickrick rather than serve blacks. He would adopt the pick handle as his political symbol during his gubernatorial campaign and thereafter, and sold souvenir picks and axes.

Maddox's showmanship and his anti-integration stance won him a following in Atlanta, where he made two unsuccessful bids for mayor. He captured the Democratic nomination for governor in 1966, despite being written off by moderates and liberals as a colorful crackpot. In the general election, he trailed Republican Howard H. "Bo" Callaway, but write-in votes for other candidates assured that neither received the required majority, throwing the election to the Democrat-dominated Legislature, which picked Maddox.

Despite his reputation, Maddox began his term in office with a vow that "there will be no place in Georgia during the next four years for those who advocate extremism or violence." But in 1968, Maddox refused to close the Capitol for the funeral of the Reverend Martin Luther King Jr. and expressed anger that state flags were being flown at half-staff.

Maddox got high marks from critics for choosing capable administrators to run state operations during his term and for making the office accessible to anyone through a program called "Little Peoples Day." And supporters loved "Old Lester" for the way he denounced the Atlanta newspapers as "fishwrappers" or condemned the latest ruling from the U.S. Supreme Court.

Barred from seeking a second term, he was elected lieutenant governor, using the post to spar with his successor, Jimmy Carter. He ran for governor again in 1974 and lost. A final comeback bid in 1990 saw him finish last in a five-person race. "I'm still a segregationist. I just told you I'm a segregationist. I've told you that 15 times. When are you going to start believing me?" he said in 1973.

Wallace was among Maddox's heroes, but toward the end of his career Wallace sought to make amends on segregation. Maddox said he still regarded Wallace as "my buddy," but told the AP that Wallace "was either a liar then or he's a liar now."

Former state representative Matt Towery, a longtime Maddox friend, said the former governor "believed what he did was proper in the 1960s. He was unapologetic for it." But Maddox "did not have a racist bone in his body when I came to know him in 1969." Republican governor Sonny Perdue ordered flags on state buildings and grounds lowered to half-staff.

His funeral will be held Friday in Marietta. His wife, Virginia, died in 1997. They had two daughters and two sons.

Comment from Robert Coles

In 1974, speaking of Georgia's Lester Maddox in a long interview with the historian C. Vann Woodward, I heard the author of *Tom Watson: Agrarian Rebel* consider the connection I had once made between those two Southern political leaders. "Yes, they were both able to speak for people who felt voiceless—out of the political mainstream: the history of Southern populism, you might say, is a mix of race politics and class politics. Maddox in particular lived his beliefs before he began selling them to voters (and they knew that to be the case). Political leaders are like the rest of us; some are sincere, even idealistic, even if many of us, evaluating them (when they were alive or afterwards), find them to be abhorrent or worse. Of course an apparent sincerity and idealism in any of us can be a cover, a shrewd and calculating one, for an ambitious, covetous lust for power, sad to say."

"THE KIND OF MAN YOU DON'T FORGET":
Robert Coles on Robert Kennedy

I first met Senator Robert Kennedy two years ago when I testified before a Senate subcommittee of which he was a member. The senators were looking into what they called "problems of the American cities." The ghettoes which continue to grow in so many of those cities were then beginning to explode with riots, and a parade of witnesses could only say, yes it is happening, and yes we must do something, and yes we must do what we know will help—but know we can't really do right now, because of the war, because of the growing conservative trend in our political life.

After I testified, the young senator from New York started asking me questions, one after another, all of them well-phrased and right to the point of my testimony, which was concerned with the development of anti-social and violent behaviour among ghetto children.

I can still remember my surprise; all senators are fed questions by their bright aides, and sometimes the questions they ask are suggested in advance by the witness himself. But Senator Kennedy did not merely respond to my testimony. He addressed himself to my further remarks, made in answer to his first polite and rather obvious questions. I was struck by something more than his charm and wit and spontaneity; he seemed to possess an almost uncanny mixture of unselfconscious compassion and real intelligence, a kind that I could only think of as *active*. A proud and powerful man, he appeared slight and talked about the ambiguities of life.

He for one was not going to take the easy way out by dismissing ghetto children as hopelessly "sick" or delinquent or whatever. He had seen their shrewd vitality, their canny ability to overcome all sorts of odds that the rest of us (with *our* lives to fall back upon) could not face, and he could not forget or quite comprehend what he saw. What did I make of that, of the inconsistency between a psychopathological or sociological view of the ghetto child's development—and, well, the writer's vision of human complexity, as it comes across, say, in Ralph Ellison's *Invisible Man* or the novels of Faulkner or Robert Penn Warren?

Nor was he interested in an academic discussion or an essentially frivolous (so far as the Senate committee was concerned) discussion of "life" and its ironies. He wanted to show that a purely negative view of poor, exiled and volatile people is convenient for those who don't want to do something about America's grave social ills. He was suspicious of our fashionable talk about "deprived" children and "disadvantaged youth" because he disliked the barely concealed condescension that the words convey, *and* he knew, on the basis of his own observations, that side by side with fear and apathy and destructiveness one can often see all sorts of psychological strengths and what Henry James used to call sensibilities.

My next encounter with Kennedy revealed yet another side of his mind. A year ago, with five other doctors, I went south to document (once again) the severe hunger, malnutrition and even starvation that exists among our rural poor. We saw vitamin deficiency diseases we all had been told in medical school no longer exist "in the western world." We saw bloated bellies, infected skin, thin and tired children who live on Coca Cola and potatoes and old bread.

We were full of horror and shame and we went to Washington to demand action from the government. We trudged along through the corridors of the federal bureaucracy, and finally reached high officials of the Department of Agriculture, which is presumably charged with the responsibility of providing food to the desperately needy. And of course we were told the political facts of life. Conservative congressmen control the purse strings and make it very hard for federal officials to bypass local sheriffs, who have no interest at all in upsetting things by providing sharecroppers or tenant farmers with food, which after all provides energy—and God knows what the "niggers" would do with *that*.

So, we went over to see Robert Kennedy, and had lunch with him. Within a matter of days an open hearing was scheduled. We spent a day giving testimony. The newspapers and television cameras gave our words wide attention. By no means was the issue satisfactorily settled; but a beginning, a very real beginning, was made. Government bureaucrats were put on the defensive, and eventually did start intervening in those medieval fiefdoms, the counties of our southern states.

I believe none of that would have happened had not the senator and his staff been more than helpful. In blunt words, they made sure our awful findings got through the layers of indifference, inertia, self-interest and worse that often characterise even the best-intentioned of our sprawling political institutions.

And finally, I have watched the senator with our poor: in the Mississippi delta, on our Indian reservations, in Appalachia, where white Anglo-Saxon Americans—old-stock farmers and unemployed former miners—live at the edge of hunger. I have seen him touring our urban ghettoes, or talking with our migrant farm workers, who are virtual slaves to an agricultural system that uses their labour callously and often enough cruelly.

I could go on to "analyse" his *presence,* his ability to "come across," and reach out and somehow persuade humble, illiterate, frightened people that someone cares, that *he* cares. But here is what a woman recently told me, a woman I have known for years. I have been studying how she and others like her get along. They are all the wives of southern tenant farmers. They all see practically no money during the year, and they all speak in those ungrammatical, untutored but strong and expressive ways that cause surprise to the same sophisticated intellectuals who accept and take for granted jazz and folk songs and ballads. What is more, they are all not only poor mothers, black mothers, uneducated mothers, but suspicious, hesitant, aloof women, and for good reason.

The white man is the "bossman," and is never up to any good. The white man is the brutal man, the exploiter. One smiles at him if he seems to mean well, and begs his mercy if he seems in the slightest unhappy about anything. And if the white man is a doctor or a social scientist, a very earnest and friendly observer, he is still suspect, and remains so over the months. Books have been written about how to reach the hard-to-reach, but like anything else, the experience of trying to do so defies the effort of description.

So, I was made a bit envious and confused by what I heard, which I've edited and connected together from several interviews:

"He's the kind of man you don't forget, no sir. He just came up here, and first thing we knew, he was just talking with us. He asked me for some water, because he was thirsty, and I was pleased to give it to him. He told us about his children, and how he wanted our children to have a better life than they've been getting. Then he just sat there and asked us a question or two—you know, about how did we live and what did we do about food and clothes and like that. The kids, my kids thought he was the nicest, kindest man they'd ever seen. They told me he was better than all the white folks and all the black folks and he was the best person they'd ever seen. Then their daddy, he wanted to know why they thought so, and they said it was the way he smiled, and he could laugh at himself all the time, and he didn't have a mean bone in him, they could tell. And most of all, I think, the kids could tell he liked them. And he didn't seem in a rush. He said he was going to stay here a little while, and he wanted to meet some people like us, and he was grateful to us for letting him.

"We were saying today, several people who live near here, that he was a real honest man. You can tell, because they stand out. Most people, they either try to put something over on you or they just don't care. They'll smile if they want something from you, and they'll be sour if they don't get it. (No, I mean the coloured, too, not just the white man.) But Mr. Kennedy, you could see that he was trying to find things out, as he said, and he wasn't going to stop there, no sir. My husband, he was in the war, you know—Korea. And he said that Mr. Kennedy, he is a fighter, and he doesn't sit back and say he knows the answers and someday he hopes it'll all get better. He goes out and does something. You can tell it about him, the way he moves. He's got energy, yes sir. And he's got a real kind heart."

From a ghetto youth in the north I heard something else: "He came through here, and all the kids, they said he was the only man you could trust, up there in the government. He's on our side, all the way. He doesn't preach at you and tell you you're no good for living here, and that stuff. He comes by and he seems to be enjoying himself. He had a good time here. He didn't say so, but you could tell it on his face, and by how he was relaxed, and he was real friendly to us.

"Some of these white guys, running for office, they come and tell you that they want you to join them and be on their side, but they're going from one street to the next saying the same thing, and you can see it as soon as they start talking, that it's all rehearsed. Kennedy doesn't put on any airs, and he *is* on our side. We know it. He doesn't have to say a word. You can see it written all over his face. Then he'll crack one of those jokes, and you can just tell how easy-going the guy is, and how he wants to do the best job he can—to help us out a lot.

"My friends, a lot of them say they really swear by him, and they don't say that about their own family, you know. One guy, he said Kennedy was the only one who could come here and make himself feel at home, and make us feel we were at home with him, and if he becomes president, then the country will be getting to be better."

Robert Kennedy will never be America's president. His death came in the middle of a hard fight for that office, and many of us who strongly supported him were doubtful he could win the Democratic nomination. America's majority is reasonably well off, and many comfortable suburban people, whose parents knew poverty and unemployment, worry instead about the cost of running two cars, or the burden of a mortgage on a second, summer home.

To such people Kennedy was at best *secretly* attractive. Somewhere "deep down" (as we psychiatrists see it) Kennedy reminded them of Franklin Roosevelt and the New Deal, and our long tradition of populist struggle. But an incredibly wealthy technological society has made all those memories irrelevant and even the passionate courage and considerable intelligence of a Robert Kennedy was having trouble awakening a nation with plenty of guns and plenty of butter to the dangers it really faces, in contrast to the various bogymen that are supposed to be around—the out-and-out reds, the crypto-reds, the pinks, the Asian hordes and on and on.

So, Robert Kennedy was shot down—it is said by an Arab born in Jerusalem. It is one world that we live in, as Kennedy knew. In recent years he had travelled all around that world, and in South Africa or Japan, in Europe or Latin America, his strong, earnest, open manner had won him friends and admiration.

He had an aristocrat's grace, a kind of confidence and generosity that come hard to the rest of us, who worry exactly where we stand in all the pecking orders that go to make up a "civilised society." But the rich can also be brutally callous or indifferent, and stupidly snobbish. Robert Kennedy had none of that decadence in him. He was gutsy. He detested "gushy talk." He was sentimental and generous, but in a quiet, thoughtful way. His mind was sharp, and unafraid of the heart's reasons.

And always, he was a wry, humorous man, who knew how to laugh at himself and invoke Aeschylus and Sophocles not because a speechwriter had so instructed him, but because, perhaps, the Kennedy family has lived and continues to live with a kind of great and tragic destiny that those Athenian writers knew so well. In the words of that ghetto youth: "He gets to you, because you feel he's deep, man he's deep, but he can smile too. That's what I call great, a great man."

Comment from Robert Coles

A bit later that young man's mother, upon hearing me declare in an informal manner the gist of the above, took pains to disagree pointedly: "I see you registering a lot of approval—but this man, he was a big-shot politico, and he fought his way up (he and his family, they all did) because he wanted to be on top. The rest of us, down here at the bottom, do the looking on, and if we're lucky we do the voting. But there's precious little praise for us, and oodles and oodles of it for the guy living way, away up there, telling us this, that, and the other. Not a bad deal, to live that kind of life, being a politician who's over and above so many of God's folks! I hope in my heart he finds peace—because he's just like everyone else (we all have our bad times, even if there are the good times to balance them). I can't even imagine myself living the kind of life Mr. Kennedy, Robert Kennedy, lived; but you know, we're all, each and every one of us, creatures of the good Lord—there's the good and the not-so-good and the bad in us, no matter our name, our place in the world."

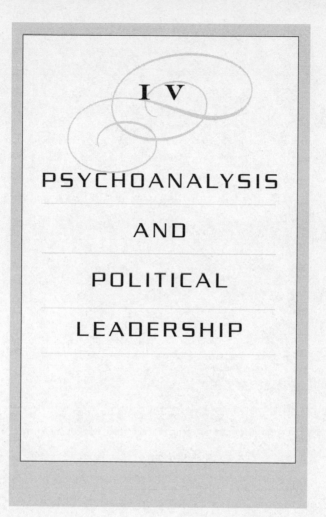

I V

PSYCHOANALYSIS

AND

POLITICAL

LEADERSHIP

NOTED CHILD PSYCHOANALYSTS Erik H. Erikson and Anna Freud, whose observations follow, had ample opportunities to observe political leadership as it affected individuals in Europe and America. Erikson studied religious and political leaders—Luther and Gandhi; and Freud bore witness as political leadership became embodied in the worries and fears and desires of those who acted as voters (England), or alas, as ardent, subservient followers (Austria).

Here, in these brief comments, Freud (Sigmund's daughter) and Erikson (neither of whom went to college or medical school) reflect on political leadership—who embraces whom, and on whose behalf.

REMARKS by Erik H. Erikson

"We spend so many hours contemplating our political leaders—we are tempted to lose sight of who they actually are. There is an aura around them that makes them shine, and I fear, many of us, their fans or their critics, become blind. If we are to understand our leaders, we need to understand our need for them (sometimes honorable, sometimes merely human, sometimes all too desperate)—I mean, our need to be *for* them, or yes, that too, our need to be *against* them."

From YOUNG MAN LUTHER
by Erik H. Erikson

Ideological leaders, so it seems, are subject to excessive fears which they can master only by reshaping the thoughts of their contemporaries; while those contemporaries are always glad to have their thoughts shaped by those who so desperately care to do so. Born leaders seem to fear only more consciously what in some form everybody fears in the depths of his inner life; and they convincingly claim to have an answer.

From CHILDHOOD AND SOCIETY
by Erik H. Erikson

Forms of leadership are defined not only by the historical dangers to be warded off by the work of organization; they must also serve the public display of popular phantasies and anticipations. Monarchs, even if foreign (and often, because they are foreign), become visible safeguard of a people's weak inner moral forces; aristocratic elites, personifications of dimly perceived new ideals. It is for this purpose that monarchs and aristocrats may and must play out on the stage of history the full cycle of irrational conflict: they must sin more defiantly and atone more deeply, and finally emerge with in-

creased personal and public stature. While they try to ac-
complish this cycle, the people will gladly serve as their whispering chorus and their sacrificial animals. For the grandiose
sin of a few promises total salvation to all.

From GANDHI'S TRUTH
by Erik H. Erikson

But it is clear that the great leader creates for himself and for
many others new choices and new cares. These he derives
from a mighty drivenness, an intense and yet flexible energy,
a shocking originality, and a capacity to impose on his time
what most concerns him—which he does so convincingly
that his time believes this concern to have emanated "naturally" from ripe necessities.

. . . .

And I would think that the inner conflicts which lead a
young person to such an unconventional leader, and to acceptance of him, come to include a deep ambivalence toward
that leader. As we saw, Gandhi sought out his followers with
a determination tempered only with diplomatic reserve, and
he did not hesitate, as it were, to take over the spiritual
parentage of these young people. Gandhi, of course, always
wanted to be sure that an applicant could be expected to do
some essential thing really well, but he also demanded a potential of total devotion in his future followers. From a man

with high academic qualifications, for example, he demanded to know only whether he would be willing "to become a scavenger." Scavenging included what in America we subsume under the word "dirty work," but it also literally meant cleaning latrines. In the name of truth and in the service of India, however, they had to accept what was his own family's plight, namely, that he belonged to all—and to none.

These young people, then, highly gifted in a variety of ways, seem to have been united in one personality "trait," namely, an early and anxious concern for the abandoned and persecuted, at first within their families, and later in a widening circle of intensified concern. At the same time, they were loyal rebels: loyal in their sorrow, determined in their rebellion. All this they offered Gandhi, displaying a wish to serve, which was determined as much by personality as by tradition. Gandhi's capacity both to arouse and to squelch ambivalence must have been formidable; but he put these men and women to work, giving direction to their capacity to care, and multiplying miraculously both their practical gifts and their sense of participation.

Followers, too, deserve a formula for the recorder or reviewer of history or life history. Whatever motivation or conflict followers may have in common as they join a leader and are joined together by him has to be studied in all the complementarity of

1. their personal lives, that is
   a. the moment when they met the leader, their state of mind, and their stage of life;

   b. the place of that moment in their life history, especially
     in lifelong themes transferred to the leader;
2. their communities, insofar as these are relevant to their
   search for an identity by participation, that is
   a. their generation's search for leadership
   b. traditional and evolving patterns of followership.

. . . .

And then, there is the leader's self-chosen suffering, which is strictly "his business," as Gandhi would say with his mild-mannered rudeness. For there must be a leader, and, in fact, a predetermined succession of leaders, so that the leader himself can be free to invite on himself any suffering, including death, rather than hide behind the pretext that he was not expendable. As we saw, in the first national Satyagraha, Gandhi's arrest turned out to be *the* critical factor, even as the Ahmedabad Satyagraha floundered over the critical issue of Gandhi's decision to fast. For once the leader decides on a "true" course, he must have the freedom to restrain as well as to command, to withdraw as well as to lead and, if this freedom should be denied him by his followers, to declare a Satyagraha against them. If such singular power produces a shudder in the reader of today—indoctrinated as he is against "dictators"—it must not be forgotten that we are now speaking of the post–First World War years when a new kind of charismatic leadership would emerge, in nation after nation, filling the void left by collapsing monarchies, feudalisms, and patriarchies, with the mystic unity of the Leader and the Masses. And such was the interplay of the private and the public, the neurotic and the charismatic, during the period when these sons of the people assumed such a mystic authority, that we must recognize even that most personal of Gandhi's decisions, namely, his *fast,* as part of an "Indian leadership Indian style."

REMARKS by Anna Freud

On Psychoanalysis and Political Leadership
"My father was not only interested in the great ones of history; often he would read of a political leader, what he said or did, and he would shake his head, or look into space (his way of thinking, and wondering), and we'd hear: 'Rulers, like the ruled, have [psychological] forces at work in their lives, which then give shape to history.' "

. . . .

"Perhaps it is all wrong to work clinically with children as I do here and not on the much bigger social problems of real deprivation. What a terrible indictment for any Society to spend money on anything else before these extreme needs are satisfied. And how can one understand it? Would it not be comparatively easy to come to the help of these districts and create employment? Is there any political reason why it does not happen?"

ABOUT THE EDITOR

ROBERT COLES is a professor of psychiatry and medical humanities at the Harvard Medical School and a research psychiatrist for the Harvard University Health Services. His many books include the Pulitzer prize–winning five-volume *Children of Crisis, The Moral Life of Children,* and *The Spiritual Life of Children.* He is also the James Agee Professor of Social Ethics at Harvard. He lives in Massachusetts.

MODERN LIBRARY IS ONLINE AT
WWW.MODERNLIBRARY.COM

MODERN LIBRARY ONLINE IS YOUR GUIDE TO CLASSIC LITERATURE ON THE WEB

THE MODERN LIBRARY E-NEWSLETTER

Our free e-mail newsletter is sent to subscribers, and features sample chapters, interviews with and essays by our authors, upcoming books, special promotions, announcements, and news. To subscribe to the Modern Library e-newsletter, visit **www.modernlibrary.com**

THE MODERN LIBRARY WEBSITE

Check out the Modern Library website at
www.modernlibrary.com for:

- The Modern Library e-newsletter
- A list of our current and upcoming titles and series
- Reading Group Guides and exclusive author spotlights
- Special features with information on the classics and other paperback series
- Excerpts from new releases and other titles
- A list of our e-books and information on where to buy them
- The Modern Library Editorial Board's 100 Best Novels and 100 Best Nonfiction Books of the Twentieth Century written in the English language
- News and announcements

Questions? E-mail us at **modernlibrary@randomhouse.com**.
For questions about examination or desk copies, please visit
the Random House Academic Resources site at
www.randomhouse.com/academic